CW01394455

THE JOYCE COUNTRY

BLOOMSDAY

16th June, 1904

'Bloomsday, 1904' by John Ryan. *Envoy,* April 1951

THE JOYCE COUNTRY

Literary Scholarship and Irish Culture

David Pierce

EER Edward Everett Root, Publishers, Brighton, 2018.

Edward Everett Root, Publishers, Co. Ltd.,
30 New Road, Brighton, Sussex, BN1 IBN, England.
www.eerpublishing.com
edwardeverettroot@yahoo.co.uk

The Joyce Country:
Literary Scholarship and Irish Culture

This volume first published in England in 2018
© David Pierce, 2018

ISBN 9781912224029 Hardback
ISBN 9781912224036 eBook

Cover designed and typesetting by Head & Heart Book Design.
Printed in Great Britain by Lightning Source UK, Milton Keynes.

To those who follow in our wake,
and in memory of my dear brother John.

Also by David Pierce

Attitudes to Class in the English Novel (with Mary Eagleton)
(London: Thames and Hudson, 1979).

W. B. Yeats: A Guide Through the Critical Maze
(Bristol: Bristol Classical Press, 1989).

James Joyce's Ireland
(London and New Haven: Yale University Press, 1992).

James Joyces Irland
(trans Jörg Rademacher and Cristoforo Sweeger)
(Köln and Basel: Bruckner and Thünker, 1996).

Yeats's Worlds: Ireland, England and the Poetic Imagination
(London and New Haven: Yale University Press, 1995).

Sterne in Modernism/Postmodernism
(co-editor with Peter de Voogd) (Amsterdam: Rodopi, 1996).

W.B. Yeats: Critical Assessments 4 Vols
(Robertsbridge: Helm Information, 2000).

The House of Music and the Cupboard Under the Stairs
(Privately Printed, 2000).

Irish Writing in the Twentieth Century: A Reader
(Cork: Cork University Press, 2001).

Light, Freedom and Song: A Cultural History of Modern Irish Writing
(London and New Haven: Yale University Press, 2005).

Joyce and Company
(London: Continuum, 2006).

Reading Joyce
(Harlow: Pearson Longman, 2007).

The Long Apprenticeship: A Writer's Memoir
(Knebworth: Troubador, 2012).

CONTENTS

List of Illustrations   *xi*

Acknowledgements   *xiii*

Abbreviations   *xv*

Introduction   *xvii*

ESSAYS

1. A NEW DEPARTURE FOR FICTION: *A PORTRAIT
OF THE ARTIST AS A YOUNG MAN*   3

2. THE HYBRID LANDSCAPE IN JOYCE   41

3. PREPARATORY TO ANYTHING ELSE: THE
OPENING TO 'EUMAEUS'   57

4. BENEDICT KIELY TRIBUTE   71

5. ANTHOLOGIES OF IRISH WRITING   89

6. HISTORY IN THE MAKING: IRISH WRITING
IN 2007–9   99

REVIEWS

7. JOYCE'S EUROPEAN CITIES

Joyce in Rome: The Genesis of Ulysses (ed. Giorgio Melchiori)
Rome: Bulzoni, 1984   129

John McCourt, *The Years of Bloom: James Joyce in Trieste
1904–1920* Dublin: Lilliput, 2000   133

Ira B. Nadel, *Joyce and the Jews: Culture and Texts*
London: Macmillan 1989   139

Thomas Faerber and Markus Luchsinger, *Joyce in Zürich*
Zurich: Unionsverlag, 1988   143

Conor Fennell, *A Little Circle of Kindred Minds: Joyce in*
Paris Dublin: Green Lamp Editions, 2011   146

8. JOYCE, YEATS AND THE MATTER OF IRELAND

John Kelly, *A W.B. Yeats Chronology* Basingstoke:
Macmillan, 2003   151

Roger Norburn, *A James Joyce Chronology* Basingstoke:
Macmillan, 2004   151

Alistair Cormack, *Yeats and Joyce: Cyclical History and the*
Reprobate Tradition Aldershot: Ashgate, 2008   161

Frank Shovlin, *Journey Westward: Joyce, Dubliners and the*
Literary Revival Liverpool: Liverpool University Press, 2012   163

Dublin James Joyce Journal Issue 1 Dublin: University College
Dublin and the National University of Ireland, 2008)   166

Voices on Joyce (eds Anne Fogarty and Fran O'Rourke) Dublin:
University College Dublin Press, 2015   170

9. JOYCE AND MODERNISM

Margot Norris, *Joyce's Web: The Social Unraveling of Modernism*
Austin, TX: University of Texas Press, 1992   177

John Nash, *James Joyce and the Act of Reception: Reading, Ireland,*
Modernism Cambridge: Cambridge University Press, 2006   180

Paul Stasi, *Modernism, Imperialism, and the Historical Sense*
Cambridge/New York: Cambridge University Press, 2012   182

Luke Gibbons, *Joyce's Ghosts: Ireland, Modernism, and Memory*
Chicago and London: University of Chicago Press, 2015   184

10. ULYSSES IN PERSPECTIVE

Terence Killeen, *Ulysses Unbound: A Reader's Companion to
James Joyce's 'Ulysses'* Bray, Co. Wicklow: Wordwell, 2004   193

Patrick McGee, *Paperspace: Style as Ideology in Joyce's Ulysses*
Lincoln and London: University of Nebraska Press, 1988   196

Andras Ungar, *Joyce's 'Ulysses' as National Epic: Epic Mimesis
and the Political History of the Nation State* Miami, FL:
University Press of Florida, 2002   207

Luca Crispi, *Joyce's Creative Process and the Construction of
Characters in Ulysses: Becoming the Blooms* Oxford: Oxford
University Press, 2015   209

11. ON COLLECTIONS OF ESSAYS

The Cambridge Companion to James Joyce (ed. Derek Attridge)
Cambridge: Cambridge University Press, 1990   221

The Cambridge Companion to James Joyce (ed. Derek Attridge)
Second Edition Cambridge: Cambridge University
Press, 2004   225

Renascent Joyce (eds Daniel Ferrer, Sam Slote and André Topia)
Gainsville, FL: University Press of Florida, 2013   226

*James Joyce Quarterly 50 Years Vol 50 No 1–2
Fall 2012–Winter 2013'*   231

12. ON A PERSONAL NOTE

*A Passion For Joyce: The Letters of Hugh Kenner and Adaline
Glasheen* (ed. Edward M. Burns) Dublin: University College
Dublin Press, 2008   237

David Norris, *A Kick Against the Pricks: The Autobiography*
London: Transworld Ireland, 2012   242

Modern Irish Autobiography: Self, Nation and Society
(ed Liam Harte) Basingstoke: Palgrave Macmillan, 2007   244

Select Bibliography   *249*
Index   *259*

LIST OF ILLUSTRATIONS

Front cover: Handcoloured postcard of Grafton Street,
Dublin, in the 1890s.

Frontispiece: 'Bloomsday, 1904' by John Ryan. *Envoy*,
April 1951.   ii

Edwardian postcard of The Exchange, Gibraltar:
image and text.   44

Back cover: Milton Hebald's statue of James Joyce in the
Fluntern Cemetery, Zurich, taken by the author in 1990.

ACKNOWLEDGEMENTS

Versions of the following essays and reviews appeared in various journals, and I would like to thank the editors for permission to reprint them here. To the *British Association for Irish Studies* for 'Anthologies of Irish Writing'. To *estudiosirlandeses.org* for 'Benedict Kiely Tribute' and 'History in the Making: Irish Writing in 2007–9'. To the *James Joyce Broadsheet* for *Joyce in Rome: The Genesis of Ulysses*; *Joyce and the Jews: Culture and Texts*; *Joyce in Zürich*; *Yeats and Joyce: Cyclical History and the Reprobate Tradition*; *Journey Westward: Joyce, Dubliners and the Literary Revival*; *Joyce's Web: The Social Unraveling of Modernism*; *James Joyce and the Act of Reception: Reading, Ireland, Modernism*; *Modernism, Imperialism, and the Historical Sense*; *Joyce's Ghosts: Ireland, Modernism, and Memory; Ulysses Unbound: A Reader's Companion to James Joyce's 'Ulysses'*; *Joyce's 'Ulysses' as National Epic: Epic Mimesis and the Political History of the Nation State*; *A Kick Against the Pricks: The Autobiography*; *Modern Irish Autobiography: Self, Nation and Society; 'James Joyce Quarterly 50 Years Vol 50 No 1–2 Fall 2012–Winter 2013'*. To the *James Joyce Quarterly* for *A Little Circle of Kindred Minds: Joyce in Paris*; *Dublin James Joyce Journal Issue 1*; *Voices on Joyce*; *Renascent Joyce*; *A Passion For Joyce: The Letters of Hugh Kenner and Adaline Glasheen*. To the *James Joyce Literary Supplement* for *Paperspace: Style as Ideology in Joyce's Ulysses; The Cambridge Companion to James Joyce* (1990). To the *Journal of Modern Literature* for *A W.B. Yeats Chronology* and *A James Joyce Chronology*. To *Reference Reviews* for *The Cambridge Companion to James Joyce* (2004).

This is also an opportunity to place on record my special gratitude and debt to Robert Baldock for his continuing support not only with this book but also with three previous books. My partner and lifelong companion, Mary Eagleton, deserves special mention for all the help she gave me in editing and revising this book. She is at the centre of every book I have undertaken. And I have been equally inspired by our son, Matthew Eagleton-Pierce, and his wife, Ammara Maqsood, in their publishing endeavours in politics and anthropology. When I finished my memoir in 2012, it never occurred to me that I would write another book, and certainly not another book on Joyce. But I have been lucky to have a supportive family and, with John Spiers in mind, supportive people around me to complete, sooner than I imagined, another labour of love. I want also to thank the following for their stimulating conversation and friendship over the years: Alistair Stead, Pieter Bekker, Richard Brown, Peter de Voogd, Rosa Gonzalez, the late Rosa Maria Bolletieri Bossinelli, Jörg Rademacher, Tim Webb, Robin Butlin and Graham Parry.

ABBREVIATIONS

D James Joyce, *'Dubliners': Text, Criticism, and Notes*, (eds Robert Scholes and A. Walton Litz) (New York: Viking, 1979).

FW James Joyce, *Finnegans Wake* (1939; London: Faber and Faber, 1964). Page number is given first, followed by line number.

Letters I Letters of James Joyce Volume I (ed. Richard Ellmann) (New York: Viking, 1966).

Letters II Letters of James Joyce Volume II (ed. Richard Ellmann) (New York: Viking, 1966).

Letters III Letters of James Joyce Volume III (ed. Richard Ellmann) (New York: Viking, 1966).

P James Joyce, *'A Portrait of the Artist as a Young Man': Text, Criticism, and Notes* (ed. Chester Anderson) (New York: Viking, 1968).

SH James Joyce, *Stephen Hero* (eds John J. Slocum and Herbert Cahoon) (1944; New York: New Directions, 1963).

U James Joyce, *Ulysses: The Corrected Text* (ed. Hans Walter Gabler with Wolfhard Steppe and Claus Melchior) (London: The Bodley Head, 1986). Chapter number is followed by line number.

INTRODUCTION

After completing *Reading Joyce* in 2007, I thought I had done with writing any more books on the great writer. After all, it was my third book on Joyce, the first being an illustrated introduction, *James Joyce's Ireland* (1992), and the second *Joyce and Company* (2006), a collection of more advanced essays. Now a decade or so later I discover I have another book, this time composed of essays and reviews, some from the past or significantly revised, others new, mostly about Joyce but some involving other twentieth-century Irish writers. Since the 1980s I have been reviewing for journals devoted to Joyce, in particular the *James Joyce Quarterly*, the *James Joyce Broadsheet*, and the *James Joyce Literary Supplement* based respectively at the universities of Tulsa, Leeds, and Miami. A collection of such reviews in book form, together with a selection of essays and lectures on Joyce and other writers, appealed to me, not only because it constitutes a form of retrieval of what I have sent out into the world at varying times and to different audiences, but also because a book has the appearance of something solid which I can hold in my hands and wave in the air. There was another, more altruistic, reason: I wanted the wider public not given to accessing or reading academic journals to have an opportunity to see what other angles on Joyce and Irish writers have been exciting readers over the years.

The period from when I began reviewing until now has been a prolific time for Joyce criticism, and it continues to be so. With the attention currently being shown to him in China and Japan, and, hopefully in the future, in India and elsewhere, Joyce has never enjoyed a higher profile on the world stage. None of this would have been possible without North America, which remains the dominant player in Joyce studies. But the European Joyce has also grown in influence in this period, not least because he continues to be claimed by different continental cities. With this in mind I have gathered together, in the first section of Reviews, books concerned with Joyce's time in Rome in 1906–7, in Trieste from 1905 to 1915 and then in 1920, in Zurich from 1915 to 1919 and then in 1940/1, in Paris from 1920 to 1940. The review of John McCourt's *The Years of Bloom: James Joyce in Trieste 1904–1920* (2000) I completed specifically for this collection. The others I revised to bring up to date or to cross-reference or in some other way to sharpen their appeal. While not specifically about Trieste, I took this opportunity of inserting into this section Ira B. Nadel's *Joyce and the Jews: Culture and Texts* (1989), since in retrospect it provides a valuable companion to McCourt's account, which itself deals with the Jewishness of Leopold Bloom and the Jewish culture of the city.

In turning to his country of birth, when I embarked on *James Joyce's Ireland* part of my intention was to reclaim more of Joyce for Ireland. It wasn't that Joyce owned Ireland, but there was a risk of his being lost to the rest of a world dominated by the United States. It seems impossible to believe today but, a quarter of a century ago, his Irishness stood in danger of being diminished or passed over in favour of a world writer whose country of origin was of secondary significance. Not that I could blame anyone who is not Irish for playing down Joyce's Irishness or for thinking his Irishness was not their concern. To some extent I agree with the American critic, Bernard Benstock, when, possibly with tongue-in-cheek, he asserted in 1972 that '*Ulysses* is no more about Dublin than *Moby Dick* is about a whale'. As if he knew it might upset people, Benstock went on to qualify the remark '- although no less'.[1] It would be hard, however, but not impossible, to read Joyce without

1 Bernard Benstock, '*Ulysses* Without Dublin' in *James Joyce Quarterly*, 10:1 1972, 100–1.

coming to terms with his Irish contexts. For myself, as I look back on what I have undertaken in *The Joyce Country*, I discover it is full of an Irish world which still commands attention.

My first book on Joyce could have been entitled 'Ireland's James Joyce', but that would have implied a form of ownership more worthy of an Irish heritage magazine. The title I chose allowed space for contemplating the world through the writer's eyes, a springboard, without all the time imagining his origins were the only thing that mattered. It was not designed to suggest that Joyce 'owned' Ireland, though one of my reviewers thought as much. Today, it is clear that the connection between Joyce and Ireland is secure, particularly since Bloomsday, the day in June on which *Ulysses* is set, has become effectively a national holiday. And there is little appetite for banishing him, as there was in Ireland until the 1960s. When Irish critics now turn their attention to Joyce they frequently do so from a broadly pro-nationalist perspective and with an edge sometimes missing in the past. This has been an important corrective to remind the world that although Joyce may express anti-nationalist sentiments, or allow such sentiments to find expression on the lips of his characters, he is as Irish as 'the lovely lakes of Killarney', as they are described in a debunking passage in *Ulysses*, or the *Tunc* page of the *Book of Kells*, which features in *Finnegans Wake* and which he so much admired.

There is merit in rehearsing the topic of Joyce and nationalism, for in many ways this accompanied him throughout his life, and it made itself felt particularly from abroad in the tension between distance and involvement. Appropriately, Joyce begins with the Christmas Dinner scene in *A Portrait of the Artist as a Young Man*, where he recreates a period in Irish history which was full of hope as well as anger and acrimony surrounding the fortunes of nationalism. As leader of the Irish Parliamentary Party at Westminster in the 1880s, Charles Stewart Parnell, who was championed by Joyce's father (and later by his son), became the spokesperson for political nationalism. When his relationship with Katharine O'Shea, the wife of one of his MPs, was discovered, he was forced out of office in 1890, in part because he had lost the support of Methodist opinion in

Britain and the Catholic Church in Ireland, and his Party of eighty-six members split in two. Thereafter, nationalist politics took a long time to recover its sense of purpose. Indeed, a return to constitutional nationalism was effectively overtaken by the Easter Rising of 1916 and the subsequent summary execution of its leaders. But in those years after the fall of Parnell, it was left to the movement of cultural nationalism to fill the space vacated by politics.

The constitutional politician, Parnell, famously declared that 'No man has a right to fix the boundary to the march of a nation'. When his statue, with arms outstretched, was completed in 1910 at the top of O'Connell Street, it was accompanied by what amounted to a clarion call for constitutionalists and non-constitutionalists alike. It was as if the march of a nation would be answered at some point in the future, or, in this case, more immediately by the next generation in 1916. Up until then, each generation of parliamentary leaders from Daniel O'Connell to Parnell took up the challenge in advancing what became known in the 1870s as Home Rule. This was very nearly delivered at Westminster in 1913 on the eve of the Great War; it was eventually agreed to by the Government of Ireland Act in 1920. Even though the Easter Rising marked a fundamental disruption in its trajectory, it is right for historians to stress the idea of continuity in the struggle for independence. Of course, with a Rising in 1916 led by Patrick Pearse and James Connolly, a War of Independence with Britain in 1919–21 led by Michael Collins, and a Civil War between those who supported and those like Éamon de Valera who opposed the Treaty, the birth of modern Ireland was accompanied by violence and bloodshed. However, we should not overlook the primordial or perennialist roots of nationalism and how all through the nineteenth century the march of the nation could be heard in the unofficial anthem 'A Nation Once Again'.

> When boyhood's fire was in my blood
> I read of ancient freemen,
> For Greece and Rome who bravely stood,
> Three hundred men and three men;

And then I prayed I yet might see
Our fetters rent in twain,
And Ireland, long a province, be
A Nation once again!

A Nation once again,
A Nation once again,
And Ireland, long a province, be
A Nation once again! [2]

In retrospect, it is also right to notice those who positioned themselves on the outside or were positioned there by others, for not everyone fell in behind the banner identified with 'the march of a nation'. From the outset there were competing ideas of what nationhood might entail, and in the period from the 1890s to the 1920s, the Fenian (physical force) legacy continued, as did the extra-parliamentary struggle associated with the Land League in the 1880s under Michael Davitt and the emergence of Sinn Fein in 1905 under Arthur Griffith. With its concern for the rights of tenants, Davitt's Land League reminds us of a longer history of land disputes from the period of agitation with the Whiteboys in the eighteenth century to 'Captain Rock' in the 1820s.[3] And it is worth recalling that in the Joyce household they would boast about the family member who was a Whiteboy. It is only with hindsight that these 'local disturbances', as they were characterised by Whig commentators at the time, anxious to lessen their impact, can be properly called nationalist (or indeed 'local').[4] So if I stress the gaps in the march of the nation, it is with a purpose.

2 Thomas Davis wrote the lyrics of this song in the 1840s. The repetition of the chorus at the end of each of the four stanzas has a powerful effect in persuading an Irish audience to feel rightly indignant that their nation is but a province.
3 For a recent historical study, which includes a discussion of the Whiteboys, see James S. Donnelly, *Captain Rock: The Irish-American Agrarian Revolution of 1821–1824* (Madison, WI: University of Wisconsin, 2009).
4 See for example George Cornwall Lewis, *On Local Disturbances in Ireland, and on the Irish Church Question* (London: B. Fellowes, 1836).

There is a trenchant comment in Benedict Kiely's novel of the Troubles, *Nothing Happens in Carmincross* (1985): 'We were misled to expect better'.[5] The rebellion at Easter 1916 was undertaken by a small group of idealists who took on the might of the British Empire and struck a blow. It was a hopeless venture and the participants knew it would issue for themselves in personal imprisonment or death. 'Sacrifice' gave them courage and it must have been a word that accompanied them to the grave. And yet, by one of those ironies of history, their dreams and sacrifice effectively won out. By contrast it would be difficult to characterise the recent Troubles in similar fashion, and this is Kiely's point. 'We were misled to expect better.' We carried from our childhood and youth the image of heroic struggle and it let us down in the present. Yeats, too, recognised as much in the early 1920s when the Irish Civil War reached his home at Thoor Ballylee on the Clare/Galway border. In his celebrated poem 'Easter 1916' the word he uses to describe their mental state is the positive word 'dreams'; now he is more critical of the participants and resorts to 'fantasies':

> We had fed the heart on fantasies,
> The heart's grown brutal from the fare,
> More substance in our enmities
> Than in our love; O honey-bees,
> Come build in the empty house of the stare.[6]

Both Kiely and Yeats, each in their different ways, give voice to something that was not envisaged by people in the nineteenth century when they sang their unofficial national anthem, for then everything looked forward. Now, with a chasm opening up behind them and in front of them, people began to draw back from a belief in the saving idea of continuity.

In 1923, when Joyce began what became known as *Finnegans Wake*, the Civil War was fresh in his mind. With the space given to

5 *Nothing Happens in Carmincross* (London: Methuen, 1986), 26.
6 'Meditations in Time of Civil War' in *W.B. Yeats: Selected Poetry* (ed. Timothy Webb) (London: Penguin, 1991), 140. A stare in Ireland is a (noisy) starling.

the warring brothers, Shem and Shaun, there is merit in considering the *Wake* as a civil war text, a text which broadens out and which becomes in the process an anti-war text in general.[7] The 'wills gen wonts' (*FW* 4.1), a phrase that appears on the first line of the second page, provides a cogent summary of much that passes for warfare in the past and in the present, and its strength relies on Joyce not being too specific. *Finnegans Wake* is indebted to Giambattista Vico with his theory of cyclical history and universal history, but Joyce never lost an attachment to a specific history and the texture of daily life and what happens when we are not awake. The movement between the universal and the particular works both ways in Joyce's last text, but here I want to stress the Irish dimension and his probing of the Irish dark.

Also in the first chapter we encounter the Willingdone Museyroom of war, the Duke of Wellington museum that is. Wellington, the Iron Duke, was the field marshal who defeated Napoleon at the Battle of Waterloo in 1815. Joyce draws attention to the soldier who managed to join effort with achievement, will and doing, in somewhat robotic fashion. At the entrance to the museum, we are told to '[m]ind your hats goan in!' (*FW* 8.9) Once inside, the reader keeps noticing the visual reminder of war in the riot of exclamation marks accompanied by the wails and shrieks of those who died from bullets or explosions: 'Brékkek Kékkek Kékkek Kékkek! Kóax Kóax Kóax! Ualu Ualu Ualu! Quaouauh!' (*FW* 4.2–3) And when leaving the museum, if you are still wearing them, you are asked to '[m]ind your boots goan out' (*FW* 10.22). 'Phew!' as Joyce, the comforter, rightly exclaims, 'What a warm time we were in there' (*FW* 10.24–5). The conversational tone is striking, but, again, it manages to convey a profound truth about human history and lessons that can be drawn from it.

Allusions abound in *Finnegans Wake*. To those familiar with Aristophanes's comedy, *The Frogs*, 'Brékkek Kékkek Kékkek Kékkek!' will recall lines of the croaking chorus mocking Dionysus.[8] One

---

7 For more on *Finnegans Wake* as a civil war text, see my essay 'The Politics of *Finnegans Wake*' in Patrick McCarthy (ed.), *Critical Essays on James Joyce's Finnegans Wake* (New York: G.K.Hall, 1992).

8 See Aristophanes, *The Frogs* (trans Gilbert Murray) (London: George Allen

minute the allusions look secure, the next minute they dissolve. The world is anchored in repetition, myth and pattern, but everything else is on the move. Once the various meanings in a portmanteau word such as 'Dyoublong' (*FW* 13.4) have been deciphered or discerned, there is still work to do in eliciting how they all work together, possibly as a chord, or, alternatively, in watching them melt into their constituent parts, their organic connection lost. The museum passage above, for example, could be read as a description of sexual intercourse and how Wellington went about his business on his 'big wide harse' (*FW* 8.21). Before entering the museum we are told that 'Penetrators are permitted into the museomound free' (*FW* 8.5). But if we pursued the theme of nationalism, we can observe a subversive writer at work, constantly taunting those who believe in the undivided truth.

Even Parnell's rallying call suffers a painful kind of distortion that looks as if it is being upheld and at the same time mocked: 'no mouth has the might to set a mearbound to the march of a landsmaul' (*FW* 292.26–7). With political manipulators in mind, such as de Valera during the Treaty negotiations, whose intervention over Document 2 ushered in the Civil War, Joyce reveals how the moral universe of 'right' can, with the change of a single letter, be returned to the cruel world of 'might', and often on account of a disagreement over a form of words. At the same time Joyce defends the right of Norwegians, then suffering from the spreading influence of Danish, to adopt the Landsmaal dialect as their national language.

That much is clear but the attentive reader wants more. 'Landsmaal' in early drafts comes after a run of words connected with language including 'languidge', and the reader senses the word is to be understood as belonging to that series and at the same time connected with a particular language and a small land.[9] In this way Joyce highlights the link between language and nationhood. '[M]earbound' follows the crossed-out word 'boundary', so we see Joyce scrambling matters, but in a way that is not immediately clear. On the other hand, the phrase

and Unwin, 1908), *passim*.
9 See David Hayman (ed.), *A First-Draft Version of Finnegans Wake* (London: Faber, 1963), 163.

'set a mearbound', which is an additional piece of complicating (or, heaven forbid, moribund) information, many readers may gloss over and read as simply a 'mere boundary'. In Irish '*méar*' means 'finger', but this is not very enlightening unless we are supposed to infer that no one has the right or might to lay a finger on the march of a nation. Without the accent, *mear* in Irish means quick, so we might interpret this as a reference to the march of an army confronting a mearbound or quick leap and being held up. At times we are not in possession of a complete picture to proceed with certainty. '[M]earbound' sounds as if it were a legal document, tied by fingers, but that must be a false trail. It is the insertion of 'a' in the first syllable that is confusing. Reverse two letters and 'sea' intervenes, for 'mear' then becomes '*mare*' in Latin, and you cannot march as such over the sea. Or we might read it as German '*meer*' or drop the 'a' and come upon '*mer*' and the sea in French. Or recall the Old English suffix 'mere' in placenames such as Windermere. If we were familiar with Norse or Norwegian or Danish or all the languages of Europe, we might recognize immediately what lay behind Joyce's use of the word. But perhaps it is nothing more than a sea boundary – or a mere boundary.

As it happens the word 'mear' occurs several times in *Finnegans Wake*, once where it signifies 'near' (as in 'so mear and yet so fahr' at 471.19) and once in a phrase celebrating the 'londmear of Dublin' (*FW* 372.2–3). In the Parnell sequence, and in contrast with the preceding phrase where 'd' (as in day, dense, decade) is to the fore, we might notice the repetition of the initial letter 'm', a nasal sound confusingly close to 'n'. So 'mearbound' is perhaps of interest to Joyce as much for its sound as for its meaning. We might be tempted to conclude that, in spite of what Joyce tells us, not every letter in *Finnegans Wake* is a 'godsend' (*FW* 269.17). Elsewhere, we read 'For newmanmaun set a marge to the merge of unnotions' (*FW* 614.7–8), where 'no man' now turns out to be Cardinal Newman, where 'march' has become 'merge', and 'boundary' has been transformed into 'marge', which is itself short for Margaret or margarine. Needless to say, the clarity of Parnell's statement has been diminished or compromised, for, once the echo of the catchphrase has been invoked, there is a problem discerning the original reference. At the same time we would do well not to assume Joyce is not on Parnell's side when it comes to the rights of small nations, Ireland included. The nature of Joyce's commitment is frequently like this, a movement between assertion and qualification, and often wrapped in his experiments with language and identity. Fortunately, Joyce seems to understand the plight of the perplexed reader for the paragraph containing the Parnell quotation ends with a cheerful observation on what he is doing in the *Wake*, expressed in a superior, upper-class English accent: 'you must, how, in undivided reawlty draw the line somewhawre' (*FW* 292.31–2).

To continue, if political nationalism in the period from the 1890s to the 1920s so often ended in forms of breakdown and cul-de-sacs, this has been less true of cultural nationalism, which ran alongside political developments. For most of the time the latter managed to establish a certain independence, and only occasionally, as with the riots in 1907 at the newly opened Abbey Theatre over the staging of *The Playboy of the Western World* by John Millington Synge, did the confrontation between politics and culture turn ugly. But inside the movement of nationalism, whether that is discussed in terms of political or cultural nationalism, there was a wider issue, which, following the historian, E.J. Hobsbawm, I would identify as a conflict between ethnic and civic nationalism. Hobsbawm distinguishes two stages in the history of nationalism, one ethnic, the other civic. Civic nationalism, which owed much to the citizen state of the French Revolution, flourished in the period 1830–70. It operated a 'threshold principle', insisting that only nations with large populations and territory were entitled to form independent states. It was followed by an ethno-linguistic nationalism in which smaller groups, on the basis of ethnic and/or linguistic ties, laid claim to independence.[10] Hobsbawm stresses the universal values of civic nationalism over ethnic nationalism. The latter form of nationalism always has the potential to shift to the right in politics, and it did so in the twentieth century, most notably in the rise of fascism in the 1930s and in recent times in the Balkans.

10 E.J. Hobsbawm, *Nations and Nationalism Since 1870* 2nd edition (Cambridge: Cambridge University Press, 2000), 102.

Hobsbawm showed little interest in Irish nationalism, but his distinction is worth pursuing in an Irish context. For there has always been a space for civic nationalism in Ireland, not least because the different cultures and religious traditions have shared so much common ground, and not just in the North of Ireland. Joyce is a fine illustration of a writer who understands the tension between the two forms of nationalism, and in many ways his work straddles the two. The mouthpiece for one-eyed nationalism in the cave of Cyclops in *Ulysses* carries the name of the Citizen. When asked by the Citizen what is his nation, Bloom replies: 'Ireland... I was born here. Ireland.' (*U* 12:1431) Joyce understands precisely what he's doing in depicting an ethnic nationalist in the guise of a civic nationalist, for it was during the French Revolution that the ideology and institution of citizenship was first formulated. The Citizen, however, became a threat to others. Equally, the deflating answer deployed by Bloom to lower the temperature in the pub has absolutely no persuasive power to those around him. In complicating the debate in this way, Joyce shows how the cave of Cyclops cannot be confined to an Irish dimension. Indeed, after the anti-immigrant sentiments unleashed in Britain during the referendum in 2016 and during the American presidential campaign, Joyce quite clearly has something to say to a world beyond the confines of Ireland.

During the period from the 1890s to the 1920s, ethnic nationalism tended to win out over civic nationalism. Joyce himself was someone who was conflicted about nationalism, and this is reflected in his work. It helped that he travelled to Europe and became a voluntary exile, for in doing so he managed to free himself sufficiently from 'the old pap of racial hatred' to be able to champion civic nationalism in the character of 'Jewish' Bloom while never forgetting Molly's ethnicity.[11] Throughout *The Joyce Country*, as is evident in my discussion of Heaney's 'Station Island' and in my reviews of Seamus Deane, Andras Ungar and others, we can identify the presence and interplay of these

---

11 *Letters II*, 167. The phrase occurs in a letter to his brother, Stanislaus, in September 1906. Joyce was referring to the Sinn Fein policies of Arthur Griffith.

ideas, for they had a powerful and continuing effect on Joyce and other Irish writers in the modern period.

However, there is more to Joyce than rehearsing his historical contexts, and in Chapter 1, 'A New Departure for Fiction: *A Portrait of the Artist as a Young Man*', I consider how Joyce introduced something new in our understanding of modern fiction and in the way we read novels. This is especially evident in the ruthless way he kept separate the line between text and interpretation. Indeed, from the outset a Joyce text presents us with a surface that acquires meaning through resistance. With the help of H. Stuart Hughes's classic study, *Consciousness and Society: The Reorientation of European Social Thought 1890–1930*, I focus on the importance of consciousness in Joyce's fiction. The consciousness I have in mind is not the fine consciousness to be found in Henry James, nor the consciousness on display in the use of free indirect discourse where the novelist moves back and forth between the interior states of mind of a character and the third-person narrator, a movement that is effected in such a way that the reader at times cannot distinguish between the two, or, rather, to take an alternative view, the reader delights in what the author, with his or her fine ear for the language, is seeking to achieve.[12] Neither am I concerned in this essay with the much-discussed technique of stream of consciousness, which often accompanies Joyce discussions. This is more appropriate when dealing with *Ulysses* than with *A Portrait*. Bloom's consciousness or Molly's consciousness is always marked by intentionality or a direction toward some goal, by the addition, that is, of 'of'. It is essentially genitival, the consciousness of something. I discuss this more fully in *Reading Joyce*, especially in connection with Edmund Husserl's theory of consciousness.[13] What intrigues me about *A Portrait*, and, in particular the opening, is consciousness *per se*.

Ironically, given all I say here, the young boy's entry into consciousness could not be better expressed or handled, but Joyce's treatment has perhaps not received the recognition it deserves by readers, critics

---

12 For a discussion along these lines, see David Lodge, *Consciousness and the Novel: Connected Essays* (London: Penguin, 2003).

13 David Pierce, *Reading Joyce* (Harlow: Longman, 2007), 291–7.

and translators. In passing, let me add that, as recent publications confirm, consciousness has been the subject of special attention by psychologists, philosophers, neuroscientists and others interested in how the brain works, but, again, my concern is not scientific or even systematic but broadly literary and cultural. My interest lies in the way Joyce (and modernists such as Virginia Woolf) provide us with an 'inside-out' view of reality, rewriting how the external world is portrayed. In Joyce's case he shows us in *A Portrait* a boy falling or emerging into consciousness. This is at the core of my discussion, and it is linked to the issue of modernity, the character of the modern novel, and, perhaps above all, to subjectivity.

I begin by comparing the opening of Joyce's novel with Laurence Sterne's eighteenth-century novel *Tristram Shandy* and Charles Dickens's nineteenth-century novel *David Copperfield*. Sterne's novel is profoundly philosophical, Dickens's novel can be read as psychological, while *A Portrait* offers something distinctly modern, an interest in consciousness. If, however, I concentrate on Joyce's originality, we cannot overlook what the three writers have in common. Sterne and Joyce are like bookends to the literary form of the novel, and at the same time, with some justification and by invoking a postmodernist perspective, they can rightly be regarded as contemporaries, one of the other.[14] On the other hand, Dickens and Joyce are, in the words of Patrick Parrinder, 'comic and visionary writers, powerfully aware both of the plasticity of words and of the mass and texture of things.'[15] And, before considering their extraordinary portrayal of the ordinary life of London and Dublin, Parrinder notices how 'they are so individual that their work defies direct comparison, though it makes a suggestive initial comparison.' My discussion in this chapter is more focused and is largely restricted to the opening page of *A Portrait*, which is where we encounter for the first time what I believe is Joyce's particular contribution to the new departure for the novel.

---

14 For more on the connections between Sterne and Joyce, see the various essays in *Sterne in Modernism/Postmodernism* (eds David Pierce and Peter de Voogd) (Amsterdam: Rodopi, 1996).
15 Patrick Parrinder, *James Joyce* (Cambridge: Cambridge University Press, 1984), 1.

With Sterne and Dickens as control figures, I analyse the shifts or transitions in the narrative voice and in the boy's perception of the world. David Copperfield is thrown into existence, but the boy in *A Portrait* falls into consciousness, unable at first to know if 'he' is 'you' or 'I'. Nearly every aspect that Joyce touches, whether that is realistic texture, narrative flow and cohesion, the stress on discontinuity, the use of epigraphs and punctuation or myths and symbols and quotation, adds something to our understanding of modern fiction. The novel, keenly championed by Ezra Pound, made its first appearance in the pages of the little magazine, *The Egoist*, in February 1914. Its technique reminds us of Imagism in literature and perhaps Cubism in the arts, but for Joyce, who always resisted being co-opted into a movement, more was at stake. Instinctively he seemed to see through the idea of Modernism as a critique of a civilisation in decline, an idea that has often dominated critical discussion in the modern period. Hughes suggests that the modern novel 'has come to play a rather more serious and self-conscious role in the enunciation of values than was the case in the two preceding centuries'.[16] Although they are sometimes unappreciated, Joyce's values are worthy of consideration, not least because they are informed by his classical temper and play a part in his identity as a writer. While it has merit, 'egoist' is not, therefore, the description that fits him best.

Even if the matter is not easy to resolve satisfactorily, the opening to *A Portrait* – and this is an aspect also on display throughout Joyce's writing – invites us to reflect in particular on the relationship between consciousness, the resistance to interpretation, and the expression of values in the broadest sense. In my conclusion, I comment on the opening to *A Portrait* having the look of something inserted after the rest of the novel has been completed. Such a move on Joyce's part, which became a characteristic method of working when composing *Ulysses*, also belongs to the craft of writing and to the new departure for the novel. There is, then, merit in reflecting on Joyce and nationalism, but, when we inquire into the new departure for fiction that *A Portrait*

16 H. Stuart Hughes, *Consciousness and Society: The Reorientation of European Social Thought 1890–1930* revised edition (1958; New York: Vintage, 1977), 21.

represents, a different approach is called for, one that does justice to the boy's consciousness before history intervenes.

In 'The Hybrid Landscape in Joyce', which began life as a conference paper at the James Joyce Symposium in Budapest in June 2006, I return to the historical theme, focusing in a small-scale way on a well-used concept in postcolonial thinking.[17] I begin with some reflections on 'Penelope' and Joyce's view of Gibraltar, and then broaden out the discussion by looking at the history of the word in English, before offering some general observations on hybridity in *Ulysses* and *Finnegans Wake*. Molly's ethnicity reminds us that Joyce's interest was not so much in a hybrid landscape but in an imagined hybrid landscape. Molly is a colonial subject with Spanish eyes, who was brought up on the Rock of Gibraltar. She is the daughter of a Spanish woman with the improbable name Lunita Laredo and of a father who possesses the suitably Penelopean name of Tweedy and who is thought to be a major in the Royal Dublin Fusiliers but who turns out to be a drum major. So natural, so lacking in hybridity, does Molly appear that we assume all kinds of things including a voice full of the broad vowels of the West of Ireland, where Joyce's partner, Nora Barnacle, on whom she is in part modelled, came from. But she could not have spoken like that. Equally, this is to forget that she is the product of Joyce's 'meandering male fist' (*FW* 123.10) and comes to life amid the shadows in the interplay between the spoken and the written and in a border region somewhere between cliché, word association, and stereotype.

In the imagined hybrid landscape Joyce enjoyed playing with stereotypes, especially evident in the characters of Molly and Bloom. In 'Preparatory to Anything Else: The Opening to "Eumaeus"', which is based on a conference paper I gave at the James Joyce Symposium in Prague in June 2010 and which retains something of its original flavour, I discuss the odd-sounding phrase 'orthodox Samaritan' in the

17 For a wider discussion on hybridity, see my opening chapter 'The Hybrid Character of Modern Irish Writing' in *Light, Freedom and Song: A Cultural History of Modern Irish Writing* (London and New Haven: Yale University Press, 2005).

opening sentence and how Bloom imagines rallying a despondent Stephen: 'bucked him up generally in orthodox Samaritan fashion which he very badly needed'. Here we observe Bloom confusing 'orthodox Jew' with 'good Samaritan'. It is part of a comic moment in what is the arguably funniest episode of the novel. Although the adjective appears in its opening sentence, 'Eumaeus' contains very few 'orthodox' sentences. Interestingly, in an early version found in the Rosenbach manuscript, which was a fair copy hand-written by Joyce, he had originally written 'good Samaritan fashion', so it took him some time to stumble on the 'orthodox Samaritan' joke.[18]

More so than Stephen Dedalus, Bloom and Molly caught Joyce's increasingly playful attention in *Ulysses*, and in part this must have been because they were characters he could work with and develop. He indicated as much to his artist friend, Frank Budgen, in October 1918 when he was at work on the novel:

> I have just got a letter asking me why I don't give Bloom a rest. The writer of it wants more Stephen. But Stephen no longer interests me to the same extent. He has a shape that can't be changed.[19]

Modern critics – and Luca Crispi is the latest – seemingly cannot stop writing about Bloom, and it is not surprising that he is a constant presence in *The Joyce Country*. His Jewishness is a particular focus, not only in books by Nadel and McCourt but also in reviews by Giorgio Melchiori and Cormac Ó Gráda. Melchiori asks why Joyce in Rome in 1906–7 chose a Jew for his central character, and suggests that Jews were then a focus of attention not only in Roman politics but also in the political writings of Guglielmo Ferrero then of interest to Joyce. According to the economic historian Cormac Ó Gráda in an essay in *Voices on Joyce* (2015), Joyce's portrait of Bloom 'owed much more to

18 *James Joyce Ulysses A Facsimile of the Manuscript II* (New York: Octagon Books; Philadelphia: Rosenbach Foundation, 1975), P570.
19 Frank Budgen, *James Joyce and the Making of 'Ulysses' and Other Writings* (1934; London: Oxford University Press, 1972), 107.

information garnered during his time in Trieste (1904–15) than to first-hand contacts with Irish Jews before leaving Dublin at the age of 22'.[20]

Translation, which occupies a site at the other end of the spectrum to a discussion about hybridity, is a topic that continues to play an active role in Joyce studies. Translators zealously avoid anything which smacks too readily of a hybrid form or a mixture of the target and source languages. 'Eumaeus' is an episode that deliberately uses multiple registers within sentences, so any translation has to attend to this slippage, movement or variety. How to translate 'bucked him up generally' reminds us of the challenges Joyce presents. In their recent Dutch translation of *Finnegans Wake*, which they innocently or humorously call a 'bi-lingual edition', Erik Bindevoet and Robbert-Jan Henkes opt for something quite radical, juxtaposing the original page alongside their translation. They accept the impossibility of literal translation and, instead, provide a system of equivalent expressions, which they call an adaptation or a reproduction in another language.[21] As they suggest, others called it 'dutchification'.[22] Translation enables us to notice at first hand how readers read, and it can therefore provide a valuable way into interpreting or discussing a Joyce text. Throughout *The Joyce Country* I often have recourse to translation and how Joyce looks to foreign eyes, especially apparent in the movement between a host and a target language.

In September 2007 I was invited to give an address at the Benedict Kiely School at the Strule Arts Centre in Omagh in County Tyrone. It was the first School to be held since his death. In revising my address I have amplified themes, developed lines of argument, and turned it to face more in a Joycean direction. Kiely was a prolific Irish writer

20 Cormac Ó Gráda, 'Lost in Little Jerusalem: Leopold Bloom and Irish Jewry' in Anne Fogarty and Fran O'Rourke (eds), *Voices on Joyce* (Dublin: University College Dublin Press, 2015), 22.
21 *Finnegans Wake* Bi-lingual edition (trans Erik Bindevoet and Robbert-Jan Henkes) (Amsterdam: Athaeneum, 2002).
22 See Robbert-Jan Henkes 'Note on the Text' in James Joyce, *Finnegans Wake* (eds Robbert-Jan Henkes, Erik Bindevoet and Finn Fordham) (Oxford: Oxford University Press, 2012), xlvi.

and his short stories remain among the best that were written in the last century. An address allowed me to offer a broad celebration of his achievement, and I have kept the tone as it was delivered to an audience composed of people from the different traditions in the North. Omagh is a special town and is blessed in that it possesses a writer who has told part of the inside story of its modern history. Not everything was destroyed by the Troubles or, indeed, by the 1998 bomb outrage in Omagh. There is a longer, and indeed more inclusive, history that takes in a kinder form of nationalism, and future generations will return to Kiely for an insight into what people felt in those years.

Surveys of other Irish writers can be found in 'Anthologies of Irish Writing' (2001) and 'History in the Making: Irish Writing in 2007–9'. After the publication of *Irish Writing in the Twentieth Century: A Reader* (1999) I was invited by the *British Association for Irish Studies* to reflect on anthologies of Irish writing and on how I went about constructing my own anthology (which I called a Reader). The other survey I undertook for *estudiosirlandeses.org*, an Irish studies internet journal then based at the University of Barcelona and now at the University of Almería. Every year for five years I acted as a general editor for the Literature section and invited reviews for particular books from contributors around the world. In addition I provided a general survey of books that caught my eye during the previous year. The chapter included here has been revised to make more of Joyce's presence, a writer with a continuing legacy who is never far from the centre of modern Irish writing.

'History in the Making: Irish Writing in 2007–9' ranges widely over books published in these turbulent years when the banking crisis and the Catholic Church's involvement in the sexual abuse of children took centre stage. History was on the move again, threatening to overthrow traditional values and destroy the country's sense of itself. As I suggested at the time, 'If anyone needed evidence that the Celtic Tiger was in terminal decline, 2008 was the year that proved conclusively that we are at the end of something – though, in truth, any year in the previous five or so gave good indications. Yet, equally it is the case that we are at the start of something both inside and outside

Ireland.' As is often the case, literature takes time to catch up with events, but there were signs that Irish writing at this time, drawing on the important place in the culture assigned to the writer as witness, was able to respond to this new world with some success. In this way the writing contributed to history in the making.

In the first section I spend time discussing in particular a number of publications including Paul Durcan's *The Laughter of Mothers* (2007), the plays of Edna Walsh, Joseph O'Neill's *Netherland* (2008), the fiction and drama of Sebastian Barry, and a lengthy, new discussion of Seamus Heaney's 'Station Island' on the occasion of the publication of *Stepping Stones: Interviews with Seamus Heaney* (2008). 'Station Island', first published in 1984, is a long sequence in which the poet undertakes a traditional pilgrimage to the island associated with St Patrick in Lough Derg. From the start, his conscience is assaulted by all kinds of memories and misgivings including his lack of involvement in politics after the murder of his cousin, Colum McCartney. But in the final section the poet gains comfort when he meets the spectre of James Joyce, who tells him to keep at a tangent and swim out on his own.

The second section focuses on Irish Writing in 2009. This was a year dominated by Irish correspondence, and I spend time discussing *The Letters of Samuel Beckett 1929–1940*, the correspondence between Elizabeth Bowen and her lover, Charles Ritchie, and a new edition of the letters of Laurence Sterne, edited by Melvyn New and Peter de Voogd. Sterne's connection with Joyce has been frequently commented upon. When he began composing *Finnegans Wake*, Joyce we know, from a conversation with Eugene Jolas, had Sterne in mind, for his book, too, was an attempt 'to build many planes of narrative with a single esthetic purpose. Did you ever read Laurence Sterne?'[23] Whenever Sterne is mentioned in *Finnegans Wake*, he is invariably in the company of Jonathan Swift, most famously when he is linked with other Irish writers in a list which invokes a tradition: 'your wildeshaweshow moves swiftly sterneward' (*FW* 256.13–4). Equally, Joyce was the first person to suggest what now seems obvious, that in the scheme of

23 Eugene Jolas, 'My Friend James Joyce' in Sean Givens (ed.), *James Joyce: Two Decades of Criticism* (New York: Vanguard Press, 1948), 12.

things Sterne and Swift had been assigned the wrong surnames, for Swift is stern, and Sterne is swift. Part of Sterne's childhood was spent in County Wicklow, where his father's regiment was stationed, and, as legend has it, he nearly died in an accident by being caught up in the mill-race at Anamoe. He never forgot his Irish roots, although he never quite overcame a certain ambivalence towards Ireland. What caught my attention in his correspondence was a reference to the real-life incident that seems to lie behind Yorick's encounter with the Monk in *A Sentimental Journey*, and how the abbé who came to the aid of Richard Oswald, a young Englishman dying of consumption in Toulouse, was of Irish descent and called not O'Leary but O'Leari. It is an incident that reminds us of Sterne's complex fate as an Anglican cleric particularly in terms of his identity and his religion; periodically, he was forced to confront his Irish past and his attitude in the present to Catholic Europe.

Beckett insisted that only those letters pertinent to his published work should be made available, so there are no letters between Joyce's daughter, Lucia, and Beckett, which is a shame, for it would be nice to hear her voice. Beckett had a complicated attitude to Joyce, whom he called not 'Mr Joyce' but 'Shem' as if the two were close. But a reference to his own writing 'stinking' of Joyce reminds us of his need to swerve away from the father figure. The letters also shed light on the domestic life of the great man. After an evening at the Joyces in early January 1938, Beckett observes, 'He was sublime last night, deprecating with the utmost conviction his lack of talent'. Bowen's personal correspondence contains a series of sharp observations into the state of post-war Britain, as well as into the social scene in London, the city she loved more than any other. As for her snobbish, Anglo-Irish attitudes, she is quite capable of self-mockery in the manner of her class, as when, coming away from a morning shopping at Harvey Nichols, she imagines the clothes she has bought might look like 'a plate of dessert'.

I have divided Reviews into six chapters: chapter 7 Joyce's European Cities; chapter 8 Joyce, Yeats and the Matter of Ireland; chapter 9 Joyce and Modernism; chapter 10 *Ulysses* in Perspective; chapter 11 On Collections of Essays; and chapter 12 On a Personal

Note. In Joyce, Yeats and the Matter of Ireland I take the opportunity to group together six different books which are concerned in part with Joyce and Yeats, either separately or together. Two books on Yeats and Joyce were published in the Macmillan author chronology series, which enabled me to reflect on their lives and how they are shaped through the eyes of two modern critics. Alistair Cormack considers the issue of cyclical history in their writing, while Frank Shovlin, in a detailed study of *Dubliners*, underlines the Irishness of the stories. The first issue of a new journal devoted to Joyce, *Dublin James Joyce Journal Issue 1* (2008), has much to recommend it with essays on 'Araby', 'After the Race', and an investigation into Alfred H. Hunter, once thought to be a model for Bloom. *Voices on Joyce* (2015) offers a wide-ranging and informative survey from different disciplines associated with University College Dublin, Joyce being their most famous pupil.

Chapter 9, Joyce and Modernism, is a topic that continues to attract very different perspectives. In *Joyce's Web* (1992), Margot Norris is concerned with raveling and unraveling. Joyce is a modern Penelope unraveling 'the modernistic formalism that consolidates his power as an artist of the dominant culture'; his texts possess 'an ideological self-correction aimed specifically at the socially empowering features of its own aesthetic modernism'.[24] Her dispute, well-captured in the image of the web, is essentially with Eliot and his characterisation of Joyce's use of Homeric myth in *Ulysses* as 'a step toward making the modern world possible for art'.[25] A form of raveling and unraveling continues in *James Joyce and the Act of Reception* (2006), where John Nash argues that throughout his career Joyce was not only responding to his audiences but also incorporating those responses into his creative work. This is especially true of early responses to *Ulysses*, as *Finnegans Wake* Notebook VI.B.6 reminds us. Nash's argument is with reader-response theory, which as he notes 'remains profoundly troubled by reading as a historical act', and with Jacques Derrida, who 'favours

24 Margot Norris, *Joyce's Web: The Social Unraveling of Modernism* (Austin, TX: University of Texas Press, 1992), 7.
25 T.S. Eliot, '*Ulysses*, Order and Myth' in *Selected Prose of T.S. Eliot* selected by Frank Kermode (London: Faber, 1975), 178.

the textuality of deconstruction over its historical formulation'.[26] His thesis is advanced in the various Irish contexts of revivalism, religion and the university question, and the new State that emerged in Ireland in the 1920s.

According to Paul Stasi in *Modernism, Imperialism, and the Historical Sense* (2012), modernist writers such as Eliot, Pound, Joyce, and Woolf not only emerged alongside imperialism, they forged something new from their own grounding in it. His chapter on *Ulysses* begins by challenging the view that the nightmare view of history is the whole story. For Stasi, 'the task in the periphery is to locate some form of agency within an omnipresent relationship of dependence'.[27] With its subtitle, *Ireland, Modernism, and Memory*, Luke Gibbons's *Joyce's Ghosts* is a sophisticated attempt to claim that Joyce's Irishness is intrinsic to his modernism. The ghosts he has in mind are the spectres and hauntings and cultural memories that inhabit Joyce's work, not only in 'The Dead' but also in *Ulysses*. Focusing on a cluster of ideas identified as vernacular idiom and free indirect discourse, inner speech, and interiority, his aim is to show how Joyce belongs to his country of origins, now defined not as provincial or parochial but as central to the emergence of modernism and to our understanding of modernity. Four such sophisticated responses to modernism serve as a reminder that history is never simply background when it comes to Joyce and, equally, that it remains a challenge to place him against his background.

Chapter 10, *Ulysses* in Perspective, gathers together four reviews of a book that is never out of the headlines. Terence Killeen's *Ulysses Unbound* (2004) has for its subtitle *A Reader's Companion to James Joyce's 'Ulysses'*. With the student in mind, Killeen tackles each episode in turn, gathering his material under various headings: plot summary, Homeric correspondences, style, commentary, biographical/historical information and glossary. What Joyce, through long years of writing and revising, had bound together the commentator unbinds, but in

---

26 John Nash, *James Joyce and the Act of Reception* (Cambridge: Cambridge University Press, 2006), 18 and 167.

27 Paul Stasi, *Modernism, Imperialism, and the Historical Sense* (Cambridge: Cambridge Univerrsity Press, 2012), 90.

this case with a lightness of touch frequently missing from other student guides. Patrick McGee's *Paperspace: Style as Ideology in Joyce's Ulysses* (1988) was written when the new theories of deconstruction, Lacanian psychoanalysis, and reader-response were at their height. Of all the books reviewed here this is without doubt the most challenging and it remains something special. I have added considerably to my original review, in part to clarify the argument for the general reader but also to expand on my engagement with the book. It opens with a declaration: *Paperspace* 'conducts a dialogue with the positions of Lacanian psychoanalysis, deconstruction, feminism, and contemporary Marxism'.[28] A deconstructive critic, McGee is keen also to assert a political dimension to his account, and thus distances himself from, among others, the editors of *Post-structuralist Joyce* (1984), whom he accuses of a fetishism of the text; from Wolfgang Iser, who stresses the gaps in reading but not in the reader; and from Colin MacCabe, whom he links with a contemporary critical bias against interpretation.[29] For McGee, 'interpreting Joyce is not *politically* negligible' (8).

Andras Ungar's *Joyce's 'Ulysses' as National Epic: Epic Mimesis and the Political History of the Nation State* (2002) is also challenging but for different reasons. His focus is 1904, the date on which *Ulysses* is set, seen now through the lens of 1922, the year when the Irish Free State came into existence. Part of Ungar's argument is that *Ulysses* 'locates the fortunes of Irish national renewal in the conjunction of its characterization of Stephen Dedalus and its incorporation of the historical argument...of Arthur Griffith's *The Resurrection of Hungary: A Parallel for Ireland* (1904)', that 'the fable... of Stephen and Bloom enacts the drama of nation and hope'.[30] Before this study appeared,

28 Patrick McGee, *Paperspace: Style as Ideology in Joyce's Ulysses* (Lincoln, NE and London: University of Nebraska Press, 1988), 1.
29 Derek Attridge and Daniel Ferrer (eds), *Post-structuralist Joyce* (Cambridge: Cambridge University Press, 1984). Wolfgang Iser, *The Implied Reader: Patterns of Communication in Prose Fiction from Bunyan to Beckett* (Baltimore: Johns Hopkins University Press, 1974). Colin MacCabe, *James Joyce and the Revolution of the Word* (London: Macmillan, 1978).
30 Andras Ungar, *Joyce's 'Ulysses' as National Epic: Epic Mimesis and the Political History of the Nation State* ((Gainesville, FL: University Press of Florida, 2002), 13.

no-one had devoted so much attention to how this might be the case, and what he brings to the topic is his Hungarian family background and an emphasis not on Homer but on Virgil (and Camões) as the epic creators and exemplars behind *Ulysses*.

No collection of recent Joyce reviews would be complete without consideration of the new field of genetic criticism. Luca Crispi's *Joyce's Creative Process and the Construction of Characters in Ulysses: Becoming the Blooms* (2015) is a fine example of genetic criticism in practice, and I have undertaken a long review specifically for *The Joyce Country*. In 2002–6, the National Library of Ireland purchased a previously unknown cache of manuscripts, which in the words of the author 'contained the earliest known *Ulysses* notebook and draft, as well as two manuscripts that chronicle a crucial, relatively late phase of Joyce's work on *Ulysses* in 1921'.[31] This cache has the potential to change the way we read *Ulysses*, but it takes someone like Crispi, who knows how to handle such material, to make it available to a wide readership. This is a richly rewarding book, which encourages us to perceive how the 'text of *Ulysses* has its origins and foundations in all of its manuscripts' (36). His thesis in brief is that the new drafts reveal a novel which has for its twin themes adultery and the lovemaking between Leopold and Molly Bloom on Howth Head in 1888. Boylan carries a stronger presence than previously thought, so much so that Crispi imagines 'Boylansday' should be added to 'Bloomsday' when we talk about *Ulysses*. In the final rush to get his book published on his birthday in February 1922, Joyce kept changing and inserting material, especially evident in his last episode, 'Penelope'. Crispi makes effective use of this new material to present an original and engaging account of how we might read the novel anew. At the same time I have taken this opportunity to offer some general observations on genetic criticism in terms of both its strengths and its limitations.

Chapter 11, On Collections of Essays, opens with reviews of two editions of *The Cambridge Companion to James Joyce*, edited by Derek Attridge and published in 1990 and 2004. The 1990 *Companion* consists

---

31 Luca Crispi, *Joyce's Creative Process and the Construction of Characters in Ulysses: Becoming the Blooms* (Oxford: Oxford University Press, 2015), 6.

of eleven critical and contextual essays by leading contemporary Joyce critics. The opening essay by Attridge on 'Reading Joyce' consists of an illuminating discussion of two passages, one from 'Eveline', the other from Book II of *Finnegans Wake* (359.31–360.06). Jean-Michel Rabaté's essay on Joyce and Paris, which really belongs to Joyce's European Cities, reminds us that Joyce invented the French heritage he modestly claimed for himself. This is an intelligent and humorous account of the 'paleoparisien' (*FW* 151.9), the arch-Parisian, who felt a primordial calling to live in the French capital. Hans Walter Gabler's essay on 'Joyce's Text in Progress' is concerned with the 'retextualisation of pre-text', how Joyce is a reader of his own text, 'Penelope' being a 'final rewriting from a re-reading of the pre-text of *Ulysses* itself'.[32] In 'Joyce and Feminism', Karen Lawrence defends Joyce against the charge of Sandra Gilbert and Susan Gubar that his language represents the triumph of a patriarchal literary heritage.

Hovering over the first edition was the theme of recycling, finely articulated by Margot Norris in her essay on *Finnegans Wake*, a work which constitutes 'the dream of his earlier texts' (169). Indeed, in advance of the rise in Joyce studies of genetic criticism, the idea of 'Ur-texts' can be observed throughout this volume. A decade and a half later, three essays have been dropped and five added. The new essays which stand out are Joe Valente's on Joyce in the light of queer theory, and Jennifer Wicke's, which provides a fresh inquiry into consumerism and Joyce. In an intelligent essay on postcolonial Joyce, Margaret Howes makes the useful suggestion that *Dubliners* possesses a diasporic imagination.

Renascent Joyce (2013), edited by Daniel Ferrer, Sam Slote and André Topia, begins with a striking assertion: 'No single perspective can do justice to such a multifaceted writer: next to the medieval Joyce, the modernist Joyce, the Irish Joyce, the European Joyce… we must learn to make room for a Renaissance Joyce'.[33] The terms

---

32 Hans Walter Gabler, 'Joyce's Text in Progress' in *The Cambridge Companion to James Joyce* (ed. Derek Attridge) (Cambridge: Cambridge University Press, 1990), 232.

33 Daniel Ferrer, Sam Slote and André Topia (eds), *Renascent Joyce* (Gainesville, FL: University Press of Florida, 2015), 2.

'Renascent' and 'Renaissance' constantly occur in a study full of suggestive insights, which includes essays on the Greek spirit in modernism, *A Midsummer Night's Dream*, the presence of Epicurean atomistic philosophy in Renaissance thought, the first French translation of *Ulysses*, and Paul Saint-Amour's stimulating essay on the depiction of the future in *Ulysses*.

The fiftieth anniversary volume of the *'James Joyce Quarterly 50 Years Vol 50 No 1–2 Fall 2012–Winter 2013'* contains an important survey of some of the best essays in Joyce studies over this period. Under each of the three editors, Tom Staley (1963–1989), Robert Spoo (1989–1999), and since then Sean Latham, the *James Joyce Quarterly* has succeeded in becoming what Spoo characterises as a 'single-author journal with an anti-cyclopean soul'.[34] Many of the leading Joyce critics are represented here including Hugh Kenner, Fritz Senn, Florence L. Walzl, Michael Groden, and Margot Norris.

Chapter 12, On a Personal Note, gathers together reviews of books dealing with correspondence or autobiographical material. *A Passion For Joyce* (2008) contains the exchange of letters between two of the leading Joyce critics of their generation, Hugh Kenner and Adaline Glasheen. Glasheen's own contribution to Joyce studies can be observed in *A Census of 'Finnegans Wake'*, which went through three editions.[35] She never lost her sense that the book was fun. As she explained to Kenner in a letter dated 24 August 1954, 'If it isn't funny, it isn't anything, is it?'[36] *A Kick Against the Pricks* (2012) is the title of a larger-than-life autobiography by the Irish Senator, Joyce scholar and gay campaigner, David Norris. To complete this section I have included *Modern Irish Autobiography: Self, Nation and Society* (2007),

---

34 Robert Spoo, 'Preparatory to a Retrospective Arrangement' in *James Joyce Quarterly 50 Years Vol 50 No 1–2 Fall 2012–Winter 2013*, 181.

35 Adaline Glasheen, *A Census of 'Finnegans Wake': An Index of the Characters and Their Roles* (London: Faber and Faber, 1956; London: Faber and Faber, 1957), and *Third Census of 'Finnegans Wake': An Index of the Characters and Their Roles* (Berkeley: University of California Press, 1977).

36 Edward M. Burns (ed.), *A Passion For Joyce: The Letters of Hugh Kenner and Adaline Glasheen* (Dublin: University College Dublin Press, 2008), 20.

a collection of informative essays edited by Liam Harte. The topic remains surprisingly under-researched, but here we can read about *The Merry Wanderer* (1725), a witty play by Mary Davys on the Irish emigrant in Britain, John Mitchel's *Jail Journal* (1854), autobiographical writings by women such as Kate O'Brien and Elizabeth Bowen, and Barry Sloan's thoughtful survey of Irish Protestant autobiographies.

The books on Joyce included here represent part of the worldwide Joyce community, but they are, inevitably, only a part. His readers, his enthusiastic readers, and some who would like to be such, grow in numbers with each passing year. Many critics address only themselves and the critical community, but there are others who would like to reach out to a wider audience. As I reflect on the reviews and essays here I hope I have not let down this wider audience, for I have taken care to explain contexts and ideas which might not be familiar to the ordinary reader and non-specialist in Joyce studies.

If there is a single thing Joyce teaches us it is patience. I expressed as much to the grandson of one of Joyce's sisters when I met him for coffee in the spring of 2016. He was delighted to hear me speak so warmly about his relation and John Joyce, Joyce's father. Their reputation preceded them and followed them, for they were for a long time not the favourite members of the family. 'All too Irish' is how a disconsolate Stephen described his father in the cabman's shelter in *Ulysses*. (*U* 16:384) My companion responded particularly to my informing him that humour was Joyce's saving grace. He confirmed what I already knew about the sport of cricket, for this is what he remembers his grandmother repeatedly telling him. I wanted to make my own small contribution to his family history by suggesting that it was cricket and humour that gave Joyce patience, the ability to laugh in the face of adversity and to watch a game of cricket unwind over the course of six hours on a summer's day or over five days if it was a Test match. Of course in real life Joyce could be ill-tempered and litigious, but anyone who spent nearly a quarter of a century and nearly half his life composing *Ulysses* and *Finnegans Wake* must have possessed patience in abundance. When I look at Joyce I do not look to him for being a good family member or a good citizen. He possesses little by the way of saintliness, and one would have difficulty in thinking he is a candidate for the priesthood of art, for there's no redemption there either. However, what I do admire is stamina, stamina not only for transforming the way we look at novels but also for what he did with words. The delight in reading Joyce, and the same is true of Shakespeare, is a delight in showing us the resources of the language we are lucky to inhabit.

ESSAYS AND LECTURES

CHAPTER 1

A NEW DEPARTURE FOR FICTION: *A PORTRAIT OF THE ARTIST AS A YOUNG MAN*

Doing things differently is the hallmark of the Joyce country. He rarely conformed to expectations, and he sometimes confused himself in the swerves he enjoyed making. He once enigmatically declared that he was against every state, but when he contrasted the state with the artist, he muddied the waters by assigning a political meaning to the word 'eccentric': 'The state is concentric, man is eccentric.'[37] Hence, the 'eccentric' man holds meaning only in relation to the 'concentric' state. Two-thirds of his life were spent outside of Ireland, but, on picking up his pen, Joyce never stopped writing about his native city and country. In the 1920s, after Irish passports became available, he never applied for one, preferring instead to travel under a British passport. He was, as he describes Shem in *Finnegans Wake,* 'An Irish emigrant the wrong way out' (*FW* 190.36). Following his death, there was nothing in his will to prevent his wife, Nora Joyce, from donating the *Finnegans Wake* manuscripts not to the National Library of Ireland but to the British Library in London. 'Déjeuner *Ulysse*' was a lunch organised in Paris by

---

37 Cited in Richard Ellmann, *James Joyce* (Oxford: Oxford University Press, 1982), 446.

Adrienne Monnier in June 1929 to celebrate the first French translation of the novel, and it was held in the company of France's leading literary figures including Paul Valéry and Édouard Dujardin, the novelist who was a key player in the emergence of the stream-of-consciousness technique. They were surprised, but perhaps should not have been, when Joyce refused to allow speeches. A private man who enjoyed socialising, he allowed few to address him as 'Jim'. As noted in the Introduction, he made an exception to Beckett, who called him 'Shem', but to everyone else he was the formal 'Mr Joyce'. As for his genius, he gave the impression that he could do anything with words, but in later life he was given to self-deprecation, and when Yeats died in 1939 Joyce expressed the view that, of the two, the poet was the greater writer.

FICTIONAL OPENINGS

Doing things differently also applied to his fiction. If we compare the opening of *A Portrait of the Artist as a Young Man* (1916) with Sterne's eighteenth-century novel, *The Life and Opinions of Tristram Shandy, Gentleman* (1759–65), and Dickens's Victorian novel, *David Copperfield* (1850), we can quickly discern not only how the three novels belong together as a group but also what distinguishes Joyce as a writer of modern fiction. Here is Sterne:

> I wish either my father or my mother, or indeed both
> of them, as they were in duty both equally bound to it,
> had minded what they were about when they begot
> me; had they duly consider'd how much depended
> upon what they were then doing;—that not only the
> production of a rational Being was concern'd in it, but
> that possibly the happy formation and temperature
> of his body, perhaps his genius and the very cast of
> his mind;—and, for aught they knew to the contrary,
> even the fortunes of his whole house might take
> their turn from the humours and dispositions which
> were then uppermost:—— Had they duly weighed

and considered all this, and proceeded accordingly,
I am verily persuaded I should have made a quite
different figure in the world, from that, in which the
reader is likely to see me.[38]

This thoroughly entertaining, 'modern' or 'postmodern' novel, which
begins nine months before the hero is born, was described by the
Russian Formalist, Victor Shklovsky, as the 'most typical novel of
world literature'.[39] In an essay exploring the connection between
fiction and history, Carole Watt has suggested that *Tristram Shandy* is
'postmodernist in every sense except the moment in which it was
written'.[40] The connection between fiction and history is always worth
pondering, but here I want to touch on something else. *Tristram Shandy*
is full of innuendo and humour, and this is especially apparent in the
astonishingly prolix opening sentence. Here the humour resides not
only in the way Sterne delays coming to a conclusion but also in the
conceit that Tristram hopes his parents gave some consideration during
the moment of conception to the person he now is. The comic note is
continued when we learn that, in the first piece of dialogue, set out in
italics and without speech marks, his mother innocently asks, *Pray, my
Dear*, quoth my mother, *have you not forgot to wind up the clock*? Mother
and father are 'bound' together to 'beget' Tristram, but this is also a
moment when the mechanical world intervenes to remind them of
their sexual needs and their role or otherwise in procreation.

At the end of the seventeenth century, John Locke outlined his view
that the individual is born with a *tabula rasa*, a clean slate. Locke held
that there are no innate principles in the mind, that 'the mind is fitted to

38 Laurence Sterne, *The Life and Opinions of Tristram Shandy, Gentleman* (ed.
Ian Campbell Ross) (1759–65; Oxford University Press, 2000).
39 Victor Shklovsky, 'Sterne's *Tristram Shandy: A Stylistic Commentary*' in L. T.
Lemon, M. J. Reiss (eds), *Russian Formalist Criticism* (Lincoln, NE: University of
Nebraska Press, 1965), 57.
40 Carole Watt, 'The Modernity of Sterne' in David Pierce and Peter de Voogd
(eds), *Laurence Sterne in Modernism and Postmodernism* (Amsterdam: Rodopi,
1996), 26.

receive the impressions made on it; either through the senses by outward objects, or by its operations when it reflects on them'.[41] His theory of knowledge commanded widespread support, so readers in the middle of the eighteenth century knew immediately from Sterne's opening to *Tristram Shandy* that he was making a serio-comic point about the father of English empiricism. The accumulation of impressions and sensations in the opening sentence is designed to undercut Locke's influential theory. Closer to conversation than to writing, the sentence is governed by a phrase that expresses a mature mind talking to us. 'I wish'. Here is a rational being already in process, his happiness and his 'genius' dependent on this moment, the mind therefore already in receipt of something in advance of any so-called external experience. The opening to *Tristram Shandy* is not only comic but also philosophical in the extreme, therefore. Even the clock, a symbol of duration and a potent image in its own way of a rational ordered universe, belongs to an intellectual context we know as associationism. Such a philosophical theory concerning the mind and how it processes thoughts not so much by reason as by association was an idea advanced in the eighteenth century by one of Locke's successors, David Hume. Sterne, of course, takes the theory to another level by humorously including in 'association' such rhetorical devices as parenthesis, irony, metaphor, bathos, exaggeration, anacoluthon, anaphora, contingency, pleonasm, to name but a few on display in this opening sentence.

Nothing escapes Sterne's 'seminar' on philosophy. The epigraph to the novel borrows a quotation from Epictetus, which includes the word dogmata or judgment:

Ταρασσει τούς Άνθρώπους ού τὰ Πράγματα,
αλλα τὰ περι τῶν Πραγμάτων, Δογματα.

It is not events [pragmata] themselves that trouble people, but, rather, their judgements [dogmata] on those events or circumstances. The novel's title leads us to expect we are embarking on a life of

---

41 John Locke, *An Essay Concerning Human Understanding* (1689; London: Penguin, 1997), 120. Section 24 'The Original of all our Knowledge.'

Tristram, but, even after nine volumes devoted to this *shandean* or whimsical journey, we never get beyond his childhood. On the other hand the novel is full of judgements and opinions, many belonging to Uncle Toby and his various comical hobby horses. However, Uncle Toby's judgements are not opinions as that word was used in the eighteenth century, where it implied a considered opinion. After noting the epigraph and turning over the page, the reader then encounters the first two words of the novel, 'I wish'. Such a phrase should be not be a matter for dispute. It is, after all, a wish, but, depending on one's philosophical position, it may be considered an opinion.

When we turn to Dickens, we encounter an equally arresting opening to *David Copperfield* which carries an echo of Sterne's *Tristram Shandy*:

> Whether I shall turn out to be the hero of my own life, or whether that station will be held by anybody else, these pages must show. To begin my life with the beginning of my life, I record that I was born (as I have been informed and believe) on a Friday, at twelve o'clock at night. It was remarked that the clock began to strike, and I began to cry, simultaneously.[42]

From the moment we alight on the title to the first chapter, 'I Am Born', Dickens has designs on our emotions rather than on our intellect. The full title to the novel, *The Personal History of David Copperfield*, is a way of enforcing this, for it is not just a history but a personal history. David is a 'posthumous child' and born with a membrane over his head, so, both figuratively and literally, the boy's past is all around him. If Dickens had called his first chapter not 'I am Born' or 'I was born' but 'I am Thrown into Existence', we would recognise immediately his philosophical position. But, a century too early and not having to hand an existentialist vocabulary of Søren Kierkegaard or Martin Heidegger, he reminds us of his own remarkable insight into the human predicament. 'I am Born' is

---

42 Charles Dickens, *David Copperfield* (ed. Nina Burgis) (1850; Oxford: Oxford University Press, 2008), 1.

a sentence which could never have been uttered by any child but which, at the same time, conveys a familiar cry of assertiveness: 'Take note, I am here.' Dickens is seeking our active involvement not in a philosophical discourse but in his story, a story that begins with a search for narrative perspective, ownership, and the appropriate kind of tone. Behind the opening we might hear *Puer Natus Est*, the Church's motet in the third person announcing for an already established community the birth of Jesus, 'a boy is born'. But Dickens insists on something else, namely the first person, attention-seeking, serio-comic, tongue-in-cheek assertion of the would-be hero of his own narrative: 'I am Born'. This is one of the most intriguing openings by a writer who shared much with his protagonist, and it signals that *David Copperfield* is to be a novel about identity, the girl who is born a boy or the boy who should have been a girl according to his aunt Betsey Trotwood Copperfield.

A Portrait of the Artist as a Young Man begins some time after the hero is born and is filtered through the presence of the father:

> Once upon a time and a very good time it was there was a moocow coming down along the road and this moocow that was coming down along the road met a nicens little boy named baby tuckoo…
> His father told him that story: his father looked at him through a glass: he had a hairy face.
> He was baby tuckoo.

Even though 'he' supplants 'I' in this introduction, the opening is much closer than we find either in Sterne or in Dickens to a boy's perspective and to a father's way of speaking to a child. It begins with a father telling his son a fairy tale (or a hairy tale), but we soon realise that the formulaic expression slips into a story about a cow meeting a little boy who turns out to be the person being addressed. This is followed by the insertion of elliptical points. Such points are presumably designed to suggest a story which is not remembered, or perhaps this is how his father would regularly begin his invented baby stories. The switch to a third-person narrator is then filtered through the boy's perspective as he notices his father's 'glass' and his hairy face. There is then another switch, this time to a half-realised reflection on the part of the boy as to his identity in the opening fairy tale.

Tracing such an opening takes longer to describe than actually to read, which is a sure sign of the narrative's density and complexity. No allowance is made, but most readers follow the narrative voice as it shifts from the perspective of the boy to the dialogue of his father to some other figure who might be a third-person narrator. We sense there might be a tension between the narrative point of view and the linguistic representation of subjectivity, but we are not sure. Equally, there is no evidence at this stage of free indirect discourse or of 'The Uncle Charles Principle', which Kenner defined as 'the narrative idiom need not be the narrator's'.[43] Sterne's opening carries a philosophical stamp and Dickens a psychological one. Joyce's opening has another kind of stamp, which is not readily subsumed under the heading of an academic subject. Its complex narrative – closer to writing than to the conversational idiom we find in Sterne – is governed not so much by philosophy or psychology or sociology, but by the emergence or the fall of the self into the world of consciousness. Put briefly, the opening to *A Portrait* is not so much concerned with an individual's identity as the awakening of the self. It could be argued that, while David's trauma is immediately observable, Stephen's fate is unknown and that being held at a distance is simply a narrative device. But there is merit to my mind in distinguishing the two fictional characters in terms of consciousness rather than personality. After all, the writing is special but perhaps the same cannot be said about the boy who makes his appearance at the beginning of *A Portrait*.

CONSCIOUSNESS AS A THEME

While Joyce is not primarily interested in contemporary philosophy or the phenomenology associated, for example, with Edmund Husserl,

---

43 Hugh Kenner, *Joyce's Voices* (Berkeley, CA and London: University of California Press, 1978), 18. Uncle Charles appears in the opening to chapter 2 of *A Portrait*, where, every morning, he 'repaired to his outhouse'.

at the root of Joyce's writing is a concern with how the world is structured and constructed. Consciousness informs all his writing. This is the new departure for fiction, one which paid special attention to the subtle workings of consciousness and how to capture it in writing. Joyce would have agreed with Locke when he claims that '[c] onsciousness is the perception of what passes in a man's own mind', and linked to personal identity.[44] But nothing quite prepares us for the modern predicament that now confronts the individual. Simply expressed, consciousness is never free from a continuous entanglement with the world. If we leave on one side the issue of personal identity, the problem lies in our (in)ability to keep separate perception and consciousness. In this regard what we encounter in Joyce is not so much Eliot's characterisation of the craft of writing in *East Coker* (1940) as a 'raid on the inarticulate' but an appreciation of the power of language in determining how the world is held together.[45]

Locke's clarity of mind meant that consciousness could be defined in largely straightforward terms. The modern world is much more aware of things that threaten such simplicity, and we find ourselves attracted to Paul Cezanne's paintings, which emphasise the *how* as much as *what* we perceive. Or, as Cezanne once famously remarked, 'Painting from nature is not copying the object; it is realizing one's sensations.'[46] Such a remark recalls the 'inside-out' view of reality mentioned in the Introduction. We are equally attracted to Pablo Picasso's use of distortion. Joyce was living in Zurich when Tristan Tzara, Hans Arp and the Dadaist movement were active, and, when he came to write *Finnegans Wake* in the 1920s, from the outset he systematically applied a 'warping process' (*FW* 497.3) to language and reality. Locke would not have agreed but today we are more inclined to believe that we are part of what passes through our minds and that we rarely if ever rise above the subject's position in language.

---

44 John Locke, *An Essay Concerning Human Understanding* (1689; London: Penguin, 1997), 118 and 302–3.
45 T.S.Eliot, *East Coker* (London: Faber and Faber, 1940), 14.
46 Cited in Richard Kendall, *Cezanne By Himself* (London: TimeWarner, 2004), 203.

CHAPTER 1

There is a passage in Hughes's *Consciousness and Society* which is germane to the distinction between Joyce and his predecessors:

> I am not writing a literary history. But in our century I think it is apparent that imaginative literature – and more particularly the novel – has come to play a rather more serious and self-conscious role in the enunciation of values than was the case in the two preceding centuries. On the major novel or play has devolved the task of making concrete and thereby more readily approachable the abstract insights of the philosophers and social scientists. Imaginative literature… has done a great deal more than this: it has surrounded its depiction of society with a penumbra of symbol and suggestion that has resisted explicit categorization.[47]

In his discussion of literature, Hughes confines himself to discussing European writers such as André Gide, Hermann Hesse, Thomas Mann, Marcel Proust and Luigi Pirandello. Although Joyce is mentioned only once, Hughes could not have expressed more succinctly an important context for understanding him. Social scientists such as Emile Durkheim and Max Weber, philosophers such as Henri Bergson, and psychoanalysts such as Sigmund Freud and Carl Jung, formulated abstract insights into the modern world, but it was left to writers to make the theory available to the wider public.

As is apparent in the opening passage to *A Portrait*, there is an emphasis on consciousness, which is signalled in the attempt at self-consciousness on the part of the boy and with what we might be tempted to recognise as the consciousness of an absent narrator. According to Hughes, the issue which tormented Joyce's contemporaries was 'how to recapture the immediacy of past experience' (65). If we knew what happened before the novel begins, or what was in Joyce's mind,

47 H. Stuart Hughes, *Consciousness and Society: The Reorientation of European Social Thought 1890–1930* revised edition (1958; New York: Vintage, 1977), 21.

11

Hughes could have been describing Joyce's opening. 'The 1890s generation', as they are described by Hughes, were 'in revolt against positivism', that is 'the whole tendency to discuss human behaviour in terms of analogies drawn from natural science' (37). The analysis of society needed a more sophisticated analysis than was to be found in Auguste Comte's positivism or Social Darwinism or various forms of materialism, and it needed an inquiry which did justice to surface and depth. Freud's psychoanalysis, to take a parallel case to the social sciences, assumes there is a gap between symptom and explanation and that what a person says, for example, can betray something else. Freud, ever alert to investigating the past in the present, developed the idea of the unconscious, Joyce the conscious, but the two are related in this central concern with interior states of mind and with how we structure the world.[48]

From the outset a Joyce text presents us with a surface that acquires meaning through resistance. In this sense we might recall the marble page in *Tristram Shandy*, the emblem of Sterne's work, which calls out to be interpreted and applied but which yet resists our interpretation. It is not always clear where to locate the origins of the resistance in Joyce, but we know that the surface meaning cannot be enough, that there is another level below the surface or somewhere adjacent to the surface. The absence of the author is potentially significant in this regard. As Stephen later informs Lynch, and he could be speaking for the author at this point: 'The artist, like the God of creation, remains within or behind or beyond or above his handiwork, invisible, refined out of existence, indifferent, paring his fingernails.' (*P* 215) Joyce is frequently linked with Flaubert in terms of fictional technique.[49] Indeed, the quotation about 'refined out of existence' and invisibility

---

48 For a brief discussion of Joyce and Freud, see Jean Kimball's essay 'Growing Up Together: Joyce and Psychoanalysis 1900–1922' in Michael Patrick Gillespie (ed.), *Joyce Through the Ages: A Non-Linear View* (Gainesville, FL: University Press of Florida, 1999), 25–45.

49 For a wide-ranging discussion on Joyce and Flaubert, see Scarlett Baron, *Strandentwining Cable: Joyce, Flaubert and Intertextuality* (Oxford: Oxford University Press, 2012).

echoes a comment by the French novelist. But there must be more to Joyce's direction of travel than simply technique. What would be the point of playing God when you are not God and when you are intent on reaching an audience for your work and intervening in the world? So hiding behind the surface of a text reflects some ulterior purpose or motivation, which requires investigation.

Hughes's comment on the 'enunciation of values' also needs further analysis in the case of Joyce. In my Introduction I stress Joyce's commitment to civic rather than to ethnic nationalism, for these, above all, are the values he espoused. The Willingdone Museum passage in *Finnegans Wake* captures Joyce's antipathy to war. He shared many of Bloom's liberal values even as he occasionally mocked them. At the beginning of his career, he admired the plays of Henrik Ibsen, the writer who dramatised the struggles of the individual confronting the limits of bourgeois society. Joyce's only play, *Exiles* (1918), is indebted to Ibsen for its setting, dialogue, and for its theme of adultery and betrayal. In a revealing passage in *Stephen Hero*, we can perhaps detect the accents of his Norwegian hero while at the same time noticing his distance from the master: 'He wished to express his nature freely and fully for the benefit of a society which he would enrich and also for his own benefit, seeing that it was part of his life to do so. It was not part of his life to undertake an extensive alteration of society…' (*SH* 151). In many ways this was Joyce's mantra throughout his writing career: through writing he would enrich society, but at the same time he pulled back from the 'alteration of society'.

Faithfulness to experience and realistic texture are the hallmark of his early fiction, and they reflect important values. In defending the stories of what became his collection, *Dubliners*, Joyce claimed that 'he is a very bold man who dares to alter in the presentment, still more to deform, whatever he has seen and heard' (*Letters II* 134). Indeed, in letters to Grant Richards in May and June 1906 (*Letters I* 61–4), when publishers and printers refused to publish or print his work, he held out, never wavering in a commitment to an ethical future where the reading public were treated with honesty and without condescension. Such attachment to describing the world around him is not to be confused with a documentary style or the real itself. 'Realistic texture' is different from 'realistic', neither of which are in themselves a true reflection of reality. Faithfulness to experience allows room for the selection of material and for all kinds of switching and bringing together of disparate elements. In the opening of *A Portrait*, the boy's age is never given. He is clearly older by the end of the first page, when he is offered a cachou by Dante, than he is at the beginning, when he is called baby tuckoo. The boy or the narrator is faithful to the boy's emerging consciousness even though the novel starts in Rathgar, a suburb on the south side of Dublin, and moves, seamlessly, to the seaside town of Bray, eleven miles south of Dublin, by the time Eileen is introduced. As for the phrase 'whatever he has seen and heard', this is like a weapon to beat the bourgeoisie or those in power, who might seek to maintain their position through forms of deception or what today we might call ideology. The youthful Joyce is on the side of those who believe in revealing the truth in personal relationships and social life no matter what the cost to one's self or to one's family – though it has to be admitted that Joyce's sense of family attachment can seem limited. Perhaps we should be grateful that his defiance carried him a long way from home.

Values, then, in Joyce is a large and complicated topic, larger than Hughes might have imagined. As for the issue of hope, this occasionally finds expression in a negative critique, which is beautifully captured in the confrontation in 'Cyclops' between the Citizen and Bloom:

> – Are you talking about the new Jerusalem? says
> the citizen.
> – I'm talking about injustice, says Bloom.
> (*U* 12:1474–5)

Bloom's retort is in keeping with an author given to doing things differently. The Citizen taunts, Bloom parries. Utopian thinking in Joyce is concerned not with the future but with the present. Paul Saint-Amour discusses the use of the word 'imprevidibility' in *Ulysses*:

> Prophecy is one of the novel's great subjects but
> repeatedly, as in the carnivalesque interruption to
> Robert Emmett's speech from the dock or in the
> reference to Mother Shipton's doubly false apocalyptic
> prediction, Joyce seeks to open a space toward a view
> of the future which is unforeseeable, one concerned
> with its 'imprevidibility' (*U* 17:980).[50]

Imprevidibility is something that cannot be foreseen. In 'Ithaca', the
question-and-answer episode in the *Nostos* or return section of *Ulysses*,
the ever-resourceful Bloom recalls marking the edge of a coin and
wondering if it might return to him after a period in circulation.
Stephen wants to know if it did return and Bloom's reply is 'Never'.
Interestingly, it might have happened, but, if it did, on reflection, Bloom
could claim it had been foreseen. In its truest sense, imprevidibility is
something that cannot be foreseen.

For Joyce, the future cannot be predicted, but, equally, the present
affords more hope than pessimism, or perhaps we should say more
realism than pessimism. 'Never' in the passage above seems to exhibit
more openness than 'No'. Beckett follows Joyce, but, if we took as
our example the sucking-stone sequence in Beckett's novel *Molloy*
(1951), we might recognise, amid the circular movement between
hand and pocket and mouth, a tragic impasse, which finds relief only
in humour. There are sad figures in Joyce such as Gabriel Conroy in
'The Dead' or Charles Stewart Parnell (whose fate was decided by
others), but Joyce resists tragic readings in part because his attitude
to the future is essentially open-ended or, paradoxically, focussed on
the present. As for the nightmare of history voiced in the 'Nestor'
episode of *Ulysses*, this is Stephen's view, not necessarily Joyce's. In
this respect, *Ulysses* could have ended in tragedy for Stephen, in
suicide for example, but Joyce abandons him to his fate, and focuses
on Molly and her optimistic view of a future with her husband,

50 'The Imprevidibility of the Future' in *Renascent Joyce* (eds Daniel Ferrer,
Sam Slote and André Topia) (Gainsville, FL: University Press of Florida, 2013).
For further discussion, see my review of this book below.

Bloom. Only someone with more than a sprinkling of hope could insert 'yes' ninety-one times into the last episode of 'Penelope', and, as Luca Crispi reminds us, change 'would' to 'will' in Molly's final feelings for Bloom.[51]

The best example of hope in the opening of *A Portrait* lies in the epigraph, which I discuss more fully below. Stephen is the modern Dædalus, who has embarked on a journey to escape the clutches of King Minos and discover freedom away from his family and abroad. The 'overture' itself lays some of the groundwork for interpreting the boy's imprisonment (if that is what it is), but this can only be understood in retrospect. The references to Davitt and Parnell, focalised through a boy who cannot know their significance, only make sense when we arrive at the Christmas Dinner scene. So the hope in the 1880s for Irish politics to free itself from Westminster control is not one that comes to fruition in the novel. On the other hand, the boy's hopes for the future lie outside his country, and if he does find an identity with Parnell it is with a fallen hero.

Making explicit his values is often for the reader to decide, but what is worth stressing is Joyce's commitment to 'converting the bread of everyday life into something that has a permanent artistic life of its own'.[52] Such a commitment has similarities with Freud's inquiry into the psychopathology of everyday life, but Joyce leaves analysis to his Viennese counterpart, preferring art to science.[53] Interestingly, his attraction to commitment is clothed in a religious vocabulary, a vocabulary he never abandoned although his religion he did. Where Freud in his early career was fascinated by blunders and what they reveal about a person's psychology, the later Joyce in *Finnegans Wake*, his ear constantly alert to the possibility of constructing portmanteau words and entertaining both similarity and difference therefore, focused not

51 Luca Crispi, *Joyce's Creative Process and the Construction of Characters in Ulysses: Becoming the Blooms* (Oxford: Oxford University Press, 2015), 175.
52 Stanislaus Joyce, *My Brother's Keeper: James Joyce's Early Years* (New York: Viking Press, 1958) 104. Joyce is referring to his early poems.
53 Sigmund Freud, *The Psychopathology of Everyday Life* (trans Anthea Bell) (1901; London: Penguin, 2002).

so much on a person's idiolect but on language as a universal system of communication. As a young man, however, Joyce was still finding out what he thought and what was in his mind. He took an interest, for example, in Yeats's occult stories. Indeed, 'The Sisters', his first story in *Dubliners*, was published in *The Irish Homestead*, a magazine for the farming community and edited by the practical visionary George Russell (AE), who encouraged him to submit more stories. But, although he might have indulged in 'unknown arts' – not to be confused with today's 'dark arts' – he never joined an occult group.

Ironically, his secular instincts he absorbed from his Jesuit teachers, who taught him all he needed concerning the intellectual framework we associate with Aristotle and St Thomas Aquinas. '[A]pplied Aquinas' *(P* 209) is how Stephen helpfully describes what he is doing. The intersection between the sacred and the secular enabled him to discover his theory of aesthetics. In this regard he learned the art of observation from the leading theologian of the Catholic Church and the leading philosopher of ancient Greece. As the opening of *A Portrait* reminds us, there is *nihil in intellectu nisi prius fuerit in sensu*, there is nothing in the intellect which was not first in the senses. But, as the novel's opening also implies, we are invited to concentrate on details and direct knowledge, and, if we can, to follow the narrative line. In this way we are reminded of the limitations and the breadth in our understanding of observation.

The reference to 'baby tuckoo' in the opening returns us again to the theme of consciousness, and reminds us of a world seen up-close, the nose pressed against the window or the birth canal or his father's glass. The phrase highlights a limited view, but, equally, we might notice how the universe of childhood is revealed for us. Such ironies can also be observed in the narrative disjointedness, which remains one of the distinctive features in Joyce's new departure for fiction. In my review below of McGee's *Paperspace*, which has *Ulysses* for its focus, I write of Joyce's refusal of a psychoanalysis, as Lacan puts it, and how he is a 'symptom' (the articulation of a contradiction between the constitutive subject and the subject-in-process). There is merit in thinking of *A Portrait* in similar terms, especially when we recall the opening page and Stephen as a subject-in-process. At the same time the reader is being asked to accompany the narrator and to identify with the boy's fragmented consciousness in trying to make sense of the world.

By way of contrast, in Ian McEwan's novel, *Nutshell* (2016), which is an imaginative retelling of Shakespeare's *Hamlet*, we are invited to see the world through the eyes of an eight-month-old foetus in the womb. The disjointedness in Joyce's account is gone, replaced by a sophisticated, fluent, adult vocabulary and by a sense of knowingness as if there is a compact between the narrator and the reader. 'So here I am, upside down in a woman.'[54] Almost immediately the narrator invokes a word missing from Joyce's opening, namely 'conscious': 'The beginning of conscious life was the end of illusion, the illusion of non-being, and the eruption of the real.' (2–3) This is nicely put because an illusion is normally seen as part of consciousness, but here McEwan is drawing attention to a realm separate from non-being, which also includes an echo of the famous line from *Hamlet*: 'To be or not to be'. As it happens, the only foetus in *A Portrait*, a novel which could well be interpreted as 'the end of illusion', is the one Stephen encounters when he accompanies his father on his disillusioning return to his home city of Cork, but now it is a taboo word cut into the 'dark stained wood' of a desk in the anatomy theatre of his father's old college. (D 89)

In a nutshell, consciousness is one of Joyce's major themes, but he tends not to address it directly, for his focus is on the struggle to become conscious. Such an approach is different from McEwan's, who provides an engaging commentary on the theme throughout the novel, but it is from a detached observer's perspective: 'We'll always be troubled by how things are – that's how it stands with the difficult gift of consciousness.' (29) This, too, is elegantly expressed and the tone is persuasive. Consciousness is rarely considered as a gift. We have seen how consciousness is characterised by Locke as 'the perception of what passes in a man's own mind', but McEwan's remark forces us to imagine how it is also a 'gift'. In a non-religious age – if that is the world now in prospect – to describe consciousness as a gift is a reminder of its

---

54 Ian McEwan, *Nutshell* (London: Jonathan Cape, 2016), 1.

proximity to the soul conceived as a gift from God, both of which have their origins outside the system of commodity and exchange. We might be tempted to invoke the work of the anthropologist, Marcel Mauss, on the gift-exchange, and how the object is indissolubly tied to the giver, but, again, I would want to consign such a thought to the margins, for that would invite considerations concerned with sale and exchange and obligation or with the idea of the soul as a gift of the Maker.[55] Consciousness *per se* is my main focus here. A 'gift of consciousness' pictures a world where the individual is already special in part because of the gift by parents but also special because of what the gift contains or signifies. A little later in McEwan's novel we learn that the unborn son alights on a common enough idea that pain produces consciousness, but he is not delayed by this thought. He recognises that there is a more profound link between being 'expressionless' in the womb and 'waiting' and, crucially, 'thinking'. (46–8)

McEwan operates in a looser postmodern world. No sooner has the novel begun than we learn that 'James Joyce's *Ulysses* sends [his mother] to sleep, even as it thrills me' (4). References, citations, quotations in this novel exist in a continuum with influences, debts and allegiances. McEwan even allows for an extension of the Yorick-like conceit in *A Sentimental Journey* and plays with the idea that Hamlet might have enjoyed listening to *Ulysses* (and encountering himself, therefore, in Joyce's novel). Equally, in the opening sentence we might well discern an echo of Dickens informing Wilkie Collins in a letter discussed more fully below about his biography, which ends on an enigmatic note with 'And That here I am'. Unless it is a moving hymn to life at the end of the novel when the waters break, struggle is not part of McEwan's world.

The opening page of *Nutshell*, which contains an echo of the opening of the 'Proteus' episode in *Ulysses* and Stephen's meditation on 'signatures' in the outside world, also makes a reference to colours, this time 'blue' as visualised in the womb, and it is linked to the colour 'green'. McEwan's embryo remarks: 'When I hear "blue", which I've

---

55 See Marcel Mauss, *The Gift Expanded Edition* (trans Jane Guyer) (Chicago: Hau Books, 2016).

never seen, I imagine some kind of mental event that's fairly close to green – which I've never seen.' (1) At the end of the novel the new born child sees blue for the first time and discovers it is 'More gorgeous than I dared believe' (197). This is not something the boy in *A Portrait* would find himself thinking or celebrating, for his consciousness has moved on from the colours his eyes have registered. By the time we arrive at 'Proteus', written a decade or so after *A Portrait*, Stephen, now a young man, is delayed by the philosophical problem McEwan is highlighting, only now the visible is not so much heard as 'Ineluctable' (*U* 3:1). In *A Portrait*, colours are more closely allied to symbols, which in turn are tied into a stronger set of narrative obligations. An earlier generation of Joyce critics focussed on 'the surface and the symbol' in his work, but this has been superseded by an awareness that his writing cannot be so easily defined.[56] In a recent essay on 'The Modernist Novel', David Trotter makes the suggestive observation about the ending to the novel how 'Although the diary's conclusion invokes the promise of achievement encrypted in his surname, it can hardly be said to resolve the dialectic between Naturalism and Symbolism. *A Portrait* is Modernism in a state of suspended animation.'[57] In that sense *A Portrait* is a new departure for fiction but also, for Trotter, held in time. To my mind, only by reinserting the symbol inside the narrative can we do justice to what is happening in a Joyce text. Otherwise, as Hughes suggests about resisting 'explicit categorization', we risk turning a text into an exercise in abstraction, which, in passing, is not something that happens in McEwan's richly inventive novel.

Critics discussing the opening of *A Portrait* often concentrate on symbols, particularly colour symbolism. In ancient Greek, the word *symballein* meant to throw together or compare, where two

---

56 See for example Robert M. Adams, *Surface and Symbol: The Consistency of James Joyce's Ulysses* (New York: Oxford University Press, 1962). Or Florence L. Walzl essay on 'The Sisters' in *'James Joyce Quarterly 50 Years Vol 50 No 1–2 Fall 2012–Winter 2013'*, which is reviewed below.

57 David Trotter, 'The Modernist Novel' in *The Cambridge Companion to Modernism* (ed. Michael Levenson) Second edition (Cambridge: Cambridge University Press, 2011), 74.

things are brought into play by the use of the prefix 'with'. Symbol, once closely identified with religious dogma, widened its scope at the turn of the seventeenth century, acquiring the idea of a token or something that stood for something else, not necessarily religious. The use of symbols in *A Portrait* belongs to a wider discussion again involving the distinction between words and things. All the five senses are considered by Joyce in turn: eyes, hearing, touch, taste, and smell. At this stage the boy is passive and things happen to him. He is experiencing the world but not fully understanding what he is experiencing. He wets the bed; one minute it is warm, the next it is cold, then the oil-sheet is changed. He does not yet understand that he is on a journey to convert the third-person pronoun into first-person, himself as object into himself as person. Symbols play a part in this process, or at least the reader alights on the use of symbols, but the boy does not. So symbols are there to be activated, either by the boy as the narrative unfolds or by the reader watching the boy bumping into experience. David Copperfield is thrown into existence, but the boy in *A Portrait* is like the Greek word *symballein*, where his consciousness is thrown together with other objects, there to be sorted and classified. If we borrowed a word from Hughes, we might agree that he is tormented by 'immediacy'.

Readers are quite naturally more informed than the boy, but perhaps we should resist being too informed. After all, for a young boy to understand the significance of a symbol takes a considerable number of years, so should we assume, as some readers do, that the 'wild rose' is a reference to Oscar Wilde or that the 'little green place' is Ireland? The two colours that distinguish Dante's brushes are anchored in something more definite, that maroon *means* Michael Davitt and green for Parnell. However, until we read on we cannot know how such information might be relevant to the unfolding narrative and why Parnell does not merit his given names. For the boy, who is acting as the focaliser here, they are just distinguishing marks on two brushes. Equally, it is not the brushes that are symbolic but the colours. And here too there are problems. Linking Parnell with green is fine for the reader (even if he did hate the colour), but it is not obvious why Davitt is associated with maroon. Moreover, rather than actually possessing symbolic status, the colours look as if such status has been assigned by someone we might struggle to identify as a character in the novel, the absent narrator or author, or, indeed, the putative reader. As for Dante brushing her clothes with two brushes, which she has marked with separate colours, this, too, needs consideration independent of the symbols. Later in the novel when an older Stephen reflects on Dante and his childhood, the symbols have vanished along with Parnell and Davitt, the 'press' has become, unaccountably, somewhere to hang clothes, Dante has become 'an old woman', and we learn something new, that she taught him geography: 'A little boy had been taught geography by an old woman who kept two brushes in her wardrobe' (*P* 91).[58]

Symbols, then, can resist interpretation, not least because of the limited viewpoint of the main protagonist and the unknown arts being practised by the author or narrator. In this respect they operate differently from how the enigma of 'gnomon' works at the beginning of 'The Sisters'. We suspect a word such as 'tuckoo' is not designed as an enigma, but we do not know if it has any symbolic significance, or if it is just a baby word used by an adult speaking to a child, a variant of 'cuckoo', or possibly even a playful rendering of Timbuctoo. We ought never to forget that some things cannot be compared. Hughes's emphasis on 'symbol and suggestion', where the two run together, offers a more rewarding avenue to explore. Indeed, to my mind, Joyce tends to work as much with suggestion as symbol. Or, rather, after we have identified various symbols and what they might mean, it is worth stepping back and taking note of suggestion in his writing.

There are more quotations in the opening of *A Portrait* than there are symbols. Symbols share something with quotations in that both

---

58 In Ireland a press was used for storing linen, food, or china and had drawers. The word 'wardrobe' was rarely used in rural Ireland. See Claudia Kinmonth, *Irish Country Furniture 1700–1950* (New Haven and London: Yale University Press, 1993), 134–44 and *passim*. As for Stephen's choice of the word 'wardrobe', this might be a way of showing his distance from his childhood; or it might be that 'press' and 'wardrobe' were used interchangeably in the Joyce household; or it might be a simple error on Joyce's part.

run alongside the narrative and are designed to be noticed by the reader rather than, necessarily, by the characters. Symbols do many things but here they tend to highlight a theme, whereas quotations tend to advance the narrative. Quotations remind us of Joyce's attraction to different voices that fill the pages of his writing. Indeed, take away the quotations on the opening page and there is little left. Joyce begins with 'Once upon a time' and then inserts a clause familiar to many parents 'and a very good time it was'. This indeed is how the Anglo-Scottish fairy tale, 'The Well of the World's End', begins. So the whole novel is embedded in one sense in a children's story, which in turn is embedded in the words of his father. This is followed by lines from a song about the wild rose blossoming, and then by dancing a hornpipe and by the singing of Tralala and clapping. All this resembles an accompaniment, which is set out like a quotation. Such quotations and examples of quotation are heterogeneous extracts lifted from elsewhere and incorporated into a singular narrative, which, against the odds, gains cohesion in the process. And we cannot forget that the boy's names are in effect quotations, his first a reminder of the first Christian martyr, the second an echo of a Greek myth. Quotations, then, help to provide a rich variety of miscellaneous contexts for the novel to contrast with the epigraph, which is enigmatic, direct and classical in origin. They are also suggestive and encourage us to notice things apart from the narrative as we read on. How to find a way through a world of quotation (or branded goods if we think of late capitalism or neoliberalism) and discover his own voice is what the boy in the novel will also explore.

In *A Portrait*, conventions of writing meet styles of consciousness meet English punctuation. 'His father told him that story: his father looked at him through a glass: he had a hairy face' *(P 7)*. Here the colon, a highly sophisticated punctuation mark in English, registers precisely one of the earliest stepping-stones on the way to consciousness, where two impressions for the child are brought into active relationship by a single mark, one dot above another. The French translation by Ludmila Savitzky has one semi-colon followed by another: 'C'était son père qui lui racontait cette histoire; son père le regardait à travers un morceau de verre; il avait un visage poilu'. But this misses all the drama between his father's 'hairy face' and his father peering at him 'through a glass'.[59] And it is not 'C'était son père', it was his father, but 'His father', a voice which is at once more immediate and more ambiguous. Some translators seem to be guided as much by explanation as by translation. Even the cow is provided with a sound, complete with brackets, italics, and a knowing exclamation mark *(meûh!)*: 'une vache *(meûh!)*'. A French reader confined to a French version of *A Portrait* might well have difficulty appreciating the new departure for fiction heralded by the opening to the novel.

UNKNOWN ARTS

Like Sterne, Joyce uses an epigraph from the classics, only his focus is on the overall theme of the novel rather than an intellectual or philosophical distinction. As soon as the title page to *A Portrait* is turned we encounter a sentence in Latin: 'Et ignotas animum dimittit in artes', 'and he lost himself in unknown arts', or, in George Sandys's 1632 translation, 'to arts unknown he bends his wits'. The context needs glossing. It is Book 8 of Ovid's *Metamorphosis* where we read of Dædalus's resolve to escape from his imprisonment by Minos on the island of Crete:

> The Sea-impris'ned Dædalus, meane-while,
> Weary of Creet, and of his long exile;
> Toucht with his countries love, and place of birth;
> Thus said: Though Minos bar both sea and earth;
> Yet heaven is free. That course attempt I dare:
> Held he the world, he could not hold the ayre.
> This said; to arts unknown he bends his wits
> And alters nature.[60]

59 James Joyce, *Dedalus: Portrait de L'Artiste Jeune Par Lui-Meme* (trans Ludmila Savitzky) (1924; Paris: Gallimard, 1943).
60 George Sandys, *Ovid's Metamorphosis Englished, Mythologiz'd and Represented in Figures* (Oxford: John Lichfield, 1632), 269.

At the very point of departure, the signs are that *A Portrait* is to be a novel of liberation and a discourse on freedom. Weary of exile, Stephen, too, embarks on a course to free himself from imprisonment. The epigraph we might then read as an announcement or a commentary by a narrator from another text, and, like the recurring imagery of flight in the novel itself, it is there to be noticed, in its own way a metamorphosis. That much is clear. However, the novel is also linked from the outset, both in the title and in the epigraph, with art. *Artes*, arts, art, artist. So, while the epigraph to *A Portrait* consciously weaves together art and liberation, only on reading the novel to the end will we know if such an aim is successful. It is, after all, an 'eccentric' novel, away that is from the centre and politically inspired. So powerful is Joyce's art that we suppress the troubling thought that his family might have been sacrificed in the process.

The epigraph is designed to be read against the novel as a whole, but many readers could be forgiven for not knowing how it speaks to the opening of the novel. Let me offer some other tentative suggestions. The theme of imprisonment on an island has parallels with Joyce's fate on the island of Ireland. On the opening page of the novel there are some early hints if not of imprisonment then of threats and adversity. Indeed, according to Hugh Kenner, the controlling emotion in chapter 1 is fear. (*P* 429) The father is perhaps slightly menacing with his hairy face and he calls his son not by his own name but 'baby tuckoo'. On first encountering 'baby tuckoo' we might not register anything unsettling. In a touching letter written in January 1931, his father recalled the tender moment that lies behind the opening: 'I wonder do you recollect the old days in Brighton Square, when you were Babie Tuckoo, and I used to take you out in the Square and tell you all about the moo-cow that used to come down from the mountain.' (*Letters III* 212) This, however, is a father's memory, not the child's. Indeed, it might be a father, recalling the opening to *A Portrait*, trying to engage once more his son's filial affection. What is the case is that the original incident in the house in Rathgar where Joyce was born is thoroughly transformed by the son in his fiction, and it is more than a change of 'mountain' for 'road'. There is a noticeable shift in the boy's consciousness in the sentence, 'He was baby tuckoo', especially if it is he reflecting on his name and identity and trying to distinguish personal pronouns and not knowing whether 'he' is 'you' or 'I'. Joyce's father recollects, but such a recourse is not available to the person who went on to give us a new departure for fiction.

In Burma, according to the *Oxford English Dictionary*, 'tucktoo' meant a large house lizard, and 'tuckoo' is what children would cry in mimicry. It would be interesting to know if Joyce or his father had come across this meaning. In the French translation by Zavitsky, 'Tout-ti-bébé' sounds like the name of a shop selling baby items. 'Le tout-ti-bébé, c'était lui-même' implies it is the third-person narrator telling us this, when the original is more ambiguous and less reassuring. Almost immediately, the boy is punished for some misdemeanour, which he may or may not understand, and he hides under the table. After all, almost as soon as eyes in childhood open, they look where they should not and innocence gives way to guilt. In the eighteenth century, as Johnson's *Dictionary* reminds us, 'conscious' and 'conscience' were much closer in meaning than they are today. Outside, there are eagles waiting to pull out his eyes.

The lines 'O, the wild rose / On the little green place' are sung by his father, we assume, but are 'transcribed' unsentimentally and coarsely by the boy as 'O, the green wothe botheth'. The insertion of 'That was his song' echoes in its construction 'He was baby tuckoo', linking father and son in a formal embrace which might in time prove mutually beneficial. However, the shaping of the adult world leaves the child, perhaps inevitably, without the means to make sense of it all. If the words of the song are from 'Lilly Dale', then the original is not particularly suited to a young boy's imitation: 'Now the wild rose blossoms o'er her little green grave', where the adult concept 'place' has been substituted for the troubling word 'grave'.[61] The song, composed by the American songwriter Hunter S. Thompson, is described by Ruth Bauerle as 'a sentimental Victorian account of

---

61 Ruth Bauerle, *The James Joyce Songbook* (New York: Garland, 1982), 183.

death'. Some readers might be tempted to associate the boy with death, but that is not my view. It is the inappropriateness of such a song that stands out, and the words, when repeated, not unlike the lemon platt, get stuck between his tongue and his teeth. The troubling continues when we recall that the one word missing among personal pronouns is the first person. The boy repeats lines from a song about a wild rose on a little green place, his mother plays a sailor's hornpipe, his father dances, and his aunt and uncle clap. 'Trala lala.' This is not so much a family at ease as an example, perhaps, of a family trying to be a big happy Irish family. The triumph over adversity is well-captured in the refrain and how it adds a syllable: 'Tralala laladdy.' To escape King Minos, therefore, the boy will have to discover a path through the unknown and through to the unknown.

Another possible way to discern the relevance of the epigraph is to reflect on Dædalus losing himself in '*artes ignotas*' or unknown arts. This seems to echo the title of the novel, that it is a portrait of an artist. Dædalus is making plans to flee the island of Crete and to escape the clutches of King Minos who is imprisoning him. As for the word 'artist' or 'arts', in the seventeenth-century translation this is closer in meaning to craftsman. This has relevance for the cross-over between craftsman and artist. Through the craft of writing, a phrase that is particularly relevant to Joyce, he is seeking an escape from his country, and in this respect his novel is an account of how his transformation, his metamorphosis, happened. With its reference to the figure of Dædalus, the epigraph also underlines that there is another template, another story-line, which Joyce is using to layer his novel with myth and identity.

Why Joyce chose to change the diphthong to the single letter is open to interpretation. *Stephen Hero* (1944), the fragmentary novel which he composed in the same years as *A Portrait*, carries the name 'Stephen Daedalus'. Some critics have suggested that 'Dedalus' carries a necessary trace of antiquity and classical mythology, but in the modern world we are closer to a reality without myth and one closer to something that is dead. Even the unknown arts of alchemy belong to another age. Alternatively, we might interpret the alteration as a

Â

sign that for Joyce the classical world can be vivified from within and given new riffs and creative twists, as he was later to demonstrate to good effect in *Ulysses*. Perhaps it was for this reason that he did not disapprove of the French translation by Savitzky, who avoided all the traps and all the wordiness of Joyce's English title when she called the book simply *Dedalus*, adding as a subtitle in small print *Portrait de L'Artiste Jeune Par Lui-Même* (Portrait of the Young Artist by Himself). It was a title – she tells us in the 1943 fifth edition – that met with Joyce's approval: 'd'accord avec Joyce' (12). After all, the word 'artist' elides too quickly into 'would-be artist' (or 'character' in Dublin parlance). Indeed, in *Ulysses* we learn that 'there's a touch of the artist about old Bloom' (*U* 10:582–3). Perhaps by the end of *A Portrait*, Joyce might have grown tired of his character being or becoming an artist. It goes without saying that the minimalist *Dedalus* misses out on all this speculative discussion.

BIOGRAPHY AND FICTION

The boy, then, is held at a distance from the reader, and his early growth in consciousness tends to be revealed in glimpses rather than through a reassuring narrator holding our hand as events unfold. And we should not overlook that we are dealing with glimpses, not flashbacks. Equally, there is no recourse to a comment such as 'When I arrived at the age of five, I became friendly with a girl who lived nearby.' Eileen Vance, the girl he plays with has a name but no identity apart from the fact that she is a Protestant. We are not sure how to interpret such a detail, but we sense it is meaningful for the boy or for whoever it was who put such an idea in his head. If the novel was set in Belfast, it might be read in terms of tribal allegiances, but in Bray, on the south side of Dublin, where Catholics only slightly outnumber Protestants, it seems to be more about difference *per se*. We can notice in passing that the word 'Protestant' in *Dubliners* often adds a certain disturbance to the surface of the text. In 'Eveline', for example, a developer from Belfast buys up the playing fields near Eveline's house and some readers might assume he is a Protestant on the basis that (Protestant) Belfast was economically more enterprising than (Catholic) Dublin at that time.[62] In 'The Dead', Mary Jane has to intervene when Aunt Kate becomes upset about the behaviour of the Catholic Church, reminding her that she is in the company of Mr Browne, who is of 'the other persuasion'. In 'Ivy Day in the Committee Room' the presence of Mr Crofton has a strange effect on those around him, but we only learn of his religious persuasion in 'Cyclops' when he is dismissively referred to as 'Crofter the Orangeman or presbyterian' (U 12:1635).

There are gaps in our reading, omissions which we are forced to fill in or supplement in some way from our own experience. What exactly is the story the father tells the boy? Or is it a story which never gets going? The decision is ours as readers to make but we do not really have the evidence to decide. We are not, though, dealing with the elusive theme of evanescence to be found in Virginia Woolf or, indeed, with 'moments of being', the title given by later critics to her autobiographical writings.[63] In his revolt against positivism, Joyce characteristically pulls back from, or pushes against, doing the work assigned to the reader. So interpretation is kept ruthlessly separate from the text. In *Stephen Hero* we learn that the protagonist was turning out essays 'as sudden defence-works while he was busy constructing the enigma of a manner' (SH 32). At the end of his final text, *Finnegans Wake*, Joyce, with perhaps the reader also in mind, writes 'The keys to. Given!' (FW 628.15) The reader is assigned the task of interpretation, but, in spite of his fondness for enigmas, Joyce provides the determined reader with enough clues to continue on the journey.

Readers, however, and researchers can take wrong directions. Eileen's father owned a chemist's shop on the main street in Bray, and when I was researching my *James Joyce's Ireland* (1992), I learned from the then owner that Eileen Vance remembered playing 'tig' with Joyce and having a child's wheelbarrow thrown at her because she was a 'prod' and he was going to burn her. Later in life she emigrated

---

62 See the guide book quoted in my Introduction: M.J.B. Baddeley, *Thorough Guide Ireland Part 1 Northern Counties* (London: Dulau, 1890), 6.
63 See Virginia Woolf, *Moments of Being: Autobiographical Writings* (ed. Jeanne Schulkind) (London: Pimlico, 2002).

to Saskatchewan in Canada and worked as a nurse and then joined a group of singers and dancers who toured Canada. In 1983 at the age of 100 she received a telegram from the Queen of England and Pierre Trudeau, the Prime Minister of Canada. In *A Portrait* we read simply that the Vances lived at number seven.

Such research can be intriguing and even fulfilling. In *James Joyce's Ireland* I reproduce a photograph of the chemist's taken in 1985 with the name of Vance and Wilson, but I do not believe any of this added to interpreting the opening to the novel. Such supplementary material might possibly help us discern what lay behind the insertion of 'Protestant' in connection with Eileen. It might even show that Joyce was being economical with the truth, and that there is a form of displacement at work here. The boy hiding under the table suggests it was a sexual misdemeanour, but in 'real life' perhaps Joyce was drawing on an incident when he was reprimanded for being a bully. Arguably, Joyce would not have minded the sexual accusation, for that is commonplace, but bullying was not something he would have liked recalling as an adult, even though this is a portrait 'as a young man'. In terms of the novel's cohesion, however, the reference to pulling out his eyes links to his father's 'glass' or monocle and anticipates the incident when his glasses are broken in the playground and he is subsequently punished by his teachers. Eyes play an important theme in the novel, a novel about how we see the world and how it can get us into trouble. But Eileen remains a figure who hovers between a memory and a symbol. Later Stephen (also) recalls playing tig with her and recalls her long white hands (*P* 31) and how, when she put them over his eyes, he thought of 'Tower of Ivory', a phrase from the Litany of the Blessed Virgin Mary.

Eileen's biographical details, then, can be recovered but her part in the novel cannot be advanced more than it is.[64] Perhaps in retrospect

64 For a discussion of Eileen's role and presence in the novel, see Michael H. Begnal's essay, 'Stephen, Simon, and Eileen Vance: Auto-Eroticism in *A Portrait of the Artist as a Young Man*' in Michael Patrick Gillespie (ed.), *Joyce Through the Ages: A Non-Linear View* (Gainesville, FL: University Press of Florida, 1999), 107–16.

or with a leap of the imagination we might interpret her as Stephen's first Beatrice, but in these early pages his aunt Dante commands our attention (though her name, written without speech marks, suggests a connection with the author of *The Divine Comedy*). What is clear is that the boy is learning about difference and about how the world is structured or mediated in consciousness. At the beginning of *A Portrait*, the girl is different from the boy, the Catholic from the Protestant. One line could be crossed, the other was more problematic. The boy expresses a wish to marry the girl when he grows up, but at this stage he is not familiar with the restraints imposed on desire by religious and cultural difference.

Gordon Bowker's solid biography contains more on Eileen and her family.[65] Joyce met her at nursery school when he was five. Their fathers shared an interest in drinking and singing. At parties Eileen recalls James donning a red cap and playing the Devil, though any misbehaving would risk James's mother pushing their heads down the toilet and pulling the chain. Dante, who regarded close contact with Protestants as 'a threat to the immortal soul' (28), was Eileen's 'enemy'. At this point, Bowker adds something which resembles the biographer's licence: 'Anti-Protestant bigotry was quite alien even to the young, impressionable boy.' As for the repeated references to eyes at the beginning of the novel, Bowker spends time expounding on the Joycean theme of guilt and blindness.

In this way, as they did in Richard Ellmann's magisterial biography of Joyce, fictional and biographical details tend to become entwined, and at the same time they acquire perhaps a spurious authority by appearing in both the life and the fiction. Perhaps that was inevitable given that Joyce runs the two together, beginning with the date – 2 February 1914 – when it began serialisation in *The Egoist*, his birthday that is. As for Bowker, he interprets the opening passage with the father peering at the boy as a 'defining memory of a blissful beginning' (20), but here I disagree. It is unclear if Joyce did have a blissful beginning. His mother was preoccupied with

---

65 Gordon Bowker, *James Joyce: A Biography* (London: Weidenfeld and Nicolson, 2011).

pregnancies, by worries about declining family fortunes, and by a husband who thought the world owed him a living. Some readers might be tempted to apply the insertion in the fairy tale opening – 'and a very good time it was' – to the Joyce household, but this I think is special pleading. We can agree, however, that his relationship with his father is crucial, but it is difficult to determine the nature of that relationship from this fictional opening. The use of the phrase 'defining memory' is, again, problematic for I suspect a childhood memory never comes clothed in the adjective 'defining'. Such a word can only be used after later reflection and then perhaps only loosely for *A Portrait* begins close-up with something that resembles nothing more than a glimpse. As for the Christmas Dinner scene, we respond to the symbolism of the fire being 'banked high and red' (*P* 23), but by the end of that scene family discord erupts, and the impression created is that there was little bliss in that household.

Commentary surrounding a text by Joyce often runs the risk of adding little to our interpretation, leading at times to more confusion. Part of the problem lies in determining what information is or is not relevant, but this is not an easy undertaking, for the associationism that Sterne sought to counter is still with us. The name Dante, which is presumably the boy's pronunciation of auntie, must have confused generations of readers on first encountering it. Texts read us as much as we read them. The role of consciousness is subject to multiple, active impressions, and, as Hughes suggests, we are not in possession of a mirror to external reality. There is another problem, for a Joyce text sometimes resembles a garment which is inside-out, with the author teasing us as it were to turn it back into a normal shape. Hence all the pages of criticism which reconstruct history and context to make the text presentable. The temptation can be irresistible but not always appropriate. Distortion aside, perhaps the best motto with Joyce is to learn from detective fiction and not to go beyond the evidence. Dante in Bowker's account confirms the impression we get from the novel; the boy's mother may or may not have been so brutal in her threats. Bowker enters a caveat about how reliable it is to know 'if the imaginative memory of his alter ego Stephen can be trusted' (20). But this is to accept Stephen is Joyce's alter ego, a view which is no longer widely held in Joyce studies. Joyce's fiction has a life of its own, and it is in many ways independent of the life. When the two are run together we almost certainly do injustice to the art and perhaps to the life.

The Prefect of Studies exits from the classroom, the boy punished and humiliated, our sentiments with the boy. It may or may not have happened to the author, so the semi-autobiographical mode of writing in *A Portrait* can be observed but not proved. This is why referring to *A Portrait* as an example of a semi-autobiographical novel can be misleading. For that we need some other kind of measurement that is available to us in, say, letters, as is the case with Dickens. Equally, if all autobiographical or semi-autobiographical fiction is involved in forms of repression, we need another account to know or verify what we are reading. The opening to *A Portrait* may contain examples of repression but the evidence for this is not very compelling. Dickens gives us psychology, Joyce consciousness.

If there is something that has the look of repression in *A Portrait* it is perhaps related to the missing years between attending Clongowes Wood as a boarder and Belvedere College as a day pupil. We know little about that period in Joyce's life. Between June 1891, when he left Clongowes, and January 1893, when Joyce was almost eleven years old, he studied at home, at which point he attended for a term the Christian Brothers O'Connell School on North Richmond Street, Dublin. In marked contrast with the two Jesuit schools, the Christian Brothers ran schools for less well-off children in Ireland. With a rich history of prejudice behind him, his father, through his fictional persona, Mr Dedalus, betrays no hesitation in declaring

- Christian brothers be damned! said Mr Dedalus. Is it
with Paddy Stink and Micky Mud? No, let him stick
to the Jesuits in God's name since he began with them.
They'll be of service to him in after years. Those are
the fellows that can get you a position. (*P* 71)

In later life the class-conscious Joyce identified with the Jesuits and made little mention of his term at the school on North Richmond Street, a street which he describes in 'Araby' as 'blind', a cul-de-sac that is.[66] However, it was hardly the equivalent of the blacking factory in Dickens's life. As for his eighteen months at home, his 'long spell of leisure and liberty' (P 71), again this is largely missing from *A Portrait*, but the decline in his family's fortunes must have told on Joyce's pride.

THE CLASSICAL TEMPER

Let me come at this question from another angle, and suggest a slightly different observation on the kind of novel we are dealing with in *A Portrait*. It is less easy today to read *David Copperfield* without recalling the material that was repressed by the author. In a tantalising letter to his friend, Wilkie Collins, in June 1856, five years after the publication of *David Copperfield*, Dickens rehearses the facts of his life: 'That I was born at Portsmouth on the 7th of February 1812. That my father was in the Navy Pay office. That I was taken by him to Chatham when I was very young, and lived and was educated there till I was – 12 or 13, I suppose. That I was then put to a school near London, where (as at the other place) I distinguished myself like a Brick.' Significantly, the time spent in the blacking factory is omitted by Dickens, and we finally arrive at: 'And That here I am.' Here I am, that is, as a writer and famous novelist. Dickens then tells Collins that it is the first time he has ever set down these particulars, adding that he feels 'like a Wild Beast in a Caravan, describing himself in the keeper's absence'.[67]

When we return to the opening of *David Copperfield* – Dickens had to be told by his biographer that David's initials reversed were his own – something happens, for 'I am Born' now resembles a statement by someone who has already arrived at a point somewhere in the future

---

66 'You allude to me as a Catholic. Now for the sake of precision, and to get the correct contour on me, you ought to allude to me as a Jesuit.' Richard Ellmann, *James Joyce* (Oxford: Oxford University Press, 1982), 27.

67 Jenny Hartley (ed.), *The Selected Letters of Charles Dickens* (Oxford: Oxford University Press, 2012), 307.

marked by the phrase 'And That here I am', someone who is now looking back. The layers multiply. We have two stories, one fictional, and one autobiographical. And in addition we have two narratives, one going forward and one retrospective. In the first one, Dickens is involved in repressing a crucial event in his life because it might reflect badly on him and he had no wish remembering how close he came to the nether world. In the second one, it is important for the purposes of the narrative and to appreciate the boy's sense of being thrown into existence that we do not know he became a famous writer. What we make of the image of the Wild Beast and the keeper's absence and how it might relate to his autobiographical novel, that belongs to a much longer inquiry into Dickens's character and Victorian sensibility.

Repression in Dickens is allied with something else. His frequently insightful biographer, John Forster, observed that Dickens 'seemed to be always the more himself for being somebody else, for continually putting off his personality'.[68] Ironically, Dickens needed to turn his gaze away from the fire of his childhood in order to capture it. But there can be no doubt about the radical unease that affected Dickens from his childhood and his sense of abandonment, which is well-captured in the image of the graveyard where the protagonist's father is buried and where the rooks no longer roost or nest. For a boy with great expectations, selling off the family's books and furniture to the local pawn shop to help pay for his father's debts cannot have been easy to dislodge from the mind.

The phrase that stands out in Joyce's Paduan essay on Dickens, written in April 1912 and around the same time as he was completing *A Portrait*, is 'creative fury': 'The number and length of his novels prove incontestably that the writer is possessed by a kind of creative fury.'[69] Such an opinion is confirmed by his daughter, Mamie Dickens, in her memoir, *My Father As I Recall Him*. Dickens did not just create; he, too, was overwhelmed in the process, for he was 'the creature of

68 John Forster, *The Life of Charles Dickens*, 2 vols (ed. A.J. Hoppé) (1872–4; London: J.M. Dent and New York: E.P. Dutton, 1966), 399–400.
69 Louis Berrone (ed.), *James Joyce in Padua* (New York: Random House, 1977), 36.

his pen'.[70] Dickens tends to overwhelm the reader, never more so than at the beginning of *David Copperfield* with 'some tall old elm-trees at the bottom of the garden', which become increasingly menacing as the theme of abandonment unfolds. But throughout *The Personal History of David Copperfield*, to insist on its full title, the facts of his life intrude into his fiction in such a way that we are reminded of two kinds of narrative, one that belongs to writing memoirs, the other to writing fiction. Thus, in terms of word count, 'memory' appears 38 times, 'remembrance' 59, recall(ed) 39, recollect/recollection 97. In repeatedly encountering such mixed modes of writing, which are evoked by such words, we wonder about the author's involvement – or repression – in writing his life.

If Joyce overwhelms, as he does in the schoolroom punishment scene or in the Christmas Dinner scene, or as we listen, terrified, to the sermon on the four last things, he soon reverts to the default position, which allows space for the reader to imagine what the boy is experiencing, without the author telling us directly. In *Stephen Hero* a distinction is made between the romantic and the classical tempers. The romantic temper is 'insecure, unsatisfied, impatient' and 'it comes to disregard certain limitations'. The classical temper 'chooses rather to bend upon these present things…that the quick intelligence may go beyond them to their meaning which is still unuttered.' (*SH* 83) Later in the novel Stephen defends his position when it is ridiculed by the College President: 'I use the word "classical" in a certain sense… By "classical" I mean the slow elaborate patience of the art of satisfaction.' (102) If we make allowances for Stephen's youthful enthusiasm for a new theory, we can discern an important moment for Joyce in understanding his developing sense of aesthetics. As noted above, Hughes might well agree with going beyond present things to discover a meaning which is 'still unuttered'. Patience is something I refer to at the end of my Introduction, for there is a meeting between the person who patiently creates and his or her audience having to pause or delay in their reading. In this way control is exercised and the classical temper felt more widely.

---

70 Mamie Dickens, *My Father As I Recall Him* (London: Roxburghe, 1896), 50.

The opening has the look of something inserted after the rest of the novel has been written, which may account for the lack of an underlying narrative of repression. Hans Walter Gabler maintains that the 'overture' of the novel, together with the Christmas Dinner scene, were written some years after the novel was begun. Part 1 as written in autumn 1907 did not include either. So, all the other chapters seem to have come first, and the opening was possibly not written until the end of the process.[71] The question that Joyce must have asked was: 'What do I need to insert at the beginning to enhance the novel I've just written?' Such a doubling back on his text became a characteristic method of working with Joyce, as Luca Crispi has demonstrated with the manuscripts of *Ulysses*.[72] This was often a special moment when critical advances could be made in experimentation and a new kind of novel emerge. As discussed above, the surface of the opening is foregrounded and we have to search for depth. The monocle in this regard has an emblematic status. It is fixed over one eye and held in place by a form of squinting and by the word 'glass'. Here is the 'symbol and suggestion' that Hughes noticed about the revolt against positivism. Here was a new way of writing that constantly drew attention to itself, to its enigmatic status, even as the reader was involved in a forward momentum. No modern writer has made us pause for so long on particular words or phrases. The novel's first word, 'once', points to something specific in time, but, as used in the phrase 'once upon a time', it signals a world outside time.

With *A Portrait* we have only just begun to find our way round the opening sequence when we are confronted by another paratextual feature with an asterisk or a row of asterisks on the second page. Some new editions of the novel have cut the elliptical points and the asterisks, but this is to lessen the subtlety of the opening pages and make light of the value of punctuation. Dashes, too, need to be kept,

---

71 See Hans Walter Gabler, 'Introduction: Composition, Text, and Editing' in James Joyce, *A Portrait of the Artist as a Young Man* (ed. John Paul Riquelme) (New York: W.W. Norton, 2007), xvii.
72 See Luca Crispi, *Joyce's Creative Process and the Construction of Characters in Ulysses: Becoming the Blooms* (Oxford: Oxford University Press, 2015).

for Joyce, perhaps with Sterne in mind, specifically objected to what he called 'perverted commas' (*Letters III* 99–100) in earlier printings of the novel. How we interpret the asterisks is, again, for the reader to decide, but this time they seem to mark a gap in years as the boy moves on. Joyce's contribution to the modern novel is allied to the arts of cutting. He thereby allows room for the text to stand proud of its interpretation. In a recent essay on Pound and Beckett, Ira Nadel refers to the 'importance of condensation and the aesthetic of subtraction'.[73] He could well have also included Joyce. Lessness was in the air, but in Joyce's case he did not need anyone else to cut anything down to size. He had already instinctively done that himself. This is something Pound recognized from the outset, Pound, the poet and critic who dramatically shaped Eliot's *The Waste Land* (1922) by effectively cutting its length in half. The new narrative returns us more directly to the act of writing and often, as we have observed, to the experience of not knowing precisely how we go about our task of interpretation. There is, therefore, no place for 'I wish' or 'I record' at the beginning of *A Portrait*. That world of Sterne and Dickens belongs to the past and to past certainties, another example of Joyce's subtraction.

At the same time Joyce's emphasis on realistic texture means that history intrudes almost immediately in *A Portrait*. So if he undermines a comfortable or secure access to reading the text on the one hand, on the other hand he enforces the close connection between consciousness and history. It is this double movement that makes for particular interest in reading Joyce: distance and involvement, a phrase I also use in my Introduction to describe his politics. His fictional resolve carried him in one direction, his attachments in another. One isolated him from the world as if he was like God paring his fingernails, the other drew on his Irish connection with the world. Almost at once in *A Portrait*, on the opening page, history intervenes: 'Dante had two brushes in her press. The brush with the maroon velvet back was for Michael Davitt and the brush with the green velvet back was for Parnell.' The

---

73 Ira Nadel, 'Pound and the Artichoke, Beckett and the Whistle' in *Ezra Pound and Modernism: The Irish Factor* (eds Walter Baumann and William Pratt) (Brighton: Edward Everett Root, 2017), 163.

grammar tells us that this remark is being focalized through the boy; the reference to Davitt and Parnell tells us the date is some time in the 1880s when the two Irish leaders were working together. What we are also being told is that history may appear to be offstage but it is rarely simple background in Joyce. In this instance the character of Dante and her brushes catch our eye as much as the two leaders. We need, therefore, to pay attention when historical figures are introduced in the text and not to assume a text is explained when the context is glossed by editors and commentators. But it is more than this, for a known history never supplants the story Joyce is telling. In my Introduction I reflect on Joyce and nationalism, but, when we inquire into the new departure for fiction that *A Portrait* represents, a different approach is called for, one that does justice to the boy's consciousness before history intervenes.

CHAPTER 2

THE HYBRID LANDSCAPE
IN JOYCE

In the first story of *Dubliners* we learn that the down-at-heel sisters live on 'Great Britain-street'. For the experienced reader of Joyce the street name is perhaps impossible to read without irony, without conjuring up an empire in decline. That particular move from text to context and back again is one we frequently make. Indeed, in the light of Joyce's other texts, we might legitimately conclude that virtually no area of Joyce's city is free from the scars of the colonial encounter. But much of *Ulysses* has an internationalism that evades a specific politics. Take the figure of Dlugacz, the pork-butcher in the 'Calypso' episode of *Ulysses*. Or Leopold Bloom, the main protagonist of *Ulysses*, whose father was a Hungarian Jew but who converted to Christianity on arriving in Ireland, whose mother, Ellen Higgins Bloom, wore an *Agnus Dei* medallion and was presumably a Roman Catholic. Bloom himself was baptised for the first time in a Protestant church near St Patrick's Cathedral in Dublin and in the cave of the Cyclops denied he was a Jew, though all the world thinks he is. Or Molly, the colonial subject with the Spanish eyes, who was brought up on the Rock of Gibraltar, and who is the daughter of a Spanish woman with the improbable name Lunita Laredo and of a father who possesses the suitably Penelopean name of Tweedy and who is not a major but a

more humble drum-major in the Royal Dublin Fusiliers. The insertion
of the phrase 'whoever she was' (*U* 18:846–7) by Molly about her
mother and how 'she might have given me a nicer name' adds to the
mystery surrounding Molly's identity. Some critics have speculated
that Lunita might have been a prostitute.

Ulysses never ceases to surprise us as readers. So natural, so lacking
in hybridity, does Molly appear that we assume all kinds of things. Some
readers, for example, will think her voice is full of the broad vowels of
the West of Ireland, where Joyce's partner, Nora Barnacle, on whom
she is in part modelled, came from. But she couldn't possibly speak like
Nora. When living on Gibraltar, one of her first lovers, the Englishman
Lieutenant Stanley Gardner, causes her to reflect on accents, and she is
perhaps slightly embarrassed about the Irish accent she inherited from
her father: 'all father left me in spite of his stamps' (*U* 18:890). According
to Bloom: 'My wife is, so to speak, Spanish, half that is. Point of fact
she could actually claim Spanish nationality if she wanted, having been
born in (technically) Spain, i.e. Gibraltar' (*U* 16:876–79). The phrase
'so to speak', reminiscent of 'speaking likeness' (*U* 16:1444), looks odd,
but seems to attract to it something about how Molly did speak. We
are not told, but one wonders if her accent did contain some Spanish
elements. It would be strange if her father's accent was as dominant as
she imagines and that her mother's accent (whatever that was) played no
part in her language acquisition. When we encounter 'jewess' and not
'jewish' in the sentence about Bloom being attracted to her 'I suppose
on account of my being jewess looking after my mother' (*U* 18:1184),
one wonders if that is because Molly cannot spell, has a poor command
of English grammar, or perhaps it is indicative of the way she talks with
an accent that might confuse the two words. She does not seem aware
of the possibly pejorative meaning of 'jewess', a lack of awareness shared
perhaps with her husband. Moreover, Bloom's observation about Molly
being 'born in (technically) Spain, i.e. Gibraltar', is not quite right. The
expression he wants is not 'technically', but, to be more precise, 'to all
intents and purposes except technically'.

We tend to forget that Molly is an invention and the product of
Joyce's 'meandering male fist' (*FW* 123.10). Joyce might have added

the word 'crude'. In the recent cache of manuscripts in the national Library of Ireland, there is a note which accompanies Molly's thought about never coming properly until she was '22 or so' (U 18:1051): '1st complete fuck at 25'.[74] In the novel itself Joyce, whose schoolboy attitudes never left him, avoids crudeness such as this. Molly, then, comes to life amid the shadows in the interplay between the spoken and the written and in a border region somewhere between cliché, word association, and male stereotyping or misconceptions.

I have in my possession (see images) a striking, street animated, hand-coloured Edwardian postcard of The Exchange in Gibraltar, with three soldiers in bright red uniform off-duty casually talking to each other, a woman in a wide-brimmed hat, pushing with some determination a pram with a baby who is sitting up with head covered, a man outside the adjacent Egyptian bazaar looking somewhat suspicious, a waiting horse and carriage, two empty wooden kiosks, and various other figures walking past the front of the Exchange. The postcard is rich in information. The sun is overhead. It could be a Sunday with people milling around. The kiosks are closed. Perhaps it is a non-trading day, Gibraltar being overwhelmingly Roman Catholic.

The Exchange itself enjoyed an interesting history, and it was used by merchants in the nineteenth century, who campaigned for greater representation from the colonial authorities. Opposite the Exchange, there was a Jewish market, for Gibraltar, which was the subject of sieges in the eighteenth century, had a significant Jewish population, along with the Genoese, Spaniards, and, later, British. By 1900 Jews numbered around 1500 out of a total population of around 29,000, a percentage much higher than in Dublin at the same time. Soldiers numbered over 5,000, a sixth or more of the population on the Rock. If Molly had been brought up in Gibraltar she would have heard English, Spanish, Genoese, Llanito, which is a mixture of Andalusian Spanish and British English, Maghrebi Arabic, Hebrew, and Ladino or Judaeo-Spanish. One of the pubs frequented by soldiers was called in Llanito *Coquenbotelie* or Cock and Bottle.

74 Cited in Luca Crispi, *Joyce's Creative Process and the Construction of Characters in Ulysses: Becoming the Blooms* (Oxford: Oxford University Press, 2015), 192.

Edwardian postcard of The Exchange, Gibraltar: image and text.

Joyce never visited Gibraltar, so he was relying on second-hand accounts, some of which were travel guides. But he might have been intrigued by what someone has written on the back of this postcard about their impressions of what was then an outpost of empire. This author is impressed by the guns and the setting and by the uniforms, as is Molly when she meets Lt Stanley Gardner of the '2nd East Lancs Rgt' (*U* 18:387):

> The policeman and postman have the same uniforms as ours, but the policeman has such a huge truncheon in leather cover. A slight tap from them would smash one's head like an eggshell. We saw a squad of soldiers march out, with the drum and fife band. My word, they were perspiring with all their arms. I cannot describe the rocks they are so high so massive, but right upon the top are some guns that command the harbour. It is certainly the key to the Mediterranean Sea: the forts are impregnable and the guns are tremendous. Just after we landed, the soldiers began practice with heavy guns, and it seemed to make the roofs shake. One of our company had a revolver, and he fired that off as well a few times.

The author could have been reading John Augustus O'Shea's *Romantic Spain* (1887), where, on setting foot on the Rock, the Irishman (who could have been reading Sterne on Tobias Smollett) unromantically declares: 'Gibraltar is but a huge garrison.'[75] As the brief description in an early-eighteenth-century gazeteer reminds us, 'Since it has been in the hands of the English, it is extremely well fortified.'[76] It remained so throughout the intervening period. It might be thought that O'Shea's fellow-countryman, Joyce, has a good eye when it comes to describing cultures he has only read about. To those unfamiliar with the Colony,

---

75 John Augustus O'Shea, *Romantic Spain: A Record of Personal Experiences* Vol 2 (London: Ward and Downey, 1887), 19. In *A Sentimental Journey* (1768) Sterne enjoys mocking the prosaic Smollett in his *Travels Through France and Italy* (1766).
76 *A New Geographical Dictionary* (London: printed for D. Midwinter, 1737). Gibraltar was ceded to Britain after the War of the Spanish Succession in 1714.

his portrait of Gibraltar rings true, but it is perhaps less credible for those brought up there. He would surely have been interested in the revolver incident, and perhaps incorporated it into the flow of Molly's thoughts. But as for all the languages mentioned by the American traveller Henry M. Field and other visitors from the period, Joyce/ Molly create the impression there are just two. In addition, Molly's memories of Gibraltar occasionally rely rather too much on images from her creator's travel guide:

> and the sentry in front of the governors house with the thing round his white helmet poor devil half roasted and the Spanish girls laughing in their shawls and their tall combs and the auctions in the morning the Greeks and the jews and the Arabs and the devil knows who else from all the ends of Europe (U 18:1585–9)

The insertion of 'the Greeks' fits into the Greek theme of the novel and might be excused or overlooked by the reader as another example of Molly's faulty memory. Perhaps the Greek reference picks up on the Citizen's comment in 'Cyclops': 'Where are the Greek merchants that came through the pillars of Hercules' (U 12:1248–9). But such an evocation seems out of place amid the detailed personal memories in the last episode of the novel – unless it is a genuine question that Molly doesn't get to answer. In Field's engaging travel book *Gibraltar*, published in 1889, there are references to Spaniards and Moors, to 'long-bearded Jews' and Turks in 'baggy trousers', and some uncomplimentary remarks on 'Levantines', Maltese, and Africans from Timbuctoo, but no Greeks grace his pages.[77] As for the phrase 'the

---

77 Henry M. Field, *Gibraltar* (London: Chapman and Hall, 1889),   28. For more impressions on the different ethnic groups on Gibraltar, see chapter 4 of O'Shea's *Romantic Spain A Record of Personal Experiences* Vol 2, which also makes no reference to Greeks on the Rock. For a richly informative critical discussion devoted to Molly and Gibraltar, see Richard Brown's essay 'Molly's Gibraltar: The Other Location in Joyce's *Ulysses*' in Richard Brown (ed.), *A Companion to James Joyce* (Chichester: Wiley-Blackwell, 2011).

devil knows', this, again, is a convenient glossing over something or a distraction for what is to come 'from all the ends of Europe'. As it happens, this last phrase carries an echo of Field's paragraph detailing the languages spoken on Gibraltar and how the locals swear at each other 'in all the languages of the East'. None of this is too destructive, for Molly is answerable to nobody except her creator.

The Spanish girls laugh and have tall combs and wear shawls, but missing are the Moroccan and North African women. The high-class, local woman in the sketch of 'A Spanish Young Lady and Her Duenna' (or governess) in the *Illustrated London News* on September 22 1889, which accompanies other exotic images of a Spanish bull-fight and the Spanish frontier under the Rock of Gibraltar, would not be an example of the Spanish women Molly is recalling. She might have been thinking about visits to Ronda and seeing 'the old windows of the posadas' (*U* 18:1594–5) or returning from Tarifa, with 'the moon shining' (*U* 18:1336), or missing the boat at Algeciras. Her Gibraltar is not technically Spanish, as Bloom imagines, but imaginatively Spanish and, complete with 'glorious sunsets' (*U* 18:1599), largely romantic. It contrasts with the reality, where, for example, the Andalusian men and women, brought in to do the menial work in the Colony, would normally have to leave in the evening when the town would revert to its customary quiet only interrupted by soldiers off-duty or firing guns. There are problems, then, with 'local colour' in 'Penelope', a charge that can almost never be leveled against Joyce in his use of Dublin.

The postcard reminds us of responses which Molly shares with her contemporaries, so her unique responses are often not so unique. And we might be forgiven for wondering if she or her expert handler do not simply convey stereotypes; they are subject to them. It would be difficult to imagine her thinking that the policeman and the postman have the same uniforms 'as ours' since this is an observation by someone from England, the mother country. While her Irishness might not be of particular interest to others, throughout this episode Molly's ethnicity constitutes an invisible presence for the reader, especially in the way it hovers over these pages without being fully addressed or acknowledged – in contrast with Bloom. It is as if we are being made aware of the imagined hybrid landscape with the stress on 'imagined'.

Like the author in the postcard, Molly, too, is impressed with uniforms, and she, too, alights throughout on the unique colonial setting of Gibraltar, a culture rarely free of the presence of the military and a culture she tends to view in binary terms. Equally, as if the hybrid theme was uppermost in the mind of the author, her thoughts carry snippets of writing that, again, remind us how Joyce came by his material, as when Molly recalls Gardner's death in, presumably, an obituary notice during the Boer War: 'Gardner lieut Stanley G 8th Bn 2nd East Lancs Rgt'. Joyce's use of 'Rgt' instead of 'Regt' adds to the impression that this is Molly in her mind 'transcribing' the notice in a newspaper and, for those with an expert eye, getting it wrong. A discussion, then, of Molly and hybridity raises issues, which, perhaps thankfully, cannot be easily resolved, and, clearly, they are different from when we ask a similar question about Bloom and hybridity. Thus, when readers sympathise with Molly, for example, what exactly are they sympathising with, and what do they make of Joyce's 'meandering male fist'? Or is it that in spite of everything she is not a victim of Gibraltar's colonial setting, and, fortunately, she has a life of her own and a history that Bloom knows nothing about?

As for Dlugacz, he can be found serving customers in his butcher's on Upper Dorset Street, and when we first meet him we do not think immediately of Joyce's Zionist friend in Trieste, who was also called by that name, or spend too much time reflecting on Zurich where the episode was composed. Equally, we need a certain amount of flexibility and an awareness of how Joyce typically moves back and forth, for if there is a Central European dimension to *Ulysses*, it resides more in the story of Bloom and his Hungarian Jewish family than in the streets of Dublin. However, there is another way altogether of thinking about this, especially evident from the vantage-point of continental Europe. In incorporating such references – never far from stereotypes – into his Irish capital, Joyce not only insists on a European dimension to his novel but, ironically, he also reminds us that his city is perhaps not so much 'hybrid' as essentially 'domestic', one which harbours an attachment more to inside stories and non-conformity than to imposing vistas and neat thoroughfares. Furthermore, it was a city which understood emigration better than immigration, which was more at home with comforting stereotypes than with the challenge of difference. What I want to reflect on here are the implications in all this, how, while the best Irish writers work the hybrid landscape, in Joyce's case in *Ulysses*, it is often an imagined hybrid landscape.

In a schematic history of Joyce's texts at least three, inevitably overlapping, stages in his understanding of hybridity can be discerned: the first is realistic texture, the second is a mixture of realism and invention, and the third is what we might call the coincidence of opposites. This is the trajectory from *Dubliners* to *Ulysses* to *Finnegans Wake*, works which in turn reflect his move from his native city to Trieste and Zurich and then in the post-war period to Paris. As he put physical space between himself and Ireland, realistic texture gives way to a greater sense of imagining his native country as even more hybrid than he had previously imagined, and this in turn issues in the realisation that, in the words of Virginia Woolf at the end of *To the Lighthouse*, 'nothing was simply one thing'.[78] In 'The Dead', Gabriel Conroy is accused of being a West Briton, where the charge has some resonance in the years leading up to Easter 1916. Bloom, who is one of only a few thousand Jews – or people with Jewish names – to walk the streets of Dublin in 1904, doesn't hesitate in calling Shakespeare 'our national poet'. And we should never forget that the Jewish community in Dublin in 1904 were mostly from Lithuania, not Hungary.

For the name of his protagonist in *Finnegans Wake*, Joyce turned to a Guide Book for Bognor in West Sussex where he read about a churchyard in Sidlesham with unusual names, which included Glue, Gravy, and Earwicker.[79] The chances are Joyce never even visited the graveyard and yet it was only a few miles from Bognor where he was staying in the summer of 1923. As he says about his fictional portrait in *Finnegans Wake*, 'Shem was a sham', where we might notice a play on Sidlesham, for the final syllable in 'Sidlesham' is written 'sham'

---

78 Virginia Woolf, *To the Lighthouse* (Oxford: World's Classic, 1999), 251.
79 *A Pictorial and Descriptive Guide to Bognor* (London: Ward Lock, 1918).

but pronounced 'shem' with an unstressed schwa. As the author of *Metamorphosis* was among the first to recognise, nothing is simply one thing. The 'wick' of Earwicker reminds us this is a Scandinavian name and linked to Birger Jarl, the founder and builder of modern Stockholm, who together with Jarl Van Hoother provides another aspect of the HCE figure. And never far from Earwicker's name is the insect, the earwig, which in turn gets inside our 'auditory imagination', as T.S. Eliot would want to emphasise.

The history of the word 'hybrid' – a word incidentally that no-one familiar with *Finnegans Wake* would invoke, for what is *Finnegans Wake* but an extraordinary refusal to recognise the world in anything but hybrid terms, so there's nothing especially revelatory about the term – the history of the word is potentially relevant to what I have to say here. The word itself began its English life in the seventeenth century to describe the offspring of a tame sow and wild boar, but it came into its own in the nineteenth century, a century when race and empire became increasingly important to the European powers. But throughout its history, in its drive to identify and classify, 'hybrid' managed to draw into the same field of play animals, human beings, and plants. As a critical tool, as part of a classificatory matrix, serving the scientific community in shaping the world, the term was neutral. A 'hybrid' was in this sense an offspring of different animals or species of plant. In Samuel Johnson's *Dictionary* (1755) the word 'hybridous', an ugly adjective which fortunately didn't make it into modern English, is defined as 'Begotten between animals of different species'. The concept, it is true, carried an ideological baggage as all classificatory systems do, but it was primarily designed to be deployed as if it did not. Such scientific use can still be found today with its employment in computers and technology, as for example with analogue and digital modes. A hybrid car is now everywhere. A 'hybrid' bill in State legislatures is one that has public and private features. More recently we have witnessed a hybrid form of warfare, which includes conventional warfare, irregular warfare and cyber warfare.

Problems arose when the term was used to describe people. And this problem we might notice was there from its inception in the seventeenth century. 'She's a wild Irish born, sir, and a hybrid', remarks the Host in Ben Jonson's lively play *New Inn* (1629) in a passage that also includes reference to pedigree (the joke is that 'she' isn't wild Irish but an English gentlewoman in disguise, just as the Host, whose assumed name is Good-stock, is in fact a Lord).[80] In a topsy-turvy world that the play delights in, Jonson's use of the word – and the OED begins its illustrative account of this word with Jonson's play – is clearly playful. A 'hybride', spelt in some editions with an e, is in this case someone who dresses up, puts on an accent, and has fun with social class and with national and sexual identity. And we cannot help noticing the disparaging use of 'wild Irish' in the play.

But invariably hovering around the term in its later uses in the nineteenth century, when applied to people, is an unmistakable pejorative sense even when that is designed to expose prejudice. In an article in *Transactions of the Ethnological Society* in 1861 – and 'ethnological' carries a powerful ideological signature in the nineteenth century – F. Crawford admits that the English are a hybrid race, but he deflects this potential for denigration with the qualification: 'and not the worse for that'. But in general to call a racial group today a hybrid or, indeed, to call an individual of mixed race a hybrid reveals the fences and proper hesitation that surround the term. And in case we thought Irish as a language was more enlightened, we should recall that one word for hybrid is 'croschineálach', which begins with a cross, while another word 'measc' is used, according to Patrick Dinneen in his *Foclóir Gaedilge agus Béarla: An Irish-English Dictionary* (1904), to refer to the offspring of an ass and a horse as well as 'confused', 'inebriated' and 'half-caste'.[81]

Interestingly, even in the non-human world, the term can carry echoes of such ideological scars. A certain species of rose is a hybrid as opposed to what? Something more pure, more itself, unmixed? That's the implication, that there is a thing which is the norm and something

<hr/>

80 Ben Jonson, *New Inn* (ed. Michael Hattaway) (Manchester: Manchester University Press, 1984), 114.
81 Patrick Dinneen, *Foclóir Gaedilge agus Béarla: An Irish-English Dictionary* (Dublin: M.H. Gill, 1904).

which deviates from that norm. Professional gardeners perhaps don't worry overmuch as other users of the language, but what about when the term is applied to animals? We don't use the word 'hybrid' with dogs or horses; instead we invoke a vocabulary of pure-bred or thorough-bred, or pedigree, or cross-breed or mongrel. And we alter our view or the price we're prepared to pay accordingly.

While his contribution to postcolonial discourse might be limited, Joyce is no stranger to many of the debates. A 'West Briton', as Miss Ivors recognised, her head full of Hyde's attack on hybridity in his famous 1892 essay on de-anglicisation, was not a 'true' Irishman. (D 88–90) The word 'hybrid' is not used in *Ulysses*, but throughout we are conscious of hybridity whether that is understood in connection with the status of Gibraltar or, in the case of the main protagonist in the novel, the uncircumcised Jew. In a passage full of spite and prejudice in 'Cyclops', the normally kind-hearted Martin Cunningham stoops to calling Bloom a 'perverted jew'. Crofton, whose religious affiliation does not merit the use of upper case and who undergoes a name change himself becoming 'Crofter the Orangeman or presbyterian', distances himself from the outsider: 'We don't want him' (U 12:1635). Needless to say, it is unclear to whom Crofton is referring in his use of 'We'. In 'Ivy Day in the Committee Room', the *Dubliners* story about an election in the period after the fall of Parnell, Crofton, who is canvassing for the Conservative candidate, is also given to few words. Joe Hynes recites a poem 'The Death of Parnell'. Crofton listens. Parnell is a figure Crofton did not support, and after it he delivers, in a story full of deflationary observations and remarks, the underwhelming verdict in the final sentence of the story: 'Mr Crofton said it was a very fine piece of writing' (D 135). Joyce lets it stand, the bottles uncorked, the flattest note in a deliberately flat story. We might be tempted to conclude that in a hybrid universe the person who is of a different persuasion can be reduced to hiding his or her feelings behind the wall of language. But it should not be forgotten that Hyde and Parnell were Protestants.

Even the animal kingdom is co-opted into this continuing piece of theatre in 'Cyclops', so that when Garryowen the dog starts sniffing

Bloom's leg, we are 'reliably' informed that 'those jewies does have a sort of a queer odour coming off them' (*U* 12:452–3). The insertion of 'sort of' reminds us of how some constructions in language also express a kind of hybrid status, for prejudice relies on imprecision at every level. Not 'a queer odour' but 'a sort of a queer odour', where 'sort' is not doing what it is supposed to do, namely sort or define. Clearly, with Hungarian Jewish ancestry, the son of a father whose family name was Virag, who changed his name by deed poll on arriving in Ireland, and who poisoned himself soon after, Bloom lacks the credentials of being considered a 'true' Irishman. Or at least this is how people in pubs and elsewhere think of him, wishing to put him down. And if his Irishness is in doubt, then so, too, for some less (for)giving critics, is his Jewishness. For Robert Adams, 'Leopold Bloom is a magic lantern Jew, as he is a cut-out Hungarian. Or to speak more analytically, Leopold Bloom's Hungarian characterization was a surface to which Joyce tried (not very successfully) to find a foundation.'[82] At the same time what Molly finds attractive in him – or at least this is what he imagines – is that he looked 'so foreign from the others' (*U* 13:1210). So what we learn from *Ulysses* is that hybridity allows scope for malicious gossip to thrive, narrative cohesion to be advanced even through error or inaccuracy, and characters given depth or a positive gloss beyond their caricature.

Finnegans Wake presents another case altogether, for what is *Finnegans Wake* if not a constant reminder of the warping process and the impossibility of purity (which in one sense can only be established by attending closely to the written word). What is Shem but a 'hybrid' (*FW* 169.09)? And, as in Jonson's play, it is the externals which count. Hence the description of Shem's 'fortytwo hairs off his uncrown', his 'loose liver' and general 'bodily getup' and how he was a 'sham', preferring tinned salmon to the real stuff caught in the river Liffey. It is all delightfully excessive and designed to mock the whole concept of hybridity and at the same time lend sympathy to the 'poorjoist'. Elsewhere in *Finnegans Wake*, Joyce coins the word 'paleoparisien' (*FW* 151.9) to describe another layer to his hybrid identity, a term that has a

82 Robert M. Adams, *Surface and Symbol: The Consistency of James Joyce's Ulysses* (New York: Oxford University Press, 1962), 106.

creative dimension for, as Jean-Michel Rabaté suggests, Joyce invented the French heritage he modestly claimed for himself.[83]

In other places in *Finnegans Wake*, Joyce's target is more straightforward as when he plays on 'hybreds' and 'hybrid' in the formal address: 'Gentes and laitymen, fullstoppers and semicolonials, hybreds and lubberds!' (*FW* 152.16–7) 'Gentes and laitymen', the people ('la gente' in Spanish) and the laity, or more precisely the Church and its hierarchy of power where the laity always took their place, whether in church itself, or in processing into or out of the church, or in funeral reports in Dublin newspapers (as happens in *Ulysses*), last behind the real men, the gentry that is and the clergy. Some people are 'fullstoppers', have all the works, all the pomp and ceremony including clearly demarcated territories; others are but 'semicolonials', semicolons, not quite full status syntactically but wishing ideologically to identify with a main clause or mother country, where half-status underscores their vulnerability, always looking abroad or over their shoulder that is. As for 'hybreds and lubberds', these are high-breds and low-breds. Behind 'hybred', spelt with a y, we can also perhaps discern the word 'hybrid'. Here is a class marker which language, as Joyce repeatedly shows, helps to sustain, for Joyce understands language and power, and he instinctively knows how to get behind and expose a culture's protective mask. On the one hand there are the high-breds; on the other, lubbers or clumsy people. Inherited wealth, we recall, is about lineage and denying that breeding, that is good breeding, has anything in common with hybridity.

In his description of Shem we read: 'Putting truth and untruth together a shot may be made at what this hybrid actually was like to look at.' (*FW* 169.8–10) Joyce is right to question: what does a 'hybrid' person look like? It would be inviting an understandably negative response to call someone of mixed race, or indeed someone who has an English father and Irish mother, a hybrid or to invoke Johnson's adjective 'hybridous'. That is to accept a *thoroughbred* interpretation of the world. Equally, Joyce is hardly standing up for hybrids. Unlike the use of 'queer' in Queer Studies, hybrid is restricted in its use, so that there is little sense of people who were or are 'hybrid' fighting back or writing back. Moreover, to describe a culture as essentially hybrid is also problematic because there is a natural reluctance today to describe a culture as 'pure'. Unfortunately, when the term 'hybridity' began to be used in postcolonial studies it potentially carried all these associations. The term 'culture', deriving in part from Latin *cultura* and the cultivation of the soil, moves easily between its many meanings and gains something by its different associations, but this is not the case with 'hybrid'.

If you were learning Irish some time in the past, you might have come across an innocuous sentence such as 'Conas tá tú inniu mo dhuine uasal fionn?' Which translates as 'How are you today my fair gentleman?' But supposing you came across the same in *Finnegans Wake*: 'Guinness thaw tool in jew me dinner ouzel finn' (35.15–6), which Joyce rightly glosses as 'a nice how-do-you-do in Poolblack'. How do you get from Irish 'inniu' to English 'jew', from today to jew? Or fionn that is white or fair to finn, the end? Not every border crossing is a flight to freedom, and some encounters are distinctly threatening. But against the use of force there is something to be said for marching across the imagined hybrid landscape under Joyce and Woolf's banner: 'Nothing was simply one thing.' Dublin after all in reverse is 'Poolblack' and looks out to the Lancashire seaside resort of Blackpool. The slogan, then, remains the best retort to nationalist extremists and racial purists, for, my quibbles about Molly Bloom and Gibraltar notwithstanding, Joyce's celebration of hybridity, whether real or imagined, is a reflection of his advocacy of peace and living together without fear.

CHAPTER 3

PREPARATORY TO ANYTHING ELSE: THE OPENING TO 'EUMAEUS'

Unless it was 'open thy mouth and put thy foot in it', I couldn't imagine a more pleasing title to an essay on 'Eumaeus' than the one I have chosen. Preparatory to anything else. Or to give it the full works knowing what we do about the episode and how it unfolds in all its impropriety and ungrammatical glory unexpectedly or should I say hopelessly before our eyes on turning the page: 'Preparatory to anything else Mr Bloom brushed off the greater bulk of the shavings and handed Stephen the hat and ashplant and bucked him up generally in orthodox Samaritan fashion which he very badly needed.' 'Thank whoever for the invention of the full stop' is the cry that goes up from the reader when faced with many of the sentences in this episode, this one included.

Let me come at this again, for it is only through repeated attempts at articulation that we can get a proper hold on this awkward, opening sentence: 'Preparatory to anything else Mr Bloom brushed off the greater bulk of the shavings and handed Stephen the hat and ashplant and bucked him up generally in orthodox Samaritan fashion which he very badly needed.' I very badly needed to read that sentence again if only to get it off my chest and out of my system. 'Nausicaa' has some sickly prose but, with apologies to the examples in Lindley Murray's grammar books for schools in the nineteenth century, you can't beat 'Eumaeus' as an example of how not to write English prose.[84]

Preparatory to anything else, I'm going to devote most of my allotted time to this opening sentence. I wanted to tackle or give the appearance of tackling the whole episode, but, as soon as I began putting pen to paper, as so often happens to readers of Joyce, I got delayed and discovered I couldn't proceed as fast as I wished. Let me begin, then, with the opening phrase 'Preparatory to anything else'. It isn't quite clear what this phrase governs. Presumably, it is the rest of the sentence, how 'Mr Bloom brushed off the greater bulk of the shavings and handed Stephen the hat and ashplant and bucked him up generally in orthodox Samaritan fashion which he very badly needed.' Before doing anything else, that is, Bloom brushed down his companion. But, expressed thus, it seems to imply more, that there's a list of things he has to do or had to do.

The French translation which Joyce apparently oversaw has this: 'Avant toute chose', literally 'before everything', or 'firstly' or 'above all', which isn't 'Preparatory to anything else'. From the outset we recognise that 'Eumaeus' is an episode that deliberately uses multiple registers within sentences, so any translation has to attend to this slippage, movement or variety. Getting this right is as important as what is said. In fact, I haven't expressed this terribly well: without stylistic variability this episode would fall flat. The translator might be tempted to iron out the infelicities of style and what Lindley Murray would call 'low expressions', and make it all sound like the Queen's English or in conformity to the Port Royal grammar, but this would be a wrong move. Equally, the prose isn't what we might call 'stilted', so that, too, would be a wrong kind of move by a translator. Nothing is quite right in this episode, and most sentences are faulty or wonky or just weird. The opening phrase is deliberately inflated or antiquated. It is not 'Before everything' or indeed 'Before anything else' but 'Preparatory to anything else'.

---

84 Lindley Murray, *English exercises, adapted to the Grammar lately published by L. Murray Designed for the benefit of private learners, as well as for the use of schools* Third edition (York: Wilson, Spence, and Mawman: 1798).

In this episode style carries all before it. On the internet there is a plot summary to 'Eumaeus' and this is how the opening is summarised: 'It is 1am on the corner of Beaver Street. Bloom helps Stephen up'. In its own way this is quite funny, a kind of Eumaean take on the style of the original. If the reader very badly needs such a summary to this episode, it is difficult to envisage how this might be constructed or indeed construed. You could not imagine Joyce beginning the first drafts with 'It is 1am on the corner of Beaver Street. Bloom helps Stephen up'. He must have always had in mind the idea of impertinence, how style and content are at variance. 'Preparatory to anything else' is in this sense equivalent to saying – and forgive me for switching between formal and informal registers – 'Before you get a take on this episode, get an earful of this.' 'Ouch', as Lindley Murray might say. And let me add that expressions such as 'Preparatory to anything else' and 'bucked him up generally' are not clichés, as Mark Scroggins asserts on his site on the internet where he discusses 'Bad Joyce'.

In an essay in *Renascent Joyce* (2013), which is reviewed below, Robert Byrnes invokes Flaubert in his title, 'Joyce's Dictionnaire des Idiotismes Reçus: Comparing the 1929 and 2004 Translations of "Eumaeus"'. He cannot be faulted for identifying 2,923 clichés in the episode. If we accept that a cliché is an overworked expression, then, strictly speaking, there are no clichés in 'Eumaeus'. What we have are twists on clichés or Joyce playing with such expressions we know as clichés. In their 'Notes on James Joyce's *Ulysses*', which is available on the net, Gerry Carlin and Mair Evans are precise: 'Probably the most stylistically conventional chapter in the novel, the narrative is composed almost entirely of clichés and second-hand "literary" styles.'[85] If we picked out the passage in the second paragraph which includes a reference to 'buttons', we can see how Joyce is doing something different from what the authors claim. As Bloom and Stephen 'proceeded perforce in the direction of Amiens street railway terminus,' we learn that Mr Bloom was 'handicapped by the circumstance that one of the back buttons of his trousers had, to

85 See https://sites.google.com/site/notesonjamesjoyce/00–notes-on-james-joyce/eumaeus

vary the timehonoured adage, gone the way of all buttons' (*U* 16:34–8). That last phrase, 'gone the way of all buttons', which sounds like something Joyce as a child might have heard from his father, turns a familiar phrase ending with 'flesh' into the comedy associated with 'buttons' and how Bloom might have struggled keeping his trousers secure with a button missing from his braces and he reduced to being 'handicapped' therefore. As for 'the timehonoured adage', what Bloom or the narrator or Bloom as narrator are looking for is 'timehonoured fashion', a phrase which neatly captures what Joyce is doing in this episode with all the twists on clichés.

There is so much freshness in this episode that I am surprised by the amount of critical commentary which labours its staleness. BBC News carries an item posted on Bloomsday 2004 by Neil Smith entitled 'Cheat's Guide to Joyce's Ulysses'. Chapter 16 is summarised thus: 'A weary Bloom takes Stephen to a cabman's shelter where they listen to the ramblings of a tattooed sailor who makes little or no senzzzzzzz'.[86] The new Folio edition of *Ulysses*, introduced by Danis Rose, John O'Hanlon and Stacey Herbert, declares: 'Part Three sees the men coming back to bleak reality over tea and buns in a cabman's shelter – the story itself is told in an exhausted, hung-over style – before the two go back to Bloom's house to discuss life into the early hours.'[87] If we leave aside whether or not Stephen did accompany Bloom home, I am troubled by the claim that the style of 'Eumaeus' is 'exhausted' and 'hung-over' or indeed that the reality is 'bleak'. Perhaps I am reading a different book, for to me this episode is thoroughly entertaining. Karen Lawrence in *The Odyssey of Style in Ulysses* (1981) has a more nuanced, if now slightly dated, approach, one that considers stupidity in the nineteenth-century novel with particular reference to Flaubert and how such a tradition influenced Joyce. At one point she writes: 'By intensifying the use of clichés, by making them come at the reader so thick and fast at every comma,

86 http://news.bbc.co.uk/1/hi/entertainment/3810193.stm
87 James Joyce, *Ulysses* (intro Danis Rose, John O'Hanlon and Stacey Herbert with illustrations by John Vernon Lord) (London: The Folio Society, 2017).

Joyce exposes their absurdity.'[88] There is merit in such an approach but it is not one I want to follow here.

So, to return to 'Preparatory to anything else', this is a reminder that we are at the beginning of something, the Odyssean *Nostos* or Return. But it is an odd sort of reminder, because such a formal introduction should lead to a meaty paragraph summarising how far we've got on our travels as a reader and so on. We might, however, agree that a line has been drawn under the 'shavings' of the previous episode, 'Circe', and that the night-town sequence and the Odyssey proper are well and truly over. The opening phrase perhaps alerts us to the ensuing episode, 'Ithaca', and to the droll style of the question-and-answer session between Bloom and Stephen. In this sense the phrase 'Preparatory to anything else' is a way of saying 'Before we come onto the catechism and Mangnall's *Encyclopedia*[89], there's a few things we have to clear up in the cabman's shelter.'

At the same time, the phrase gestures toward a position outside what is to follow. Because it is in many ways an impertinent phrase, it perhaps gives me a certain licence to extend that impertinence with the claim that everything in the episode of 'Eumaeus' that follows is governed by 'Preparatory to anything else'. Before we get down to business or whatever it is we have to do, here are the things we must attend to. Thus, everything after 'Preparatory to anything else' constitutes a list. Indeed, the episode is nothing other than a list of thoughts or a reprise of what we already know or have already encountered in the novel. In that sense it provides another example of recycling that Margot Norris writes about in *The Cambridge Companion to James Joyce*. 'Eumaeus' we can readily agree is not 'Cyclops' but it does contain material we might itemise or want to itemise. Unlike 'Cyclops', however, the episode consigns to a list things already covered and ticked off. So, whenever we encounter something that looks like a list, such as the touristy version of Ireland, it is a list that has already been used as a list.

---

88 Karen Lawrence, *The Odyssey of Style in Ulysses* (Princeton, NJ: Princeton University Press, 1981), 75.

89 Richmal Mangnall, *Mangnall's Encyclopedia and Miscellaneous Questions* Third edition (London: Longman, Brown, Green, Longmans & Roberts, 1857).

There's nothing particularly newsworthy about anything that follows 'Preparatory to anything else'. The freshest one-liner in the episode is Stephen's much-quoted remark about changing the subject seeing that one could not change the country. (*U* 16:1171)

With the publication of Umberto Eco's characteristically wide-ranging and erudite study, *The Infinity of Lists* (2009), the idea of lists came back into vogue, but we shouldn't forget that sentence structure or phrases also conform in part to a list.[90] Consider, for example, the opening sentence as a list: 'Preparatory to anything else Mr Bloom brushed off the greater bulk of the shavings and handed Stephen the hat and ashplant and bucked him up generally in orthodox Samaritan fashion which he very badly needed.' This might be clearer if I were to read that in such a way as to bring out a list of phrases one after the other in sequence:

> Preparatory to anything else
> Mr Bloom brushed off the greater bulk of the shavings
> and handed Stephen the hat and ashplant
> and bucked him up generally
> in orthodox Samaritan fashion
> which he very badly needed.

This is a list not so much of things to do but of actions on the part of the narrator or character. Six things are listed: before, then brushing, then the handover, then bucking up, then how he did that, then a comment by either the narrator or Bloom 'which he very badly needed'. It is a list of clauses in a sentence posing as an 'orthodox' sentence. There is a nice rhythm, with five of the lines beginning in iambic fashion and the final line slowing down on account of the full stress on 'which'. But the effect is disorienting, not only on account of the misplaced relative clause at the end but also on account of adjectives such as 'orthodox' or a phrasal verb such as 'bucked him up'. Equally, the stress on 'the greater bulk' of

90 Umberto Eco, *The Infinity of Lists* (trans Alastair McEwen) (London: MacLehose Press, 2009).

the shavings seems designed to distract the reader or slightly shift the scene-setting focaliser by coming at things from inside Bloom's anxious state of mind. We might be reminded of Eco's remark that in the modern world 'the list is conceived out of a taste for *deformation*' (245).

As for the 'orthodox Samaritan', this is a delightful confusion, and comes so early on in the episode, for we've only just got into the first phrase preparing us for something when we've got stuck already on a 'Jewish' bloomer. The Italian translation by Giulio de Angelis follows Auguste Morel's French translation and has 'alla maniera del buon Samaritano', after the manner of the good Samaritan.[91] This, unfortunately, misses the humour of 'orthodox'. We know that Bloom is a good Samaritan, kind to animals and blind striplings and so on, but he is also the butt of humour, as the original phrase suggests. What Bloom confuses is 'orthodox fashion', as in to do something in orthodox fashion, the good Samaritan of the Gospels, and Jews who are orthodox. I could be wrong but I don't believe there is such a thing as an 'orthodox Samaritan'. As we see from what happens later in 'Eumaeus', Bloom's defence of Judaism against the Citizen in 'Cyclops' continues to agitate him, and, in relaying that incident to Stephen, he repeats what he said at the time, how Jesus was a Jew. *Ulysses* is a Greek-Jew novel and Bloom is a Greek-Jew character, but Bloom is also, again unconsciously, describing himself in the phrase, an 'orthodox Samaritan', that is someone who exists between Judaism and Christianity, on the borders where the Holy Land and the great religions meet. In the cave of 'Cyclops' Bloom is referred to as a 'perverted jew' (*U* 12:1635). This phrase also plays on the idea of conversion, a converted Jew (or Christian) and a person who suffers an insult, but now the context is decidedly nasty and full of prejudice. Not surprisingly Bloom is unnerved. What's in a name is a question that runs throughout the novel, but from the opening sentence of 'Eumaeus' we are treated to a humorous response to such a question.

According to Teresa Caneda, the Spanish translation by Fransciso

---

91 James Joyce, *Ulisse* (trans Giulio de Angelis) (1960; Milan: Arnoldo Mondadori Editore, 1967). James Joyce, *Ulysse* (trans Auguste Morel with assistance of Stuart Gilbert) (1929; Paris: Gallimard, 1957).

Tortosa 'en el modo ortodoxo samaritano' is odd, unnatural, baroque-sounding, and would have been better to use 'a la manera' or 'de la forma'.[92] But I assume Tortosa was attempting to capture something of the oddness of the original. An earlier translation by José María Valverde has 'le adecentó de la manera más ortodoxamente samaritana' or helped him in the most orthodoxly samaritan fashion. But this misses the play on orthodox (as in orthodox Jew). The problem with 'Eumaeus' is that the style is peculiar but not necessarily stilted or old-fashion. Hugh Kenner declares strikingly it is 'a stylistic homage in Bloom's style to Bloom'.[93] This is another reason it is especially difficult to get right in translation. Bloom's language in this episode is full of other associations which he is at the mercy of, or full of other associations, which he is at the mercy of. Stilted English suggests something else. Interestingly, in the Rosenbach manuscript Joyce wrote 'good Samaritan fashion', so it took him some time to stumble on the 'orthodox Samaritan' joke.

The phrase 'bucked him up generally' is such an extraordinary expression that it can make any other association slightly beside the point. It is the addition of the adverb 'generally' after the phrasal verb that does this. It is perfectly fine to refer to bucking someone up and even add 'as best one could'. It is the position of the adverb, as much as the adverb itself, which makes for oddness. Tortosa has 'le animó', encouraged him, or we might retranslate that back into English as 'animated him'. 'And animated him generally' catches something of the antiquated style of the original, but you can also deduce it is not the original, which takes up into it a current English expression only to distort it in the process. 'le remit d'aplomb' is Morel's sober French translation, literally returned him upright. But, apart from some great one-liners, we hardly ever observe Stephen doing anything with aplomb. So perhaps this is not the best translation.

Reflecting further on the opening phrase 'Preparatory to any-

92 James Joyce, *Ulises* (trans Francisco García Tortosa) revised edition (Madrid: Cátedra, 2003).

93 Hugh Kenner, *Joyce's Voices* (Berkeley, CA and London: University of California Press, 1978), 38.

thing else', we realise that it, too, is already governed by something else. We are already circling close to the orbit of Bloom's slightly anxious mind. He is not quite sure of his ground but he would like to get acquainted with Simon Dedalus's son, a young man who has a degree and writes poetry and speaks foreign languages but who is also taciturn and fairly unapproachable. 'Preparatory' is therefore not so much what it says but what it betrays, a form of ulterior motivation. It is already part of another discourse, in this case psychological, and unable to get far on its own. Bloom is thinking ahead, laying out what he needs to do. First I will dust him down, then I will take him for a coffee or cocoa, then I can have a chat with him and perhaps invite him back to the house.

'Preparatory' leads not forward in this case but back to 'anything else', not something else, but anything else. It is the kind of phrase you might hear in a vegetable market, when the trader asks you after getting you various things such as a pound of tomatoes and half-a-pound of mushrooms. 'Anything else?' 'Qualquier cosa' is how the Spanish translation renders this phrase, 'toute chose' the French. But I wonder what you'd hear in a Spanish or French market? 'Algo mas?' sounds more like something you might hear in Spain. The phrase has a lifted quality, lifted that is from common speech, and it acts like a container or, indeed, a shopping-bag in which all kinds of things can be stored or collected. Indeed, the information that is revealed in 'Eumaeus' has the look of something miscellaneous rather than essential. This leftover quality is something I find rather engaging for it is as if the only gloss we need when reading 'Eumaeus' is the novel we've already read up to this point.

Throughout the episode we keep being reminded of previous events or passages or phrases we've encountered before. 'bucked him up generally' recalls Buck Mulligan and his attempts at bucking up Stephen in 'Telemachus', as when he tells him: 'Chuck Loyola, Kinch, and come on down' (*U* 1:231–2). Bloom doesn't know any of this and yet here we have an echo of something that we might be tempted to call the work of the Arranger.[94] And yet it is not like the Arranger who pops up to greet us in a phrase such as 'as said before'. By 'Eumaeus' it is as if Joyce can dispense with the idea of the Arranger and simply involve us the reader in his game. If you want to think of the first episode of the Telemachiad and Buck Mulligan, that's fine, Joyce seems to be saying. I allow it. This is my anything else chapter, including a reader's take on his or her reading. Or consider the phrase 'Funny, very!' (U 16:600) In 'Eumaeus' this has acquired an exclamation mark. In 'Aeolus' we read 'Clever, Very' (U 7:674) as one of the subheadings without the exclamation mark. First time round it is the Arranger. Second time round it looks as if it is Joyce having fun with the Arranger. We are, as I say, in the 'anything else' mode.

'Funny, very!' comes at the end of a passage about Skin-the-Goat, the keeper of the cabman's shelter, and his possible role in the murder of the Chief Secretary to Ireland in the Phoenix Park in 1882. Mention of the incident produces a meaningful exchange of glances between Bloom and Stephen: 'His inscrutable face which was really a work of art, a perfect study in itself, beggaring description, conveyed the impression that he didn't understand one jot of what was going on. Funny very!' Again, what we have here is the humour of bad English recalling something familiar to the attentive reader of the novel. And part of the humour centres on the fact that nothing, not a jot, is going to be resolved in this episode, and certainly not the truth or otherwise about Skin-the-Goat. Indeed, after such an inscrutable sentence, the role of the keeper in that historical episode is even less clear. 'Eumaeus', then, is a perfect study in itself, an episode which also goes some way to beggaring description. As for Bloom,

---

94 This is a term that has become widespread among critics in discussing *Ulysses*. The anonymous Arranger intervenes not as a third person narrator but as a slightly unnerving, supra-personal figure, 'arranges' things, cautioning or advising the reader. David Hayman was the first critic to identify this figure as the Arranger. See his '*Ulysses*': *The Mechanics of Meaning* (1970, 1982). Hugh Kenner has many interesting observations on this figure in *Ulysses* (London: Allen and Unwin, 1980). No-one, as far as I know, has yet come up with an equally convincing term or, rather, series of terms to identify the various figures who compose the Arranger, for there are clearly many.

in one sense, he, too, doesn't understand a jot, an iota if we think of
the Greek motif, of what is going on, for he is but a character in a
novel which delights in its fictional status while invoking history for
its realistic texture.

There are so many comic moments in 'Eumaeus' as it reprises
aspects of the novel, but one of the funniest moments for me is the
sentence that ends with the word 'getup'. Not to be outdone by W.B.
Murphy's exotic Bolivian postcard showing native women scantily
clad outside a primitive osier, women who are perhaps given to eating
horse liver raw, Bloom shows Stephen a photo of his wife, Molly:

> the accomplished daughter of Major Brian Tweedy
> [who] displayed at an early age remarkable proficiency
> as a singer having even made her bow to the public
> when her years numbered barely sweet sixteen. As for
> the face it was a speaking likeness in expression but it
> did not do justice to her figure which came in for a
> lot of notice usually and which did not come out to
> the best advantage in that getup. She could without
> difficulty, he said, have posed for the ensemble, not to
> dwell on certain opulent curves of the. (U 16.1441–8)

The word 'barely' has all the innuendo we associate with display,
while the figure coming in and then coming out reminds us of
Molly's curves, which are much commented on in the novel. Equally,
the final sentence should end with something about her figure but
it finishes abruptly or embarrassingly with the definite article. A
definite point we might say. A full stop reflects a shocked Bloom,
unable to quite bring himself to say 'breasts', the character viewed
from within and without. The Shakespeare and Company edition
has three elliptical points; the Rosenbach manuscript has what looks
like a single point or nipple with a space on either side. I am not
over-keen on the three elliptical points, for that seems too coy on
Bloom's part. It is also a reminder of how Sterne's *A Sentimental
Journey* (1768) ends with Yorick reaching out of bed in a dark room

and, presumably, catching hold of the Fille de Chambre's genitalia (which, depending on the edition, is set out either as a dash or an empty space). Such a reminder here seems misplaced. Luca Crispi has recently argued for the correctness of three elliptical points, but I still read this little moment as a single point, a full stop.[95] Of course, the reader is excluded from knowing at this juncture what Molly looks like, simply that the face was a 'speaking likeness' and that her figure was not revealed at its best in what she was wearing. Bernini's statues have sometimes attracted the phrase 'a speaking likeness', that is they give the impression of the figure about to speak, but this is different from a face having a speaking likeness to the subject. Bloom is perhaps reminded of his morning visit to the National Museum to see the statues of nude figures, and now he confuses a face that speaks and clothes that suppress.

But it is the 'getup' that delights me, a word that appears in the Rosenbach manuscript as 'get up'. At a stroke it drops into an informal register, which we cannot be sure is not Molly's word or Bloom distancing himself for Stephen's benefit from the high-flown view of his wife. Bloom is proud of Molly displaying herself to the world, but he is also slightly uneasy about this or where it might lead. So 'getup' suddenly enters his thoughts with what is for him (and for us) a word that inevitably carries a double meaning. It is a nice slip, a reminder of the early bawdy joke in the novel about who's getting it up, and it connects directly with Boylan getting it on or up with Molly. In, out, on, up. Words not only have a history but also a hinterland of association. Ever attentive to the body she inhabits, Molly in the next episode wonders 'have we too much blood up in us or what' (U 18:1122), where the insertion of 'up' again calls out for attention. Not in us but up in us. According to our guide, remote corners of Donegal might be 'getatable' only with difficulty and one of the denizens in the shelter has a 'seedy getup', but Molly can't wait to get out of her 'getup'.

'Preparatory to anything else….' As we delay on this opening sentence we can perhaps observe the careful way Joyce prepares

95 Luca Crispi, *Joyce's Creative Process and the Construction of Characters in Ulysses: Becoming the Blooms* (Oxford: Oxford University Press, 2015).

us for the episode which follows. In this way he plays fair by the reader. We would expect the shopping-bag that is 'Eumaeus' would contain references to most of the previous episodes, and we are not disappointed to learn at the end that Bloom and Stephen in their '*tête à tête*' – a phrase that Lindley Murray would have struck out as he would have done with all the other italicised foreign expressions in this episode – should include a reference to 'usurpers' and 'sirens'. This is a reminder if we ever need it of the Odyssean story on which *Ulysses* so generously draws. And for one sentimental moment the ancient Greek hero, the unconquered hero, comes into view, discussing with his son in private what he's been up to those ten years he's been away from home. Anything else?

CHAPTER 4

BENEDICT KIELY TRIBUTE

It is a great pleasure to be here in Omagh for the Benedict Kiely Weekend. It is also a great honour and a privilege to give this opening keynote address and to welcome everyone to the first Benedict Kiely weekend to be held since his death. It promises to be a memorable weekend with an appropriate mixture of serious reflection, serious enjoyment, and serious entertainment. It couldn't but be especially as our weekend here at the new Strule Arts Centre occupies a site between Sharon Shannon, the accordion player, who was on the programme at Dun Uladh last weekend, and Nuts about Squirrels, which I believe is the topic for the last weekend in September at Gortin Forest Park. Our weekend is slightly more high-brow being a literary event with poetry readings and creative writing workshops, but for all that we shouldn't get carried away. After all, Kiely was a writer who was himself positioned somewhere between traditional Irish music and a natural world teeming with life and interest, a writer who possessed a keen ear for the language and a keen eye for the world around him. Or if we were to extend the imagery slightly, we might say of Kiely that he was a forager like the squirrel and a celebrator like the traditional musician.

Positioned thus on this year's September programme for west Tyrone would surely have amused him. Music and the natural world.

Benedict Kiely between music and squirrels. He would then have been tempted to give it a slight twist to activate that sophisticated punctuation mark in English the colon (which he often used in a rhetorical as opposed to a strictly grammatical sense). 'Music and squirrels: the fiction of Benedict Kiely.' That would have appealed to him and set him off on another story, a memory from childhood, or his schooldays in 'sweet Omagh Town' or exploring the countryside around these parts, the streams and rivers and interlocking hills, the country cottages, the Big House, the estates emptied of wood and men by the Great War, the flax-dams and the clothes worn by the fashionable in the great cities of the world, or he might have recalled an incident from the last of the hiring fairs in the 1930s, or a snatch from a nationalist song or something to do with the 'counties of contention', the title of one of his early polemical books. Start with the streets of Omagh or Red Squirrel Week and you end up with the world or, better still for there was nothing PC about Kiely, the 'Beauty Queen of Iowa', which was a title to one of his stories.[96]

I never had an opportunity of meeting in person the 'gentle poet from the black Northern hills', as his fictional persona, Brother MacKenna, is described in *There Was an Ancient House*,[97] but I feel I know him through his writings and through his talks on RTE radio. 'The most urbane voice on Irish radio in the twentieth century' is how I describe him in *Light, Freedom and Song* (2005), my cultural history of modern Irish writing. I suspect he would have enjoyed this moment listening in to someone from across the water singing his praises amid the surroundings of his home town in an accent that is neither Scottish nor Irish but, when it is not RP, southern English. He was of course a 'gregarious' writer, if I can use that term in a positive sense and not in the sense that we find it in Kiely's 1960 novel *The Captain with the Whiskers*, where it is employed to discourage special friendships.[98] A journalist cannot but be gregarious, but Kiely's gregariousness was

96 All the stories mentioned here can be found in *The Collected Stories of Benedict Kiely* Introduction Colum McCann (London: Methuen, 2002).
97 *There Was an Ancient House* (1955; Dublin: Wolfhound, 1977), 71.
98 88.

so special that he gave the impression that he knew almost everyone in Ireland worth knowing, north and south of the border and across at least three generations – Brinsley MacNamara, Patrick Kavanagh, Brendan Behan, John Montague, Friel, Heaney to name but a few. He clearly cultivated friendships, not only here in Ireland but among his American acquaintances.

At the same time, he would have appreciated my status as an interested spectator, for he understood the way of the world, how it never quite conforms to the expected, and I thank the organisers for inviting me to participate in this celebration. And just in case you think my accent confirms my status as an outsider, perhaps I should add that I took my first steps in County Clare in the summer of 1948, that I attended an American Wake in the mid-fifties in a house now owned by the uillean piper Davy Spillane, and that my Irish family hosted some of the last house dances in the west of Ireland where an unknown Micho Russell from Doolin would play all night amid the crush of the set dancers, the uneven flagstones and the rising dust. Everything we might be tempted to say, including loss and all sorts of fleeting memories, comes along with us from the past.

The byways, lanes and boreens, the ancient footpaths, the minor roads and crosses, the streams and rivers – this is Kiely's chosen world. His father 'chained' Ireland, that is, he worked for the Ordnance Survey and used chains to measure the country. Benedict, his youngest son, engaged in a different sort of mapping or chaining. Get off the trunk roads and motorways, and life isn't so clear-cut or chiselled out or indeed measured. As he often reminds us in the course of his writings, the rivers Camowen and the Drumragh meet in Omagh and they then become the Strule. The Strule in turn runs north into the Fairywater and emerges as the graceful Foyle. In 'Down then by Derry' he wonders about the differences between the great rivers of the world such as the Amazon and the Seine but he is not overawed. Local rivers, he concludes, find their destiny in infinity:

> United, the waters of Drumragh and Camowen went
> on under the name of the Strule, sweeping in a great

horseshoe around the wide holm below the military
barracks, tramping and tossing northwards to meet yet
another river, the Fairywater, then to vanish glistening
into a green-and-blue infinity. (388)

The military barracks recall the divided North, but the rivers flow
into each other, circling round natural obstacles on their way not to
the sea but to infinity. They are 'United', being rivers of connection
flowing through counties of contention, and we hear the triumph
in that first word 'United'. Years later, in his last memoir *The Waves
Behind Us*,[99] published in 1999, as if he can't let go, he rehearses again
the course of these flowing rivers in a chapter entitled 'Beginning to
Write'. Joyce, too, couldn't let go, beginning his last book *Finnegans
Wake* with 'riverrun, past Eve and Adam's, from swerve of shore to
bend of bay, brings us by a commodious vicus of recirculation back to
Howth Castle and Environs'. (*FW* 3.1–3) As if to remind us that rivers
in cities have their source elsewhere, Joyce starts his most complex
book with a lower case. Civilisation took root along rivers but rivers
remain to unite us or to be followed by the naked eye. The upper case
took time to enter the language.

'Howandever', to quote one of his deliberately awkward
conjunctions, if we were to leave on one side for a moment his
biographical details and family history and attachment to home, we
might want to reflect on the common ground Kiely shares with other
Irish writers. As I suggest in *Reading Joyce* (2007), this is particularly
evident in the role that ritual plays in the imagination of the modern
Irish writer:

> If you're asked as a writer to draw water from the
> well of Irish life, you'll find like Joyce that what you
> return with again and again is ritual. Yeats begins
> with the ritual of storytelling in *The Celtic Twilight*
> (1893), Synge with the ritual of weddings and wakes

99 *The Waves Behind Us* (London: Methuen, 1999), 61–3.

in his plays, Roddy Doyle with the ritual of abuse, John McGahern with the ritual connected with the seasons. Rituals give us a culture, and, in Ireland particularly, culture, whether urban or rural, gives us rituals. (80–1)

The observation appears in a chapter on 'The Sisters', and I continue by writing about attending funerals and wakes in the west of Ireland and how the term 'faithful departed' stamps itself on the living as much as the dead. Joyce begins his career as a writer with a wake and ends it with a title that includes the word 'wake'.

On display throughout Kiely's work is not only a filial, wake-like attention to those who went before him but also an interest in the allied rituals of recitation and storytelling. Few modern writers are so given to recitation, and this has nothing to do with signs of a misspent youth poring over *Irish Fireside Songs* or *Our Boys*, the Christian Brothers' magazine, or with parading his knowledge, or indeed with betraying his post-modern credentials. We might remember the charge made against Brother MacKenna in Kiely's semi-autographical, Jesuit novel *There Was an Ancient House*, how he 'talks too much about books'.[100] Literature was a temptation for Kiely and he couldn't resist it. Indeed, although he suffered at the hands of the censor in Ireland, he went on to devote his whole life, when not writing, to talking about books, and what emerged was something unique.[101] For his fiction reaches all the time into the rich storehouse of European literature and Irish balladry. Proust and Shakespeare rub shoulders with a traditional singer like Paddy Tunney, and with ballads such as 'Sweet Omagh Town'. It would be pedantic to count all the quotations from other writers or Irish songs, but if you did it would probably exceed your expectations.

As with Joyce, keeping up is what his reader is often required to do, but it is supplemented by something else in Kiely. When you

100 Benedict Kiely, *There Was an Ancient House* (1955; Dublin: Wolfhound, 1979), 69.
101 Three of Kiely's books were banned in Ireland: *In a Harbour Green* (1949), *Honey Seems Bitter* (1952) and *There Was an Ancient House* (1955).

encounter a sentence that contains the phrase 'with my dog and gun o'er the moorland heather' – and more often than not he sets out the lines not as verse but as prose, as if he wants to emphasise the theme of continuity – before you realise it, if you're familiar with Irish traditional song, you're singing the song to yourself:

> To seek for pastime I took my way
> Where I espied a lovely fair one
> Her charms invited me a while to stay.[102]

Quotation works differently in Joyce as can be discerned for example in his early story 'Two Gallants'. Corley and Lenehan are walking along Nassau Street and then they turn into Kildare Street:

> Not far from the porch of the club a harpist stood in the roadway, playing to a little ring of listeners. He plucked at the wires heedlessly, glancing quickly from time to time at the face of each newcomer and from time to time, wearily also, at the sky. His harp too, heedless that her coverings had fallen about her knees, seemed weary alike of the eyes of strangers and of her master's hands. One hand played in the bass the melody of *Silent, O Moyle*, while the other hand careered in the treble after each group of notes. (D 54)

Thomas Moore's song, 'Silent, O Moyle', concerns Lir's daughter, Fionnuala, who is transformed into a swan and forced to wander for 900 years over the lakes and rivers of Ireland until the coming of Christianity. It is a song of exile, its symbolic status increased by 'the eyes of strangers' and by references to the Irish harp and to the position of the harpist outside a club where English officers and the Anglo-Irish would meet. The song is designed by Joyce to enforce an ironic message about the condition of Ireland at the turn of the

---

102 *The Captain with the Whiskers*, 70. The song in question is 'The Mountain Streams Where the Moorcocks Crow'.

twentieth century where young men wander the streets of Dublin not just unaware but also heedless of the exiled status that surrounds them. When the character of Maria in 'Clay' becomes confused and sings again the first verse of 'I Dreamt that I Dwelt in Marble Halls', we fill in (or look up) the missing stanza, which begins with 'I dreamt that suitors besought my hand'. Her romantic dreams at an end, her fate sealed, we interpret accordingly.

Joyce and Kiely constantly remind us that singing is part of the culture in Ireland. However, such songs in *Dubliners* serve to advance the narrative or reveal the plight of characters; they are not there primarily to show a common culture shared by all. That is not Joyce's intention. By contrast, Kiely's use of quotation often serves to summon up a common culture an Irish audience shares with the author. He is in this sense the celebrant at a Mass rather than the priest in the pulpit. In its purest form quotation constitutes a form of bonding not an invitation to observe irony or detachment. In its most savage form it hits out against those who would seek to destroy or interfere with that common culture. In *Nothing Happens in Carmincross* (1985), a novel set in the 1970s during the period of the Troubles, Mervyn recalls a newsflash about a seventeen-year-old Catholic girl having her head shaved and green paint poured over her for consorting with British Army soldiers:

> The green bald girl was taken to Altnagevlin hospital, Derry, where her condition is described as satisfactory: if I had you, lovely Martha, away down in Inishowen or in some lonely valley in the wild woods of Tyrone, I would do my whole endeavour and try to work my plan for to gain my prize and feast my eyes on the Flower of Sweet Strabane. (178)

The colon here works to join and to separate. On the one side there is the news report of a young woman suffering at the hands of the IRA; on the other side we read lines from a beautiful traditional song, 'The Flower of Sweet Strabane', set out like prose. The colon, the click inside the narrator's head, conveys the venom Kiely feels for the perpetrators. He doesn't want to enter into an argument with those who feel betrayed by the girl's actions. The colon shuts down that line of discussion. It is a hard-hitting judgment, full of anger by someone within the nationalist community, on those seeking to destroy a culture shared across the sectarian divide, a culture shared with a past that belongs to everyone. And, without any authorial comment, he continues with another news report from Iran about two men and two women being stoned to death for, among other things, adultery. The quotation thus acts as a substitute for a comment and the reader is given space to respond. Singing and recitation, we might well conclude, call attention not to an empty classroom ritual but to a living culture, a culture which, as Joyce also perceived, still has the potential to snap into place when called upon.

Kiely is also quite capable of reflecting the comic side of his inbred facility to recite. Consider the moment in his much-admired story 'The Night We Rode with Sarsfield', when the young boy, before he had internalised anything about the politics of Orange and Green, recites in the house of a Presbyterian neighbour the poem celebrating the rearguard action of the Jacobite leader Patrick Sarsfield at the Siege of Limerick in 1690. His older sisters, who realised a line had been crossed, 'never recovered from the shock' (484). It should have been a moment of triumph for the boy, how he repeated word-perfect the six-stanza 48–line ballad, which for his sisters offered a way of blotting out his efforts at singing a rebel song about heading off to Dublin in the green. But that wouldn't have produced a story, or at least not one of interest to the peace-loving Kiely. On the other hand, we might wonder how the young boy could be so innocent as to praise Sarsfield in the house of 'a good Orangeman' with the 12th July coming on and the sash hanging up to air 'for the great Walk and the great Day' as he recalls in *And As I Rode by Granard Moat* (1996), his book of songs and place.[103] How could he, especially as the Presbyterian couple, a brother and sister,

103 *And As I Rode by Granard Moat* (Dublin: Lilliput Press, 1996), 175.

had been kind enough to share with his family the roof of their house in the violent years following the Great War and the birth of the Irish Free State. The boy's innocence fills the pages of the story. Boyhood is linked by the generous-hearted Kiely with the past that surrounded his own childhood in the 1920s before the advent of a cruel sectarianism. It was a time when a graceful Orangeman, without conceding any ground, could appreciate the humour that divided a community.

Over the decades or centuries, there must have been many such examples of slips, gaffes, or just saying the wrong thing when Northern Catholics and Protestants found themselves in the same room. There is of course an elaborate set of rules and codes in the North to help people negotiate their way through life, beginning with given names and surnames, schools, places of work, hospitals, and the different cemeteries where Catholics and Protestants are interred. Identity in the North has been fiercely fought over and at times has been a matter of life and death. In this story Kiely reminds us of something else, how the occasional party pieces that go wrong can sometimes betray not only the neighbourliness that once existed between neighbours across the sectarian divide but also the sense of ritual perceived now not as a clash of cultures but as an encounter between different traditions, one in the shadow of the other. Whether the story is about longing or belonging is a natural question. Equally, perhaps the story points to a longing for a past where people mixed more. Mixing, we should recall, was so important to Kiely. When he was a boy, Omagh was a garrison town but its soldiers fraternised with the locals, unlike in the time of the recent Troubles when that proved impossible.

Or, to continue, is the clear-eyed Kiely recalling something about the nature of tribal identity and how belonging comes into play in a divided society? The story begins with a seven- or eight-year-old boy recalling how he put back gooseberries on the bushes by 'impaling' them (476). Kiely lets the image stand and doesn't return to it except at the end of the story, but the reader is alert to the potential image of violence in the word 'impaling'. Equally, playing gooseberry, if we were to pause over that opening image, is an awkward reminder of feeling on the outside of things, of not belonging, which is precisely the fate of the Catholic minority in the North. The story also reminds us we should be grateful for the boy who grew up in ignorance of the conventions governing Northern society, able to recall such an embarrassing moment in one sense without embarrassment and to approach the whole scene through humour and not satire. Rituals, then, give us a culture, and the gentle Kiely was a writer who knew how to offend when he needed to, but, more importantly to my mind, he also knew how never to offend gratuitously.

As for the ritual of storytelling, we might well agree that Kiely is one of modern Ireland's great storytellers, ever alert to the passage of time and the dark secrets of the heart. In the long winter evenings before the coming of electricity, what was there to do years ago but listen to music, get on each other's nerves, and tell stories? *Irish Fireside Tales* or *Beside the Fire* are favourite kinds of title for collections of Irish stories in the nineteenth century, the setting being in harmony as it were with the subject-matter and disposition of the stories themselves. Such stories, told in hillside cottages, might have been garnered from the ancient repertoire of myths concerning Oisin and Finn, or Diarmuid and Grainne, or Cuchulain of Muirthemne. Or they might have been traditional tales about the fairies or fields or wells, or more salacious stories such as we read about in Eric Cross's 1942 collection entitled *The Tailor and the Ansty*.[104] Not surprisingly, as we learn in one of his most impressive stories, 'Homes on the Mountain', the family possessed a whole series of pamphlets entitled 'Irish Fireside Songs'.

Kiely taps into this hillside culture of storytelling, 'the heroes in the dark house' as one of his stories is called, and he reminds us of its continuing power. In the 1970s the County Kerry shanachie, Eamon Kelly, could hold a radio audience for twenty minutes and more with stories about the Gobán Saor, that mythical mason and builder of mountains and round towers. 'It is a long time since the Goban Saor was alive', so begins one of the stories about the Goban Saor in Patrick Kennedy's *Legendary Fictions of the Irish Celts* (1866).

104 Eric Cross, *The Tailor and the Ansty* (1942; Cork: Mercier, 1990).

'That was the house where I put the gooseberries back on the bushes by sticking them on the thorns', so begins 'The Night We Rode with Sarsfield' (476). 'My father, the heavens be his bed, was a terrible man for telling you about the places he had been', so begins one of his finest stories 'A Journey to the Seven Streams' (200). Kiely is a traditional teller of tales, except the stories he tells possess a certain angularity and a more modern appeal. It is joined with something else. In his hands we are reminded of a leisurely tradition that's been brought up-to-date, conscious of its past and indebted in no small measure to an unsentimental take on the world.

In passing, I suspect it is because he positions himself in the space between an oral and a literary tradition that there are few soft centres in his short stories. This was the accusation we might recall made by Francis Stuart against Frank O'Connor in stories such as 'Guests of the Nation' (1931) and 'First Confession' (1951).[105] What Stuart had in mind was the 'new mood of complacency and satisfaction…at having, as well as its own brand of government and Church, an equally national and cosy literature'. There is nothing cosy about Kiely. As you try and connect replacing gooseberries at the beginning of the story we've been discussing and the boy's gaffe at reciting a ballad about Sarsfield in a house whose owner is named after William of Orange, there is no place for sentimentality nor, indeed, for the comfort of symbolic cohesion. As Kiely notices in the story, 'plucked fruit is plucked forever' (481). Once said some things can't be unsaid. It is worth repeating: Kiely is not the provincial writer, as he might be seen by some, but the surviving countryman, the 'wordweaver'[106] with his dog and gun heading back up to the 'mountain streams where the moorcocks crow'.[107] 'God's Own Country', a story about an insufferable and conceited American bishop

105 Francis Stuart, 'The Soft Centre of Irish Writing', *The Irish Times* October 1976. Reprinted in my *Irish Writing on the Twentieth Century: A Reader* (Cork: Cork University Press, 1999), 832.
106 A television programme about the writer was broadcast in 2005 under the title *Wordweaver – The Legend of Benedict Kiely*.
107 'The Mountain Streams Where the Moorcocks Crow' is the title of a traditional song associated with the singing of Paddy Tunney.

making a pilgrimage to an island off the west coast of Ireland, ends with
the f-word blurted out by a local cameraman who has been filming the
trip. All the way through the story the reader has been waiting for this
one genuine moment, and Kiely doesn't disappoint. This is God's own
country, but not as the Bishop might imagine it.

Every writer has an essential story to tell. It might be thought
that uncovering such an underlying story wouldn't be easy to discern
in Kiely's case, for as an author he has been prolific: four collections
of short stories numbering over seven-hundred pages, ten novels, a
monograph on the nineteenth-century novelist, William Carleton, a
critical study of Irish fiction, three books round the island of Ireland,
a collection of Irish short stories for Penguin, a book on his adopted
city Dublin and another on Yeats's Ireland, and not forgetting a
children's story book *The Trout in the Turnhole* (1996).[108] But as we
look back on his career we can trace a line running through it. Above
all else, the essential story seems to me to be about connection. This
is the great theme of his life and work. From his boyhood in Omagh
to Dublin as an adult, from North to South and back again, from the
Irish song tradition to the European literary tradition, from popular
culture to the world of books, from newsprint to the experience of
ordinary people, from raconteur to storyteller, Kiely was a witness
to the generous spirit that never stopped seeing connections and
drawing inferences. He was someone who knew from the start that,
if you work at a connection and not get distracted, you can find
something important to say. As he says in the Sarsfield story 'This
ground is littered with things' (479), and we can't help recalling
Walter Scott's description of this area of Ireland in 1825 as 'the
narrow ground'.[109] It might be narrow but it is full of memories,
cluttered, and for that reason important. They could be dismissed as
just clutter or litter, something that's for the tip or wheelie-bin, but
that's Kiely's point. Keep looking and very soon, as *Finnegans Wake*
also reminds us, litter has the capacity to generate literature.

108 *The Trout in the Turnhole* (London: Merlin, 1995).
109 *The Complete Works of Sir Walter Scott: With a Biography* Volume 7 (New
York: Conner and Cooke, 1833), 436.

Kiely is the wisest of modern Irish writers and he has gathered together his own 'litters from aloft' (*FW* 17.26). As with Joyce, nothing is waste or indeed wasted. If he tells us anything it is, on the one hand, that the world we carry with us needs cherishing and remembering and, on the other hand, that at the heart of our humanity beats the sympathetic imagination. Only fanaticism was alien to this poet from 'the black Northern hills' who was, as we learn from his Jesuit novel, 'unable to find a brother's fault'[110]. 'We were misled to expect better', as his protagonist, the old-style nationalist Mervyn, remarks in *Nothing Happens in Carmincross*, a remark which in some respects, as I suggest in the Introduction, sums up a whole history.[111] Mervyn has in mind the heroic past, a past that includes for Kiely 1916:

> That was when fighting for Ireland had been a clean business, the handful of brave men with muskets and rosary beads standing up to privilege and the might of empire. Patrick Pearse surrendered in 1916 to prevent further slaughter of the citizens of Dublin: the heroes of the 'Seventies aren't so choosy. John O'Leary, the Fenian whose nobility had affected the poet Yeats, said there were things a man might not do, not even to save his country: he meant telling lies, being dishonourable, not being a gentleman. Blessed are the gentlemen for they shall make no mark in urban guerrilla warfare. (19)

Betrayal lies close to the heart of Kiely's critique of the violence perpetrated by the modern IRA, a betrayal of the brave individuals who took on the might of the British Empire in 1916. In *Nothing Happens in Carmincross*, he manages to keep the narrative flowing in spite of the outrage we know is coming. On board the plane carrying him back to Ireland for his niece's wedding, he is seated next to someone who has lost both legs and his bladder in a rail accident, and

---

110 *There Was an Ancient House* (1955; Dublin: Wolfhound, 1977), 71.
111 *Nothing Happens in Carmincross* (London: Methuen, 1986), 26.

the stewardesses have to constantly empty his bottle. The encounter is treated with some humour by the narrator. 'Look, excuse me, but I spent a year or so in hospital once myself and perhaps I could look after my friend's little needs.' (14) This is a reference to the year Kiely as a young man spent in hospital in Dublin with a back injury. His more private thoughts then take over. 'His legless neighbour is a perpetual pisser, 'as a tap somewhere else' (14). The last phrase echoes a remark by Sam Weller in Dickens's *The Pickwick Papers* how Job Trotter, who is given to shedding tears, has 'got a main in his head as is always turned on.'[112] The reader senses the humour at the beginning of the novel is going to serve a serious purpose, for the novel's focus is on living with consequences, with the terrible consequences for those caught up in unimaginable violence, who might need constant care, unable for example to go to the bathroom on their own. In Kiely's sights is the deliberate maiming by bombs and bullets, and no-one is better at capturing images of atrocities as when after a bomb exploding we read: 'One man came out with his arms out. He was on fire from head to toe. He died like that. The way he stood. In the shape of a cross.' (215)

Proxopera (1977), a novella which carries the subtitle '*A Tale of Modern Ireland*', was written during the bleakest period of the Troubles when hope against the dark forces of history seemed particularly forlorn. In a later book of memoirs, *The Waves Behind Us*, and published in 1999, Kiely claims that 'the deepest evil of the secret bomber may be that he casts a blight on humanity on the very ground he crawls on.'(3) *Proxopera* concerns the proxy bomb and how an elderly man, Granda Binchey, is forced to drive a bomb into his local town while his family are held hostage. This is arguably more reprehensible than the secret bomber who places a bomb in a crowded place and disappears back into the community. The proxy bomb involves a hostage taking and the threat of destruction to a whole family, so it is more personal with the potential on the part of the hostage-taker of misgiving and feelings of guilt to be aroused and/or suppressed.

112 Charles Dickens, *The Pickwick Papers* (Oxford: Oxford University Press, 2008), 196. The 'main' is a reference to a water main pipe.

As a tale of modern Ireland there are very few redeeming features, and we witness Kiely struggling with his chosen material. The 'opera' in the title reminds us of the 'spectacular'; it is like an opera we might go and see in a theatre. Spectaculars were, and are, beloved of terrorist groups. The spectacular bomb or spectacular incident hits the news headlines and speaks to governments or the authorities, for it is in its own way a language, part of the violent conversation or dialogue with those in power. Only occasionally in this novel does Kiely escape from the heat of his condemnation, as when he pays tribute to the homely creamery can (in which the bomb has been placed):

> Once upon a time a creamery can had been a harmless or lovely even a musical object. Up and down the street in the town in which he was reared, the horses and carts from the farms would travel, bright with jingling cans, taking fresh milk to the creamery, taking away the skim milk for cattlefood.... No shuddering shattering death in those bright cans. Nowadays motor-trucks took the cans to a modern factory.[113]

This is followed by a passage which is supposed to represent what is going on inside the old man's head as he is driving along with the bomb. As his blood freezes we learn that:

> What right have these brainless bastards with their half-baked ideas to crash in on the lives of better people, to bind and gag old women, set children whimpering, and himself bearing death and ruin to the town he loves. Ireland? What Ireland? Ulster? What Ulster? Multiplying like body-lice, the other crabs, in the hairy undergrowth, one madman produces another. (363)

113 *The State of Ireland: A Novella and Seventeen Stories* Introduction Thomas Flanagan (New York: Penguin, 1982), 363.

It is difficult to read such a passage as the words or thoughts of someone whose blood has frozen and who is shivering. This sounds like Kiely himself giving vent to *his* feelings. Kiely could have drawn out how the paramilitaries use the idea of proxy to promote their ideas, not just planting proxy bombs but also assuming they speak for, by proxy, the wider community. Paramilitaries gain strength by imagining they are acting on behalf of a vision, the future, or a people currently under various illusions. Getting them to confront the reality of themselves and their own feelings might issue in something other than a resort to violence. Kiely undermines his case by insisting on his own disdain and horror. As for the image of lice and crabs, this again lessens his attack, for whatever paramilitaries are, whatever nasty deeds or *opera* they are involved in, they remain human beings. It is one of the few blemishes in his work and driven by something noble. On the other hand, without *Proxopera*, he might not have come upon a (better) way of handling his antipathy to the Troubles that emerged seven years later in *Nothing Happens in Carmincross*. The image of the man on fire running out of the building in the shape of a cross never leaves us.

Like Joyce, Kiely forgot nothing, and when he began writing he returned to the past, to William Carleton, the great pre-Famine novelist from Clogher in County Tyrone, who too brought all his past with him when he arrived in Dublin, and to the ancient walkways of his own childhood in Omagh near where the seven streams meet. 'Look and see, look and remember, and then you will discover what is within' — to adapt Virginia Woolf's famous remark about life and fiction; this too would be a suitable motto for Kiely.[114] Seeing and remembering. Squirrel things away and when the occasion arises, as in what he called the 'graceless times' of the recent Troubles, use it. Like a squirrel his writing reminds us of food to be stored against the bleakness of winter or history, a sharp reminder of the value of foraging among what is to hand or what comes naturally.

'Everything is everywhere' observes the narrator in *The Captain with the Whiskers*. In a sense this was true for Kiely. Wherever he travelled, all

---

114 'Look within and life, it seems, is very far from being "like this".' *The Common Reader* (1925; Harmondsworth: Penguin, 1938), 148.

over Ireland, the four years he spent in the States, in Britain, in Europe, he found that everything is everywhere: disputes, upsets, characters, stories and story-telling, memories and odd juxtapositions, and always those inside stories. He was a leisurely observer who delighted in the human world or the 'chuman' world, to quote Peter Keown as he pats the bonnet of the 'hybrid' car in 'A Journey to the Seven Streams' (202). *Nothing Happens in Carmincross* constitutes his most passionate plea on behalf of the human world against the 'graceless times' (158). Not now 'everything' and 'everywhere' but 'nothing' and one of its implied qualifications, not 'everything' but 'something'. Now insert history and the passage of time and see what happens. Not 'Nothing Happens in Carmincross' but 'Something Happened in Carmincross'. Not everything, fortunately, but something. In quiet or forgotten places, things can happen and get out of hand. But Kiely reminds us not of tragic coincidence, that the 1998 Omagh outrage took place thirteen years or so after the publication of his fierce novel (which was set in the early 1970s), nor that the outrage took place on his birthday in August. No, what he underlines is that the forces of history are at work all around us and that sometimes writers are more percipient than others. Kiely was not only percipient but outraged, and he spent a whole novel never getting it out of his system.

It is a good place on which to end this tribute and keynote address. Suddenly that is. Without more ado. Omagh, 'the county town of Tyrone, well-built and prosperous-looking, but not a tourist-resort', as the town is described in Baddeley's 1897 *Thorough Guide Ireland*.[115] Not a tourist-resort but, as Kiely reminds us, a place to return to. In *The Cards of the Gambler*, his Faustian novel written in 1953, well over a half-century ago, with God and death in mind, Kiely anticipated his own return: 'Every man at the end should return to the place he started in'.[116] In his youth, a certain single-mindedness appealed to the young seminarian anxious to serve in some higher goal, but, like Joyce, he is at his best on the journey home.

---

115 M.J.B. Baddeley, *Thorough Guide Ireland Part 1 Northern Counties* (London: Dulau, 1897), 178.

116 *The Cards of the Gambler* (1953; Dublin: Millington, 1973), 151.

Kiely's work has an enduring appeal. Those of us of a certain age who are alive today have the advantage of hearing his voice, the voice that gave pleasure to his many listeners of the RTE Sunday Miscellany programmes in the 1970s and 1980s. And as we read the printed stories we find that voice accompanying us all the time. He enjoyed nothing better than getting into his stride with an unusual remark and then adjusting the view as he waited for us to adjust our sets. And then there are all the asides that pepper his writing: 'God knows', 'as every child, male or female, sometimes desires', 'the heavens be his bed' (following a reference to his dead father), 'and why wouldn't he'. Fortunately, none of these asides were edited out by an over-zealous copy-editor, for they remind us of something characteristic about the man, which we might define as a certain defensiveness or angularity as if he couldn't stop making connections with his audience and his own status as a writer. Those asides are there to be appreciated. 'Don't let's get too pompous', he seems to be saying. 'The world is constituted thus and no more, and I'm only drawing it out, simply recalling what's already there.'

Omagh is blessed that it possesses in Benedict Kiely a writer who has told part of the inside story of its modern history. Not everything was destroyed by the Troubles or, indeed, the 1998 bomb outrage in Omagh. There is a longer, and indeed more inclusive, history that takes in a kinder form of nationalism, imperial wars in far-flung places such as Spion Kop, as well as the tragic loss of lives in the Great War and the Second World War. Military history is one history Benedict Kiely was especially alive to since he had grown up with the men who did indeed march away, their heads full of the American wild west and seeing the world. But in remembering those swept away by history, he shows how the writer can shine light on obscure lives and remind us of the power of the imagination in returning us, not always tragically, to the local habitation where all of us begin.

CHAPTER 5

ANTHOLOGIES OF IRISH WRITING

In the classical world an anthology in the singular case was a flower-gathering and, in the plural, collections of short Greek poems, which an editor made up into a 'nosegay'. When the word came into English usage it had a tendency or a capacity to switch between the flowers of the earth and the cultural meanings now associated with the word. In Samuel Johnson's *Dictionary* (1755) three meanings are identified: (i) a collection of flowers; (ii) a collection of devotions; and (iii) a collection of poems. The idea of anthologies as 'flowers' is especially marked in modern anthologies of Irish literature, as is evident from Frank O'Connor's *A Book of Ireland* (1959) to Patricia Craig's *The Oxford Book of Ireland* (1998). [117] I should say at once that the charm of such books is difficult to resist.

O'Connor's was one of the first books I owned and I still return to its neatly arranged 'culture-bites' with much pleasure. It is divided into broad headings: Places, History, Pastoral and Town Life, People Great and Small, Humour Romance and Sentiment, Customs and Beliefs, Poems Songs and Ballads, Religious and Philosophical. In addition it is supported by postcard views of Ireland in the 1950s. *A Book of Ireland* was just the right size to put into a jacket pocket and thus provide an

---

117 Frank O'Connor, *A Book of Ireland* (Glasgow: Collins, 1959); Patricia Craig, *The Oxford Book of Ireland* (Oxford: Oxford University Press, 1998).

accompaniment to whatever one was doing during the day. *The Oxford Book of Ireland* is a little too big to carry round, but is cleverer and the choices more subtle and arresting. Patricia Craig, however, follows in O'Connor's footsteps and, as it says in the blurb, 'captures the essence of a complex and fascinating land'. What both of these anthologies have in abundance is pleasure, pleasure in their subject, pleasure in their choices, pleasure in providing pleasure for the reader. 'Come dance with me in Ireland', O'Connor's translation of the fourteenth-century poem in Irish, appears in the prologue to his anthology, and Craig might have used the same to introduce her more restrained Northern view of Ireland. In a dark house before the coming of electricity (and this is O'Connor's world especially), the candle could be relied upon to give comfort and to light up everything in its path. These anthologies do likewise, lighting up a culture that was once held in common. At times you might even forget the cruel passages Ireland has endured in its history and politics.

During the second half of the eighteenth century, the nosegay tradition veered towards collections of 'beauties'. *The Beauties of Sterne*, first published in 1783, was a collection of 'the best' of Sterne's writing. To publish Sterne in this way is precisely what appeals to the cultural historian, who can learn much about changes in sensibility not only on account of the selection but also by comparing the changes between the first and subsequent editions. *The Beauties of Sterne* (or Shakespeare for example) created a convention among the emerging middle-class reading public in the eighteenth century, for whom publishers provided multi-volume collections of poems. In *A Collection of Poems in Six Volumes* (1782), James Dodsley, a leading London publisher, highlighted the importance of preservation in his opening remarks to the first volume: 'The intent of the following Volumes is to preserve to the Public those poetical performances, which seemed to merit a longer remembrance than would probably be secured to them by the manner wherein they were originally published.'[118] The emphasis on preservation – this is the era of Thomas Percy's *Reliques of Ancient English Poetry* (1765) and, in the Irish context, of Charlotte Brooke's *Reliques of Irish Poetry* (1789)

118 J. Dodsley, *A Collection of Poems in Six Volumes* vol 1 (London: Printed for Dodsley, 1782), 1.

– led in time to a concern with representation and then within that to the issue of canonicity. But Dodsley shows little of the anxiety that drives and confronts the modem anthologist, contenting himself with the observation: 'It is impossible to furnish out an entertainment of this nature, where every part shall be relished by every guest: it will be sufficient, if nothing is set before him, but what has been approved by those of the most acknowledged taste.' (2)

Pleasure, preservation and canonicity form a useful trefoil when thinking about anthologies. For anthologists, anxious to achieve particular effects by arrangement, pleasure is often what sustains much of their endeavour. Today, preservation, or reliques as our predecessors in the eighteenth century might have called it, tends to attract less attention, but it cannot be ignored altogether by the modern anthologist. What deserves preserving now tends to be related to perceptions about the importance of literary canons, which inevitably raises issues concerning exclusion and inclusion. In *Molly Keane's Ireland: An Anthology* (1993), Molly Keane reveals: 'In reality, one is haunted, almost from the start, by what is left out.'[119] Derek Mahon is less apprehensive in *The Sphere Book of Modern Irish Poetry* (1972): 'If X isn't there it may be because people don't read him now and I don't think it is a great loss; if Y looks for his name in vain, perhaps he's one of the many rising poets who haven't yet found their individual voices.'[120] In his use of 'he' Mahon also reveals that the woman poet was unimaginable as much as inadmissible, although, in his defence, in 1972 'he' often did service for 's/he'. In a recent, brave anthology *Ferocious Humanism* (2000), W.J. McCormack throws off the yoke altogether and declares that he has assembled 'a frankly and avowedly interpretive selection of Irish poetry' from Swift to Yeats and beyond.[121]

The note that accompanied the publication of that remarkable

119 Molly Keane, *Molly Keane's Ireland: An Anthology* (London: Harper Collins, 1993), xvii.

120 Derek Mahon, *The Sphere Book of Modern Irish Poetry* (London: Sphere Books, 1972), 15.

121 W.J. McCormack, *Ferocious Humanism: An Interpretive Anthology from Before Swift to Yeats and After* (London: Dent, 2000), xiv.

achievement, *The Field Day Anthology of Irish Writing* (1991), edited by Seamus Deane and others, was comprehensiveness. The same note is to be found in Justin McCarthy's ten-volume anthology *Irish Literature* (1904): 'Irish Literature is intended to give to the reading world a comprehensive if only a rapid glance at the whole development of literary art in prose and poetry from the opening of Ireland's history.'[122] Confidence in the comprehensive coverage in *The Field Day Anthology of Irish Writing* (1991), however, was soon dissipated in the row over exclusions of women, and one consequence of which was the publication in 2002 of *The Field Day Anthology (Volumes IV & V) of Irish Women's Writing and Tradition*, edited by Angela Bourke and others. The storm was a reminder of the limitations in ever thinking anthologies could somehow escape the movement of history, politics, or gender. It was also a reminder that the idea of comprehensiveness would always be open to dispute and perhaps such an anthology would never be attempted again, or never with so much ambition again.[123]

What the controversy also raised was an issue which many anthologies – and this includes my *Reader* – cannot really address in spite of their form: the problematic way history is divorced from the contexts to which it properly belongs. Each extract in my *Reader*, for example, sits alongside others as if in a series, facing out, but for the most part without any sense of a natural or organic connection with its neighbour. The sequencing threw up some suggestive contrasts and comparisons, but this tended to be more by chance than planning. In this regard my *Reader* was exceptional because it was tied to a diachronic-synchronic grid which was perhaps too precise. This might be thought radically historical and an advance on other anthologies in the nosegay tradition which pluck extracts from their context. But that was the problem, for history is more than dates in a calendar. Interestingly, what allows my choice of outline to breathe is the use of decades, for all the extracts are set within a larger, more natural,

---

122 Justin McCarthy, *Irish Literature* vol 1 (Philadelphia: J. D. Morris, 1904), vii.
123 For a clear-eyed discussion on constructing anthologies, see Mary Eagleton, 'Who's Who and Where's Where: Constructing Feminist Literary Studies', *Feminist Review*, No. 53, summer 1996, pp.1–23.

framework. Thus, it normally makes more sense to say that a play belongs to the 1930s than to, say, 1932.

Notwithstanding these reservations, the structure I settled on provided me with an important angle on the material, and it also made something else possible. The strength of the *Reader* partly resides in its democratic disposition and outlook; it refuses, or pushes against, a hierarchy of significance. If it had been a tenth of the size, I would have been forced to be more selective and exclusive in my choice of extracts. So size had benefits and made itself felt in another way, for it lessened the possibility of my being accused of a narrow ideological perspective or special interest. One (English) reviewer claimed I had produced a *Reader* which was essentially pro-Unionist, but I thought that was difficult to prove. No pro-Unionist anthologist would have included Seán Ó Tuama's 'Abair Do Phaidir' (Say a Prayer), a controversial poem which pays homage to the violence which created the Irish Free State (see 1065–6). It is a Reader where my own views are largely submerged. Always my method as a teacher was to define the terrain, and let students develop their own interests and come to their own conclusion. In my cultural history of modern Irish writing, *Light, Freedom and Song* (2005), written in the years following the *Reader*, I focus on the Irish dark and on what I call the great themes of loss and struggle, but in my *Reader* I resist propagandising on behalf of my own ideas and theories. However, I do guide students in the task of gathering material by inserting in the Appendix how the extracts can be grouped under a number of headings including Religion, Politics, Irish Ireland, the North, Violence, the City and Country, Cultural Critique, Colonialism/ post-colonialism, Folklore, Gender, Women Writers, Childhood, the Outsider, Life Writing, Prison Writings, Irish Writers in Britain (1267–1281). Working with themes helps to provide the *Reader* with something more manageable. Let me also add something else from a critical point of view. It is an obvious point but worth repeating. The *Reader* carries an implicit ideology, which can be identified in terms of my support for Ireland's contribution to world history and literature. This is the Joyce country, the modern muse at its most articulate. And if I err on any side, it is with preservation and with widening the canon.

Examples of changes of mind on the part of anthologists of Irish writing can be found in such able critics as David Marcus and Dermot Bolger. Over the years Marcus helped to provide in the *Irish Press* a platform for new Irish writers with a weekly page of short stories and poems. His own prodigious work as an anthologist and his refusal to sit permanently in judgement has been much admired, and what he leaves out in one anthology he can always include in his next anthology. Bolger is alive to the constant movement which is contemporary Irish writing and not apprehensive about things getting out of hand. In the revised edition of *The New Picador Book of Contemporary Irish Fiction* (1993/2000), Bolger welcomes Maeve Brennan, the Irish American short-story writer, who was missing from the first edition only because her work appeared in Europe in 1999, two decades or more after publication in the *New Yorker* and elsewhere in the United States.[124]

To focus more directly on *Irish Writing in the Twentieth Century*, I used the subtitle *A Reader* to distinguish the compilation from an anthology. As indicated, my primary consideration was not so much comprehensiveness or ownership or sitting in judgement but simply a big reader for the classroom: what material would make for good discussion in a class of students working on modern Irish writing in English? Brendan Kennelly appreciated something of this from the start, suggesting the book should be in every school in Ireland. Once I had settled on the format – strictly chronological, by decade and then divided into Documentary and Imaginative – the material began to shape itself. I knew from the outset that the core text needed the skeletal structure provided by the work of Irish dramatists: Shaw, Synge, Yeats, Lady Gregory, Brendan Behan, Beckett, Brian Friel, Teresa Deevy, Tom Murphy, Stewart Parker, Sebastian Barry, Marina Carr and Martin McDonagh. My choices derived from a mixture of principles, prejudices (some known, some unknown) and classroom experience. O'Casey fell by the wayside, something I now very much

---

124 Dermot Bolger, *The New Picador Book of Contemporary Irish Fiction* (London: Picador, 1993/2000).

regret. As for short stories the task of the anthologist is particularly acute because of the richness of the seam in Ireland, but some authors made it immediately onto the list: Edith Somerville and Violet Ross, George Moore, Liam O'Flaherty, Frank O'Connor, Sean O'Faolain, Elizabeth Bowen, Mary Lavin, John McGahern.

Surprisingly, poetry was more problematic because the choices seemed less obvious not only with regard to poet but also poem. I was keen not to underplay Yeats's presence, but I had a certain advantage in that the Yeats poems included can be read against a wider history, which is always something I've responded to in great writers. Of course, the accusation was made after publication that the Yeats selection did not provide an overall view of the poet, a criticism I willingly accept. Yeats needs to be read as a whole and my *Reader* was tied, as already stated, to a grid which was too precise. On the other hand I could have done more with the selection to make it more coherent, but my mind was elsewhere. In the shadow of Yeats came the flowering we associate with Austin Clarke, Patrick Kavanagh, John Hewitt, Seamus Heaney, Michael Longley, and Eavan Boland. Extracts from novels needed particular care, largely because extracts are just that, namely incomplete and therefore less easy to manage in class. Some extracts, though, such as the sucking-stone sequence from Beckett's *Molloy* (1954), can be read on their own independent of a narrative context.

The guideposts for the Documentary material delayed me for some time. I could have gone in several different directions but I was directed by various prompts and intuitions. Vincent Cheng, one of my American readers, insisted I include material from the 1890s. Hence the presence in the *Reader* of Hyde, Russell, Yeats and Moran. That intervention was important and it has proved particularly beneficial to scholars and students around the world who have limited access to research libraries. Once established, the pattern of polemical debates over such issues as cosmopolitanism, cultural nationalism, and the place of literature in the culture needed to be continued across the intervening decades right up to the 1990s Documentary section. This last section conveys something of the current lively debates about gender and nationalism, colonialism/post-colonialism, history and politics. It consists of twenty extracts taking up ninety pages, or some 70,000 words, and in many ways can be regarded as an anthology in itself. Another area of general interest – life writings – also took my attention: Peter O'Leary, Forrest Reid, Peig Sayers, O'Casey, Behan. Prison writings also appealed to me, not least because over these last three decades the fate of Irish prisoners and their sense of abandonment cannot, or should not, be overlooked. Indeed, with his centenary in mind, I had intended using Oscar Wilde's 'The Ballad of Reading Gaol' (1898) to act as a preface for the whole volume.

To convey an idea of the constant sifting process at work throughout the century under discussion, I included some informative surveys of Irish writing by Andrew Malone, Ernest Boyd, O'Faolain, Frank O'Connor, Thomas Kinsella, Sean O'Tuama, Brendan Kennelly. Irish-language examples were there from the start, even if I was unsure initially how to handle this material. Governing my thinking was the question: how does a tutor interest students in the language spoken in Ireland before Thomas Kinsella's gapped tradition opened up in the middle of the nineteenth century?[125] As is apparent in the work of Nuala Ni Dhomhnail and Cathal Ó Searcaigh, the material in translation is striking and edgy and refuses to function as if it were simply an object for the reader's patronising attention. I should add that, as Terence Dolan, author of *A Dictionary of Hiberno-English: the Irish Use of English* (1999), told me, the *Reader* can also be used as a useful resource for how English is spoken in Ireland.

I began work on the *Reader* after attending the Frankfurt Book Fair in 1996. I was there for the launch of *James Joyces Irland* (1996), a Swiss-German translation of my *James Joyce's Ireland* (1992). With a giant inflatable cartoon figure of Jonathan Swift's Gulliver flapping in the wind near the entrance, the Fair took for its theme 'The Irish Diaspora', and I somehow knew, as I listened to Irish novelists and critics such as John Banville and Edna Longley, that I had to include

---

125 See W.B. Yeats and Thomas Kinsella, *Davis, Mangan, Ferguson? Tradition and the Irish Writer* (Dublin: Dolmen, 1970), 62–3. Kinsella argues that modern Irish culture is the product of the 'gapped tradition', which was in part a consequence of the loss of Irish.

the Fifth Province: Irish-American, Canadian-Irish, Irish-Australian, the Irish in Britain. Here were Irish voices waiting to be heard in their own countries but also across the seas of the world. Some of the figures emerged from the background immediately: Eugene O'Neill, John O'Hara, F. Scott Fitzgerald, James T. Farrell, J.F. Powers, Thomas Flanagan, William Kennedy. Others came into view after further research: Betty Smith, Edwin O'Connor, Mary Gordon, Tess Gallagher. Irish-Australians from Joseph Furphy and Miles Franklin to Vincent Buckley and Thomas Keneally are especially perceptive about their fate, 12,000 miles from Ireland. Only in recent years have the Irish in Britain got their anthology.[126] I avoid using the over-used term 'identity', but in stressing the Irish Diaspora I betray a lingering attachment to the notion of an identity-in-dissolution. In the poetry of Maura Dooley, a second-generation writer born in Britain, you can just hear the Irish strains on the point of vanishing, of being assimilated into another culture.

I was fortunate to have an Irish publisher keen to listen to my suggestions for a big book. I wanted the reader browsing through the pages to say 'This, and this as well, and this too, and this and this.' I wanted to convey a sense of accumulated excitement. I took the opportunity to include somewhat inaccessible material often referred to in discussions about Irish Literature such as Hyde's 'The Necessity of De-Anglicizing Ireland' (1892) and John Eglinton's 'The De-Davisization of Irish Literature' (1906). There was my fondness for material that is little-known or under-appreciated which has the potential to challenge and interest us. Jim Phelan has perhaps more extracts than he deserves, but that's what happens in the final stages of putting to bed a big project like this; some things somehow manage to avoid the scissors. I was pleased to include Nesca Robb, and Fred Ryan, and Cathal O'Byrne, and Rosita Sweetman, and Sir Christopher Lynch-Robinson's extract about the last generation of Irish RMs, especially given that, folded within it, is the Proclamation of the Republic.

After publication I almost immediately began to regret omissions

126 See Liam Harte, *The Literature of the Irish in Britain: Autobiography and Memoir, 1725–2001* (London: Palgrave Macmillan, 2009).

and enthusiasms of the moment. Kathleen Coyle, the neglected novelist from Derry, whom I write about length in my *Light, Freedom and Song* (2005) and who only came to my attention on finishing the *Reader*, is missing. Aidan Matthews's title story from his collection *Lipstick on the Host* (1992) kept insisting on inclusion, and the only thing that stopped me was that I couldn't manage to get an extract that did it justice and the whole was too long for inclusion. But, with its debt to the Molly Bloom soliloquy in *Ulysses*, it is a story I particularly admire. The Irish-Scottish links are insufficiently represented. As for the removed Joyce pages (323–346), that's another story involving a dispute about copyright, but disfiguring a book in this way will never be forgotten or forgiven.[127] By way of amends for omissions and sitting in judgment, in an Appendix 'Select List of Authors' (1323–1328), I provide a list of authors which is much larger than the list of authors I include in the *Reader*. In this way I have signaled my commitment to that wider body that goes under the collective name 'Irish Writing in the Twentieth Century'. As I indicate in my Introduction to the Cork *Reader*, when asked by students which books would I recommend to build up a knowledge of Irish writing, I normally replied: many.

---

127 I write about this at length in my memoir, *The Long Apprenticeship: A Writer's Memoir* (Kibworth: Troubador, 2012).

CHAPTER 6

HISTORY IN THE MAKING: IRISH
WRITING IN 2007–9

If 2006 was Beckett's year, 2007 was Louis MacNeice's, the year of his centenary. There was a symbolic moment in September during the conference dedicated to him at Queen's University Belfast when the leading Northern Irish poets gathered at his graveside in the grounds of the Church of Ireland Church at Carrowdore in County Antrim. Even though he has been dead for some forty-five years, MacNeice's presence continues to be felt strongly. 2007 also witnessed his *Collected Poems*, edited by Peter McDonald, an edition which prints MacNeice's poetry in groupings corresponding closely to the collections published by Faber between 1935 and 1963. Faber also reprinted an edition of MacNeice's autobiography *The Strings Are False*, with an introduction by Derek Mahon, and, forthcoming, there is to be an edition of *Autumn Journal*, the poem MacNeice wrote on the eve of the Second World War and which continues to be of interest especially to Irish and Spanish readers. In another edition, *Selected Poems*, Michael Longley makes a strong case for reading MacNeice as our contemporary.

A new novel by Belfast-born writer Lucy Caldwell has a title taken from a MacNeice poem: *Where They Were Missed* (2007). There are few novels written by an author in her early twenties which are as accomplished as this one. Like MacNeice, Caldwell has a keen eye for hauntings, for what's been lost, for false strings, only now the loss is wrapped in the continuing trauma of sectarianism and the Troubles. In attending to the great Irish theme of loss, Caldwell reminds us that families carry not only their own history inside them but also a wider history that accords with but is not identical to what happens there. This she shares with other contemporary Irish novelists, as well with Joyce, whose Christmas Dinner scene in *A Portrait* briefly yokes together the fate of a family and the fall of Parnell. As she quite properly remarked in a short interview about the novel: '[I]t has a rawness and an energy and innocence that I'll never be able to capture again.' And, equally properly, she then quickly adds: 'But then again in a funny sort of way every single thing that you write feels as if it's the first thing you've ever written.' Her protagonist's name, Saoirse, is Irish for freedom or liberty, and Caldwell opens her account as a novelist with the old Irish cry even as she attends to the loss that accompanied such a cry in history.

Walk the Blue Fields by Claire Keegan is a fine collection of short stories.[128] In some stories such as 'Surrender' she recalls John McGahern. But in a story such as 'Night of the Quicken Trees', which is set in the turf bogs of Dunagore near Doolin in County Clare, we might find ourselves thinking of Benedict Kiely's story 'Homes on the Mountain' and how utterly strange some country people can seem as if ancient Ireland was still alive and well.[129] For there is a Southern gothic seam in Irish culture, and it is especially evident among those who live in remote parts. In turn, the grotesque can attract imaginative writers and commentators alike. Kiely manages to avoid the gothic potential in his story but Keegan cannot resist the temptation, at least here. Her best stories, however, are the two at the beginning of this collection – 'The Parting Gift', an understated story of emigration, and 'Walk the Blue Fields', a story about another ritual, that of a wedding. However, it is a wedding story with a difference, for the story focuses as much on the priest conducting the service as

128 Claire Keegan, *Walk the Blue Fields* (London: Faber, 2008).
129 For Benedict Kiely's stories, see *The Collected Stories of Benedict Kiely* (Introduction Colum McCann) (London: Methuen, 2002).

on the bride and groom. When one of the guests refers to the priest's 'cock' as an 'ornament' (43), we know we are in the presence of a storyteller with a way with words.

Tim Robinson's *Connemara: Listening to the Wind* can also be mentioned here.[130] This study is closer to home for Robinson, with Roundstone in Connemara at its centre. His prose style is something to be relished, and few writers are better at capturing the landscape of the West. His favoured mode of walking, he tells us, is not 'a single-minded goal-bound linear advance but a cross-questioning of an area' (364). Lying on the terrace of his house overlooking the bay, the summer sunset in full swing, he notices how Connemara 'tends to undefine itself from minute to minute' (362). It is in keeping that the writer who has helped define a whole landscape for us should deploy the word 'undefine' to describe such a moment. If 'undefine' stands out, it does so because we are observing the naturalist at home in his habitat and surroundings, listening to the wind. It is also in keeping that Robinson, who understands the concept of legacy more than anyone, has left his house and books to the University of Galway for future use by students researching the natural history of this part of the world.

Paul Durcan's new collection *The Laughter of Mothers* (2007) is in one sense a book about golf, but in another sense it is about his mother.[131] 'The Story of Ireland' opens with a dramatic, off-beat statement: 'The single most crucial factor in twentieth-century Irish history was golf' (533). Such a sardonic comment follows in the wake of Wilde, Joyce and Beckett, but none of these would have been capable of such an expression or conclusion, for Irish humour has moved on. And Durcan continues with another striking pronouncement: 'Had it not been for golf, the country would have relapsed into barbarism.' The last thing we might associate with golf is barbarism or indeed, perhaps, the civilising instinct. The satire is not just unexpected; it also gives the appearance of being free

---

130 Tim Robinson, *Connemara: Listening to the Wind* (London: Penguin, 2007).
131 See Paul Durcan, *Life is a Dream: 40 Years Reading Poems 1967–2007* (London: Harvill Secker, 2009).

from constraint. So the use of 'relapsed' evokes not only a medical condition but also in Catholic Ireland lapsed Catholics, missing Mass and falling by the wayside.

Inevitably, though, a darker side accompanies this volume, and, as we turn the pages, we witness it gathering force, for this is a remarkably frank and tragic reading by Durcan of his own life and, more especially, that of his mother's life, a woman who qualified as a lawyer but was unable to pursue her own career and became the wife of a judge. 'Daughters of the Civil War' is a forceful reminder of the fate of his mother set against the Irish Civil War, only for her the disillusion of that period is more personal and recalls in the use of the word 'leg-ironed' another civil war and another kind of slavery:

> How could we have known, we who were the
> daughters of the Civil War,
> That before we were young women we would be
> old women?
> That we would not have time to climb the mountain
> Before the cold fog of marriage leg-ironed each one
> of us. (562)

The poet's aunt, Sara Mary, also suffered, for, while her siblings had careers, she was left behind to care for the turkeys and hens and run the family public house. When she died, Durcan in characteristically wayward fashion yokes together a public outrage from the Troubles, the slave owner Fraulein Miller's stale cakes, and his aunt's hostility to nationalism. However, these kinds of equivalences between very different historical contexts, as also with 'leg-ironed', sometimes work but not always:

> On the morning she died two heroes of the IRA,
> September 16th 1974,
> Separately arriving at the houses of two judges in
> Belfast,
> Shot them both dead in front of their daughters

As they were eating their breakfasts, cornflakes and
sugar,
So that old daily Ireland might be a nation once
again;
All that pure pedigree, miller's fraulein, racial opining.
(545)

Durcan, who spent periods in his youth in psychiatric institutions
and at one time faced having a lobotomy, is an acute observer of the
contemporary scene from an outsider's perspective, and in his verse we
can see and at times almost touch the great theme of loss in modern
Ireland. No one does irony quite like Durcan, the insider's outsider.

In terms of banking and the economy, 2008 marked the end of
something; the new beginning might be heralded by the election of
the first African American to the White House. So, while the focus
of my discussion is quite properly 'Ireland', we find ourselves almost
immediately talking this year about the global situation. At the cultural
level, however, the downturn is being played out in ways that require
patient observation and thinking outside the box. Writers and film-
makers might feel compelled to jump in and give us the world as it
is, but often contemporary reality eludes them. We sometimes need
the passage of time before a story can be adequately told or indeed
discerned. Equally, critics in the field of cultural analysis will need to
do more with the traditional concept of determination than simply
suggesting that **X** caused **Y** or that in a time of recession people turn
to fantasy to fill the void within or without. All around us, therefore, at
every level there is a rewriting going on, and this makes for a certain
excitement as new configurations or possibilities forge themselves.

In terms of the wider historical picture, among the first things
to be distinguished are the overlaps from the preceding period and a
sense of continuity therefore. In Irish culture, to take a recent example
from the field of drama, the emptiness on display in Edna Walsh's plays,
such as *The Walworth Farce* (2007), and *The New Electric Ballroom* (2008),
suddenly seems not so much prescient as immediate and descriptive of
the world surrounding the theatre. At the beginning of *The Walworth*

Farce, as we listen to a tape-recording of 'An Irish Lullaby' and 'A Nation Once Again', the message insists on itself: this is a play about post-romantic Ireland, where rituals serve as a distressing and unsentimental reminder of both what was lost and what cannot now be recuperated. 'Shite' says Dinny as, without more ado, he switches off the tape-recorder to begin the farce (7). In history, as Thomas Davis's unofficial anthem from the nineteenth century attests, there could once be heard the optimistic strains of a future, of a clear national identity, a nation once again as the rallying call of the song has it and which I discuss in my Introduction, but by the end of this play we cannot escape the conclusion that we have been witnessing not a farce but an excursion into a modern tragedy and an exploration, inside a council flat in South London where everything is 'worn and colourless and stuck in the 1970s' (5), of the Irish dark. Or to quote one of a series of mocking phrases on 'A Nation Once Again' in *Finnegans Wake*: 'Innition wons agame' (*FW* 614.7–8). Benedict Kiely imagined 'We were misled to expect better', but now that has become something bleaker: 'We were never misled, and we don't expect it to get better'.

With its echoes of William Trevor's short story 'The Ballroom of Romance' (1972), Walsh's next play, *The New Electric Ballroom*, evokes a different sense of loss. The play begins with talk and with the desultory observation that '[b]y their nature people are talkers' (5), but it ends more dramatically with 'Blackout. Silence. The End.' (46). Hanging on a wall on the stage three sets of retro clothes stare out at us: a cashmere jumper and rara skirt, a 1950s red blouse and pleated skirt, and a glitzy show-business man's suit. Punctuating the play are memories of possible romance enjoyed by the three sisters at the Electric Ballroom in rural Ireland and other dreams of fulfilment. In this play, unlike Trevor's story, we imagine at first that it is we who are looking on but in fact it is the other way round, for with its mixture of claustrophobia and dreadful provincialism this is a cruel world that confronts us. On the other hand, with 2008 in mind, another complicating thought prompts itself, and it has to do as much with the power of context in our reading and re-reading as with any sense of the discontinuous present. For while the credit crunch across the globe has ironically thrown us all together, Walsh registers not only personal alienation but also a particular Irish history, which seems destined at this juncture to play itself out inside a wider recessionary context.

The twin themes of loss and struggle have accompanied modern Irish history since its inception, and perhaps it is for this reason that an Irish writer living largely in the diaspora should give us one of the most engaging and intelligent novels about American loss after 9/11. *Netherland* by Joseph O'Neill has received widespread acclaim on both sides of the Atlantic. The novel supplies its own contexts, both fictional and documentary: the (once Dutch) city of New York after 9/11, a childhood in The Netherlands, an epigraph from Walt Whitman (and the theme of male friendship therefore), perhaps echoes from the Great American Novel such as F. Scott Fitzgerald's *The Great Gatsby* (1925) and Ralph Ellison's *Invisible Man* (1952) (as in the figure of Mehmet Taspinar, the Turkish angel, in one and Ras the Exhorter in the other), and so on. But, even as we find ourselves having to supply such a context (and we might now add to the list the credit crunch, for it is more than a post-9/11 novel as it was initially marketed), O'Neill's Irishness should not be overlooked. For this is a novel about loss and struggle, loss of a friend, loss of the past, loss of direction, a marriage in dissolution, and then the struggle for meaning, for a narrative that would make sense beyond simply the world of gangsterism and intrigue, a novel about the struggle for family life amid separation, above all a struggle for friendship. Like the pervasive imagery of water in a novel about submersion, loss and struggle go hand in hand suggesting that the exiled writer was being driven by even stronger currents or by a more inclusive and older structure of feeling.

At one point in the novel, Hans, the protagonist, explains he is 'given to self-estrangement' (46). It is a slightly old-fashioned way of putting it, as if he was in the same creative writing class as the young boy in Joyce's first story 'The Sisters'. He is thinking about the game of cricket and how his new-found team-mates from the West Indies and the Indian sub-continent have no difficulty adapting themselves to the new environment and to a less than hospitable field on Staten Island that they claim for cricket. Chuck Ramkissoon, the Gatsby figure, has dreams of creating a New York Cricket Club and making money in the process. As the novel constantly illustrates, it is an impossible dream, and yet, as O'Neill also reminds us, there is something in it. Cricket after all was widely played in nineteenth-century North America and, with the huge numbers of immigrants from countries where the game is pre-eminent, it could be revived again. Hans even insists, at least to himself, that cricket is a civilising game – and this in spite of disputes about umpiring decisions, one of which comes to overshadow the novel as it unfolds.

The idea of using cricket as a structuring device in the novel is at once a daring and a clever move on O'Neill's part. Indeed, although he is, like his character, given to self-estrangement, O'Neill still manages to get inside American culture through this alien corridor. With some justification, we might recognise it as *Netherland*'s answer to *Underworld* (1997) and a riposte therefore to Don DeLillo's trumpeting of baseball in the famous opening to that novel. As if he were consciously 'writing back', there is something playful about O'Neill getting one of his characters to spend time surveying New York's boroughs for a piece of land to purchase and then build post-colonial dreams. In a long footnote in *Light, Freedom and Song* (2005)[132] in a chapter on 'Joyce and Cricket', I outline the nineteenth-century American interest in the game and quote from Jones Wister's *A 'Bawl' for American Cricket* (1893), an early account explaining why the game of 'base ball', played by professionals, won out over the 'amateur' game of cricket. O'Neill, whose Irish grandfather, as we learn from his investigations in *Blood Dark Track* (2000), was imprisoned in the Curragh during the Second World War for IRA activities, is more daring and confrontational for, while I was interested in 'beyond a boundary' and the colonial encounter between Britain and Ireland, his focus is inside the boundary and how cricket abroad serves as a home for exiles, a place of longing, and even 'an environment of justice' (116).

The sense of loss in *The Pride of Parnell Street*, a new play by Sebastian Barry which was staged by the Tricycle Theatre in London

---

132 See page 289.

and at the Dublin Theatre Festival in autumn 2007, is filtered through monologues, which work their cumulative magic in characteristic Barry style. Unlike other plays, the loss now is more contemporary and for the most part focused on northside, working-class Dublin. In some ways the play is close to Roddy Doyle's world. Joe, deflated after the Irish soccer team's exit from Italia '90, returns home to beat his wife and, from then on, life on the streets, outside the family that is, beckons, a life of bitterness and drugs and knives and prison. It is an ugly world, but, as the 'pride' in the title reminds us, Barry is ever alert to the possibility of redemption whether that is through an intense love of landscape, the use of a lyrical phrase, moments of tenderness or reconciliation at the end. *The Pride of Parnell Street* lacks the tragic reach of his earlier plays, but for all that there is something being constructed here for what feels like a larger retrospective exhibition. The contrast with Bridget O'Connor's play *The Flags*, a play which was revived at the Royal Exchange in Manchester in autumn 2007, is noteworthy.[133] O'Connor's play tells the story of two life guards, JJ and Howie, who find themselves on duty on the 'second worst beach in Ireland' (3). As such a phrase suggests, there is nothing romantic here – unless it is the humour, which is everywhere on display. The best moments recall the work of Martin McDonagh, but it has its own qualities as if a new voice was attempting to be heard on the second worst beach in Ireland.

Barry's highly regarded novel, *The Secret Scripture* (2008), which was shortlisted for the Man Booker Prize in 2008 and which won the Costa Prize in 2009, returns us more surely to an Irish context.[134] The territory is familiar to those who know Barry's work, only now it is fiction and not drama that is the form. The setting is a psychiatric hospital in County Roscommon where Roseanne McNulty (née Clear), a patient perhaps nearing her centenary, has a series of meetings with her psychiatrist Dr Grene, who is himself grieving over the death of his wife. Roseanne recalls, not always accurately, growing up in Sligo, memories of her own family and relationships. The narrative or course of her life, we surmise early on, is shaped, overshadowed or

133 Bridget O'Connor, *The Flags* (London: Faber, 2006).
134 Sebastian Barry, *The Secret Scripture* (London: Faber and Faber, 2008).

silenced by trauma. Throughout, the mood music of loss is heard in the two alternating centres of consciousness, where monologues never quite manage to become dialogues.

As in his earlier plays such as *The Steward of Christendom* (1995) and *Our Lady of Sligo* (1998), there is an often exquisite lyricism in Barry's writing about loss and, for those who have not encountered his previous work, *The Secret Scripture* possesses a real charm. The achievement, though, is perhaps less impressive on second reading. You never know with Barry if he is giving us his point of view or that of his characters. For example I assume this sequence of reflections expressed by Dr Grene is related to the overall theme of the novel: 'The fact is, we are missing so many threads in our story that the tapestry of Irish life cannot but fall apart. There is nothing to hold it together. The first breath of wind, the next huge war that touches us, will blow us to the Azores' (183). Barry's long-standing, self-appointed task has been to recuperate voices of those who lost out in the emergence of modern Ireland, such as those like the protagonist in *The Whereabouts of Eneas McNulty* (1998) who had fought for the Crown and who had worked for the Royal Irish Constabulary before Independence in the 1920s, or those who, for most of the duration of the new State, had been locked away in asylums as happened to Eneas's sister-in-law Roseanne in this novel.[135] But, to broaden the discussion away from the issue of families in this particular novel and their hidden skeletons, I am not sure if this is the secret scripture that contemporary Ireland has lost. The Yeatsian vocabulary and imagery that Dr Grene deploys, especially evident in phrases from 'The Second Coming', certainly has power, but whether it persuades is open to question.

The sympathetic imagination works differently with me. Some things cannot be retrieved without doing injustice to other struggles in history, and, even if they could be recuperated, we would still have other losses to prick our conscience. Ruins of the Big House are dotted all over the Irish countryside; 40 years after Ireland's entry into the European Union, the creamery as an institution has virtually

---

135 Sebastian Barry, *The Whereabouts of Eneas McNulty* (London: Picador, 1998).

disappeared. So to live in the present is to live with a sense of loss, some of which is worth lamenting, some not. In spite of Barry's at times searing indictment of Roseanne's treatment by Church and State in the new Ireland that emerged after Independence, the point is worth making: all those hidden from history in Ireland share something of the history of loss, but the missing-from-history idea can take us only so far. Keeping the faith has a much longer reach than this and should not be abandoned so readily. There is something worrying about one of Roseanne's last entries in her jotter: 'I once lived among humankind, and found them in their generality to be cruel and cold' (268). The note is not so much plangent or even sentimental as slightly false, either on Roseanne's part or on Barry's, and the effect is to distance the reader from her plight and diminish her representative or tragic status.

The Secret Scripture, then, constitutes a study not only in alienation but also in the relationship between politics and style, a relationship which seems to me more rewarding to investigate than the frequently noticed twist at the end of the novel. Also central to the novel is an exploration of the Irish dark, which to Barry is close to mystery or silence or deceit or concealment or 'something deep in the water' as the black-listed Sligoman Eneas McNulty affirms on discovering his brother Tom and his wife Roseanne have separated (*The Whereabouts of Eneas McNulty*, 187). However, although families may indeed conceal their histories from themselves and others, I do not believe the Irish dark is irrational or that dark. What holds the tapestry of Irish life together is the complex interlocking of loss and struggle, which is a necessary tension and, at the same time, a refusal to buy into Yeats's Second Coming in 1919 or end-of-world despair in 2008. Barry's exquisitely crafted prose invites assent, but somehow my mind continues to resist the secret scripture it contains. Almost perversely, I find myself searching for the light and the positive gloss that inheres in the 'days without end' idea in his 2016 novel of that name, a novel that somehow manages to be life-affirming amid all the horror associated with the Indian Wars and the American Civil War.[136]

---

136 Sebastian Barry, *Days Without End* (London: Faber, 2016).

Dennis O'Driscoll's interviews with Heaney in *Stepping Stones* (2008) is a thoroughly engaging book, full of interest, not least because Heaney's speaking voice and his written prose are as beguiling as his verse. [137] As O'Driscoll confirms in an essay on Heaney's politics in *The Cambridge Companion to Seamus Heaney* (2009), there has been a continuing interest in the poet's political position. Sean O'Hagan, in reviewing *Stepping Stones* in the *Observer* on 16 November 2008, took Heaney to task over his politics and on his unwillingness to comment while the Troubles were in progress. According to O'Hagan, 'What Heaney did not do, of course, was take sides, either as a poet, or, as his fame increased, a reluctant statesman.' The charge is one frequently made against Heaney, but perhaps it is not entirely fair. 'Whatever You Say Say Nothing', to take one of his early poems as an example, was first published in *The Listener* in October 1971, two months after the introduction of Internment. It was accompanied by a photo of desperate Catholics fleeing their burnt-out homes in Belfast, a photo reproduced in *Light, Freedom and Song* on page 245. So, in one important respect, Heaney is not saying what the poem's title says. The position the utopian Heaney has characteristically sought is 'the far side of revenge', a position which is beyond but not above the sectarian politics of his native province. However, we should be in no doubt of his nationalist sympathies, nor indeed that he is himself, as he once wrote about John Hume in 1969 before the Troubles began in earnest, like a 'questing compass-needle of another hidden Ireland'[138]. At the time of the Hunger Strikes in 1981, Heaney's own mantra, as he reveals in *Stepping Stones*, was a remark by Czeslaw Milosz that he quotes in 'Away From It All': 'I was stretched between contemplation of a motionless point and the command to participate actively in history' (260). Such a position we may well agree might be precious, but it should not be confused with a failure to commit.

Reading this collection of interviews reveals a poet on a journey south through his native province, a journey to shake himself free of the

---

137 Dennis O'Driscoll, *Stepping Stones: Interviews with Seamus Heaney* (London: Faber and Faber, 2008), 77.
138 Cited in my *Irish Writing in the Twentieth Century: A Reader*, 766.

nets which might have held him back. Heaney has often been linked with Yeats, but perhaps we should make more of the final section of 'Station Island' where Heaney comes face to face with Joyce.[139] As he told O'Driscoll, the Catholic Joyce is there to help 'my unbelief' (249), not the Protestant Yeats. St Patrick's Purgatory on Station Island in Lough Derg is an ancient site of Catholic pilgrimage, and Heaney imagines he is a penitent in the company of other penitents, but he also finds himself involved in confronting his past and his accusers. As he moves from one station to the next, he is burdened by two thoughts.'It is a road you travel on your own.'And 'I have no mettle for the angry role' (65).The focus of 'Station Island' is the journey through life, its vicissitudes and its adversities, a focus that also includes morality and how one conducts oneself accordingly. In this way, conscience, and the assault by conscience and on conscience, runs through the poem. As if we were also following in the footsteps of Jesus in the Stations of the Cross, on every page we come across the brutal language of accusation and violence: 'set upon' (63), 'the challenged one' (64), 'hammering' (64), 'unforgiving iron' (65), 'wounds' (66), 'trapped' (67), 'iron cross' (69), 'helpless smile' (72), and so on. Then in section VII the poet encounters his cousin, Colum McCartney, who was murdered by Loyalist paramilitaries in 1975 at the age of 22. With the sound of knocking ringing in his head, knocking at the door below, the poet tries to understand the death of his cousin, but he is prevented by some startling images, one of which, set out as a single line like a coffin, eventually obliterates time:

Through life and death he had hardly aged.

The thought has a stilling effect on the reader, not unlike a *pietà* by a Renaissance sculptor or a painting of a corpse by Mantegna. The 'perfect, clean, unthinkable victim', a phrase which cannot be rushed, confronts the poet, who is himself held back by his imperfections and surprised by his own admission:

139 Seamus Heaney, *Station Island* (London: Faber, 1984).

'Forgive the way I have lived indifferent –
forgive my timid circumspect involvement.' (80)

It is Heaney's *mea culpa*, but it is not an excuse for others to condemn
him for non-involvement in politics. Feeling guilty is not the same
as being guilty, and, for whatever reason, Heaney, who, in an earlier
poem, 'Exposure', colourfully called himself an 'inner émigré', tended
to overplay or expose his guilt.[140]

The poem culminates in a final section when Heaney meets not
St Patrick or God but Joyce, who provides him with some kind of
balm and even redemption, a counter to what has gone before. As
Heaney steps down from the jetty after returning from the island,
he feels like a 'convalescent' (92) and grasps the helping hand of
someone who seemed blind, walking with an ash plant. He recognises
the voice, a voice 'eddying with the vowels of all rivers'. The figure
is described as 'cunning', the adjective used by Stephen Dedalus
in *A Portrait* when he is determined to embark on exile from his
country with 'silence, exile and cunning' (*P* 247). And then, recalling
perhaps the conversation between Davin and Stephen in the novel,
we are presented with what amounts to an act of encouragement
from one writer to another: 'Your obligation / is not discharged by
any common rite.' After all the self-flagellation comes relief: 'You've
listened long enough. Now strike your note.'

The encounter between Heaney and the spectre of Joyce is both
strange and unexpected, especially in regard to roles. The poet is also
involved in an exercise in rewriting or extending what we read in Joyce.
The slightly morose and inward-looking Stephen is now reassigned
the role of encourager, attempting what Bloom tries in the 'Eumaeus'
episode of *Ulysses*. The reference to the 'Feast of the Holy Tundish'
recalls the episode in *A Portrait* where Stephen corrects his English
Jesuit teacher over the use of the word 'funnel' and how in Ireland it is
called a 'tundish' (*P* 188). At this point Heaney adds a reflection from
the vantage-point of a later history, 'Who cares…any more?' And he

---

140 Seamus Heaney, *North* (London: Faber, 1975), 73.

goes further: 'The English language / belongs to us.' It is a moment of triumph over the history of colonial rule, something to which Heaney would, presumably, assent. But then comes Joyce's verdict on the whole nationalist agenda:

> That subject people stuff is a cod's game,
> infantile, like your peasant pilgrimage. (93)

The allusion to a *peasant* pilgrimage, which recalls the story of 'The Lough Derg Pilgrim' by the pre-Famine, Ulster novelist, William Carleton, reminds us also of Stephen's disparaging comments about Irish country people in the novel. It can be allowed to stand as part of Stephen's character, and perhaps it is an assessment with which the secular Heaney, putting aside his 'questing compass-needle of another hidden Ireland', might also agree. But the fierceness of the 'subject people stuff' is striking, in part because it looks like Heaney updating Joyce from his experience of the Troubles in Northern Ireland. However, what unites them in the closing moments of the poem is the phrase that also appears at the end of *A Portrait*: 'Old father, old artificer' (P 253), and the hope that he, the traditional father-figure of Dædalus from Greek mythology, might stand them both in good stead. When Ireland failed them, writers could turn to the Greeks for sustenance. As with the interviews in *Stepping Stones*, 'Station Island' is compulsive reading and, rightly, deserves our attention.

2009 was a year for reflection, filtered in part through the publication of letters and correspondence. In 2008 I wrote about the economic downturn, but this has been augmented by the loss of something as profound. Ireland is facing another period of radical adjustment, the outcome of which will continue as uncertain possibly for years to come. What gives a certain edge to recent events is that bishops can resign and reforms be announced, but all that is on the basis of something painful, which is continuing. For cultural historians and those dealing in time-lines longer than the present, the revelation of abuse has come not so much as a shock as a recognition that the 'Troubles' has a wider application than simply being about politics or the North. Equally, the enormity of the abuse has highlighted once again the role of the Church in post-Independence Ireland. One conclusion we might legitimately draw is that the concentration of power and the lack of transparency have contributed in no small measure to the current malaise. Of course, many have long since stopped looking to the Church for guidance, so there is some other kind of vacuum or hollowing out now beginning to clamour for attention. It will be for later historians to determine whether what is happening forms part of a larger crisis associated with loss and the struggle for a new identity.

If the scandal of recent sexual abuses highlights the deformity in relations between the private and the public, then the correspondence of Samuel Beckett underlines the importance of the private as a defence against the public world. Indeed, there is no better place to return us to ourselves than by attending to the Irish writer who, above all others, hated cant and pomposity and who constantly knows how to surprise us. 'How can one write here', Beckett confides to Tom McGreevy on returning to teach at Trinity College, Dublin, 'when every day vulgarises one's hostility and turns anger into irritation and petulance?'[141] To my mind, it was appropriate that *The Letters of Samuel Beckett 1929–1940* were published to mixed reviews, for Beckett never fails to defeat expectation. If anyone was hoping to behold a writer in the making or in full flow, they would have been not a little disappointed. By way of contrast, D.H. Lawrence in his letters frequently reaches the same pitch of heightened prose that we encounter in his novels, but this is the not the case with Beckett in the 1930s. That said, there is enough of interest for the student of Irish Studies to ponder and value.

On display throughout these letters are Beckett's difficulties in writing, of putting pen to paper, in his home country. In turn, those difficulties become the whetstone not only for Beckett understanding his plight but also for developing his imagination. In that 1930 letter

---

141 Samuel Backett, *The Letters of Samuel Beckett 1929–1940* (eds Martha Dow Fehsenfeld and Lois More Overbeck) (Cambridge: Cambridge University Press, 2009), 49. 5 October 1930.

just quoted, it isn't that he is hostile to the world but that the world vulgarises his hostility. This is the Beckett country we are familiar with, where plight and imagination become inseparable. We are inside the folds of his personality. This is Beckett one step removed not from reality but from the world, both of which – both reality and the world – are then redefined. In 1932, as if anticipating one of the leitmotifs of his later work, the despairing Beckett tells McGreevy, 'Nothing seems to come off' (121). Wherever he turns, he meets with little success and receives what he thinks is more than his fair share of rejections from publishers and editors of literary journals, but he cannot allow the matter to rest there, turning rejection slips into humour at the expense of those who didn't see a Nobel prize-winner for Literature in the making. Chatto and Windus is recast as 'Shaton and Windup', a phrase that wouldn't be out of place in Lucky's speech in *Waiting for Godot*, and it is one of those quips to lift the heart of all aspiring authors undergoing similar treatment. The publishers thought his novel, *Dream of Fair to Middling Women*, was wonderful, he tells McGreevy, but 'they couldn't they simply could not' (125). For non-native speakers of English, the humorous distinction here between 'couldn't' and 'could not' is worth pondering, for in certain contexts, as here, the distinction is not about formality or informality but about a hardening in attitude and how this gets to be represented in writing.

Beckett insisted that only those letters pertinent to his published work should be made available, a comment which can be applied to all the subsequent volumes in the series. It would be difficult (or nice) to know what constitutes the line between relevant and irrelevant – or pertinent and its opposite – when it comes to any author but especially to Beckett. So I am not sure Beckett got this one right. In Beckett, the private acts as a bulwark against the world and, paradoxically, provides not only a defence against, but an entry-point into, the public world. In this sense he redefines the line between the public and the private. His correspondence, for example, is full of problems with digestion and the limitations of the body, and it is fitting that we should read about what is happening to him physically, for this constitutes the material and crucible of his imaginative vision. 'Dies diarrhoeae' (124), a day of diarrhoea, he writes amusingly at one point echoing the 'Dies Irae' of the Requiem Mass of the Dead. Elsewhere, as yet another reminder that he was ill-at-ease with himself, we read of panic attacks he suffered at night.

As expected, the letters shed further light on his relationship with Joyce, though not on his relationship with Joyce's daughter, Lucia. An early reference to his writing 'stinking' of Joyce reminds us of his need to swerve away from the father figure, and, appropriately, it is expressed in terms of odours (81). In a phone call from his hotel in Paris in 1937, he stumbles across a domestic scene of the great man shaving and being protected by his wife: 'I rang up Shem now and was engaged by Norah [for Nora] while he finished his shave' (562). 'Shem', the son in *Finnegans Wake*, and the figure most closely associated with Joyce himself, is the name Beckett used for 'Mr Joyce' when speaking with those like McGreevy inside the circle. After an evening at the Joyces in early January 1938, he observes, 'He was sublime last night, deprecating with the utmost conviction his lack of talent' (581). The following week, Beckett is stabbed in a street in Paris and hospitalised. The 'lovable' Joyce was very solicitous for his fellow countryman, arranging for his medical care (though there's no letter about this here), sending him bunches of Parma violets and going to visit him. That same month, it is clear that Beckett is well on the way to recuperating when he writes about his chronic inability to understand a phrase like 'the Irish people' or 'to imagine that it ever gave a fart in its corduroys for any form of art whatsoever' (599). The sentence ends with the painter Jack B. Yeats, whom he much admired.

Some readers might be tempted to conclude that Beckett's antipathy toward Ireland in these letters is the final word on the subject. In *Beckett and Contemporary Irish Writing* (2009), Stephen Watt concurs with Deirdre Bair: 'Beckett had no pride in his Irishness; national identity meant nothing to him'.[142] According to Watt, by December 1931, 'Beckett could no longer tolerate Dublin and escaped to Germany and then Paris' (198–9). The letters tell a more nuanced

142 Stephen Watt, *Beckett and Contemporary Irish Writing* (Cambridge: Cambridge University Press, 2009), 199.

story, where frustration is accompanied by yet more irritation. The idea of a series is important here, for no single attitude emerges. His confidant in these letters was a fellow Irishman, the poet and art critic Tom McGreevy, who also acted as confidant to Yeats's wife George in the 1920s. But while George Yeats sometimes betrayed her feelings of frustration about her husband to McGreevy, Beckett is reporting on his plight as a person and an aspiring author to someone who shared much of his worldview. [143]

It is difficult to believe Beckett would ever allow a sentence such as 'I have no pride in my Irishness' to be his final word on the subject. He hated grand statements, preferring reticence to articulation in certain matters including attitudes to the country which, as Stephen Dedalus also believed, could not be changed. (*U* 16:1171) McGreevy would have understood this and allowed his friend to sound off. Let me put this another way. If Beckett took no pride in his Irishness, why did he spend so much time in correspondence with someone like McGreevy and mixing with an Irish writer like Joyce or talking up the work of an Irish painter like Jack B. Yeats? And there is enough in these letters which speaks of his pride in what the country has to offer the visitor, such as Galway ('a grand little magic grey town full of sensitive stone and bridges and water' 127), or seeing Clonmacnoise for the first time ('indescribably beautiful' 324), or walking in the Dublin mountains and discovering 'a lovely small Celtic cross' (489).

I felt somewhat unsure reading the first volume of Beckett's correspondence as to how many relevant letters were missing, and I cannot say I was fully reassured by the editors in their introduction. Tipping the balance towards a more comprehensive coverage leads to a different problem as exemplified by the publication this past year of the second volume of T.S. Eliot's letters. [144] Many of the letters, written between 1925 and 1927, are business letters written by Eliot in his capacity as editor of *The Criterion* and director at Faber and Gwyer (later

---

143 For a photograph of McGreevy and Beckett in London in the early 1930s, see my *James Joyce's Ireland*, 203.
144 T.S. Eliot, *The Letters of T.S. Eliot Vol 2 1925–1927* (eds Valerie Eliot and Hugh Haughton), (London: Faber and Faber, 2009).

Faber and Faber). Fortunately, there are glimpses of humour in the midst of all this, and in one of the letters we learn something more about his relationship with Joyce. In the summer of 1923 Joyce was on holiday in the seaside resort of Bognor in Sussex. The previous year the two writers had published their most famous books *The Waste Land* and *Ulysses*. How would the leading American modernist living in London address the leading Irish modernist living in Paris? The answer: light-heartedly, with a dig at his own text as a letter written on 29 June 1923 suggests: 'I want to get a car one day when I am at Fishbourne and fetch you over and show you some of the waste lands round about Chichester.' As it happened, Joyce did his own exploring round Chichester, but this was largely undertaken through reading what was to hand in a book such as the Ward Lock guide to the area. It was there that he came across in the churchyard in Sidlesham the name of Earwicker, the name he lifts for the main protagonist of *Finnegans Wake*. If the Roman remains at Fishbourne had then been known, I suspect both Joyce and Eliot would have found room for them in their writing, but Joyce would have been happy just reading about them in a newspaper.[145]

The title of *Love's Civil War: Elizabeth Bowen and Charles Ritchie Letters and Diaries from the Love Affair of a Lifetime 1941–1973* (2009), edited by Victoria Glendinning with Judith Robertson, is slightly at odds with the tender love story on display inside its pages. Not entirely, however, for the title does mirror a lengthy correspondence over three decades between the Anglo-Irish novelist and the Canadian diplomat, who conducted their relationship in secret. Interestingly, Bowen and Ritchie spent very little time together, but there is a sense that they made up for this by writing, at least in Bowen's case. Her letters reflect a keen observer of life around her and are full of her love for him, while his diary entries are inward-looking and fairly terse.

Ritchie signs himself with an initial, E, while in her letters he is always you. Forms of address can betray so much in love letters. 'The fact is that happiness and tenderness and love don't evaporate from the place where they've been strongly; one's left with something

---

145 For more on the name of Earwicker and the churchyard at Sidlesham, see my *Reading Joyce*, 314–8.

stronger than memory, a feeling of something still going on – don't you think?'[146] In the Index there are no separate entries for 'reality' or 'presence' or 'absence', yet perhaps there should be, for these are Bowen's overriding themes, in these letters as in her novels. As for the physical side of love itself, we learn she had 'a love of touching the nape of the beloved's neck or of having the nape of my neck touched' (347), which is followed by a series of elliptical points. I couldn't determine, here and elsewhere in the book, if these points are cuts by the editors or suspension marks by Ritchie.

Because Bowen is such a sharp observer of the social scene, there is little or no sense when reading these letters of prying into things that don't concern us. Certain attitudes, such as those toward social class, we are familiar with or we could guess what she thought. She was alarmed by the Labour Party landslide victory in 1945, which gave her a 'psychic shock' (53), agreed with the Swiss, in the lead-up to the subsequent general election in 1950, that the British being socialists bored everybody, and, from her patrician background, she was in favour of the Conservative Party taking on Big Business. At the same time, because of her Anglo-Irish identity she was able to recognise her own position, which she could subject to humour. 'I'm that awful paradox, a dowdy snob' (153), she admits at one point. Coming away from a morning shopping at Harvey Nichols, she imagines the clothes she has bought might look like 'a plate of dessert' (226). London is her abiding passion. Of all the many cities she writes about, Madrid, where she stayed in October 1954, is least admired in this book, a city that assaults the senses, where church bells smash the silence to smithereens and 'all the people look most fearfully common' (193), which she puts down to the Franco-Fascist atmosphere. It is a rare lapse, for in general 'doing the rounds' in the manner of the Anglo-Irish normally allows her to see something of value on which to report.

Throughout these letters there are nice moments, sometimes quite unexpected. She is struck, dining with the Duke of Leinster in London

---

146 Victoria Glendinning with Judith Robertson (eds), *Love's Civil War: Elizabeth Bowen and Charles Ritchie Letters and Diaries from the Love Affair of a Lifetime 1941–1973* (London: Simon and Schuster, 2009), 131–2.

in 1946, how Ireland's premier duke is ending his days in a 'baroqued-over St John's Wood kitchen' (98). Visiting Edinburgh in 1950, Bowen wonders about 'the whole "British" concept', given the need for Scots to have their own Home Rule (167–8), an observation that will delight those campaigning for an independent Scotland today. As for writing and other authors, she particularly admired Flaubert's letters and his ability to capture the sensation of writing (see 361), and she read with interest *David Copperfield*, a novel that gave her 'an almost terrifying illumination about her own writing' (440). There are in addition valuable portraits here of other Irish writers including Molly Keane and Iris Murdoch. What surprised me were the occasional comments about the leading psychological novelist of her generation not being interested in people or in her own 'interesting personality' (181). The letters betray something else, and that too is intriguing, such as when she claims in a letter written in 1950: 'I might "live for others", but I could never live for my work' (176).

Those with an interest in Irish Studies should not overlook the *Letters of Ted Hughes*, which appeared in paperback in 2009.[147] Hughes's friendship with Seamus Heaney is well-known, but the ten letters to the Irish poet Richard Murphy are worth noticing for their varied insights into Hughes's verse, into the work of other writers and also into the Irish landscape. The period he spent in Ireland in 1965 provided Hughes with a way out of the impasse in his writing, and it was to lead to the poems in his celebrated volume *Crow* (1970). The influence of Yeats on Hughes is also to the fore in the letters, not least in Yeats's stress on reading aloud. When he was young, we learn that Hughes encountered Yeats's first volume of verse *The Wanderings of Oisin*, and in a letter in 1992 he recalls what it meant to him: 'I was swallowed alive by Yeats' (625). In passing, we can detect that the rhythms in Hughes's early verse also betray a debt to the Irish poet. What particularly attracted him to Yeats was the use of myths and legends, as well as his passionate devotion to the occult and to the esoteric tradition in Western culture.

147 Ted Hughes, *Letters of Ted Hughes* (ed. Christopher Reid), (London: Faber and Faber, 2009).

The only occasion I had an opportunity of talking with Hughes was inside Waterstones bookshop in York in the early 1990s. We spent about twenty minutes conversing, and most of that time was taken up with the occult. I must have been at work on *Yeats's Worlds* (1995), which includes a chapter on the occult. For me the topic was simply of academic interest, but I could tell from his line of questioning that Hughes was a believer. I was unnerved, wrong-footed, my free-thinking soul somehow exposed or snared. The stacks of books on the floor, the black, uniform bookshelves offered no relief, I was struggling, and there was no escape into a looser kind of passing conversation. Hughes was as concentrated as his poetry (which I greatly admire). Not surprisingly, in the letters he defends Yeats against those critics such as W.H. Auden who would dismiss the occult as 'embarrassing nonsense' (426). I cannot now recall if we spoke about anything else.

As someone who lives, surrounded by history, in York, the correspondence that has given me the most pleasure this last year, published in two volumes and edited by Melvyn New and Peter de Voogd, has been that of Laurence Sterne.[148] Sterne is essentially a York or a Yorkshire writer, but he does have links with Ireland. He was born in Clonmel in County Tipperary, and spent his early years in Ireland when his father was stationed there with a British regiment. In the village of Annamoe in County Wicklow, where Synge was later to spend his summers, can be seen the remains of a mill-race that once swept up the young Sterne and nearly killed him. In 1765, as an adult, when taken to task for ridiculing his Irish friends at Bath, Sterne, now the famous author of *Tristram Shandy*, resorts to the clincher: 'Besides, I am myself of their own country: – My father was a considerable time on duty with his regiment in Ireland, and my mother gave me to the world when she was there, on duty with him' (430–1). The tongue-in-cheek attitude suggests he

148 Laurence Sterne, *The Florida Edition of the Works of Laurence Sterne Volume VII The Letters Part 1 1739–1764 and Volume VIII The Letters 1765–1768* (eds Melvyn New and Peter de Voogd) (Gainesville, FL: University Press of Florida, 2009).

wouldn't go to the stake over his identity, but Ireland is nonetheless real for him. This can be seen in little things in *Tristram Shandy* by his use of names, for example, such as Corporal Trim, or in the choice of tunes such as the Williamite 'Lillibulero', which is whistled by Uncle Toby whenever difficulties arise or he has to express an opinion. And it is not surprising to learn in these letters that Sterne was offered clerical appointments in Ireland by his friend the Bishop of Cork and Ross (638).

But what intrigues me most reading these letters and their accompanying intelligent notes is the real-life incident that seems to lie behind Yorick's encounter with the Monk in *A Sentimental Journey*, and how the abbé who came to the aid of Richard Oswald, a young Englishman dying of consumption in Toulouse, was of Irish descent and called not O'Leary but O'Leari (306ff). The incident clearly moved Sterne, especially 'the great fellow feeling he shew'd to our friend' (307). So Sterne's changing attitudes and altered disposition toward Catholicism seem to belong in part to his sojourn amidst European Catholicism, a Catholicism which was itself shaped by the Irish driven into exile in the seventeenth and eighteenth centuries on account of their religion. The local curé initially refused to allow the young man a church funeral because he was not a Catholic but, as the editors suggest, he seems to have relented when Sterne offered him money. The curé confirms Sterne in his prejudice against Catholics but it is the abbé with the French-Irish name who finds his way into fiction. Always with Sterne it is through contact that feeling comes, and it is feeling that changes the world, in this case, of anti-Catholic prejudice, to which he himself was subject. One suspects he could have made more of the Irish connection in *A Sentimental Journey*, but Sterne gives the impression that Irishness is behind him, part of the past, an already discovered or known country, ripe for humour, while European emancipation, in the shape and, presumably intended, symbol of the caged bird, is ahead of him, somewhere in the future.

The present Troubles continue to provide material for creative writers to ponder. *Five Minutes of Heaven*, a television drama shown on BBC2 in April 2009 and now released as a film, was a particular highlight for me. The play/film, which was written by Guy Hibbert and directed by Oliver Hirschbiegel, starred James Nesbitt as Joe, the younger brother of a Catholic murdered in 1975 by Alistair, a member of the Ulster Volunteer Force, who is played by Liam Neeson. Years later Joe and Alistair come face to face in a television show (an imagined scene at the Truth and Reconciliation process), and this encounter is the subject of the film. Sensibly, the emphasis is on encounter, not resolution, and this is given a further twist by the fact that Nesbitt, who comes from Ballymena and who as a boy took part in Protestant marches on 12 July, plays a Catholic, while Neeson, who played Michael Collins in the film of that name, took the part of the Protestant killer. Everything contributes, then, to the tension in the drama. As if the murder was still fresh in his memory, Joe seethes, while Alistair, who has changed as a person, characteristically expresses the best line in the play: 'The years just get heavier.'

Renewed interest in the North, especially from a Protestant perspective, shows little sign of abating. *Irish Protestant Identities* (2008) is a useful collection of essays, three of which can be noted here.[149] In 'Assessing an Absence: Ulster Protestant Women Authors 1900–60', Naomi Doak argues for a revision to the conventional view that Protestant women writers came only from the Ascendancy. In an essay listing her chosen authors, she also shows how Ulster literary biographies will need to attend more closely to the issue of gender (and, equally, social class). A second essay that caught my eye was Peter Day's 'Pride Before a Fall? Orangeism in Liverpool Since 1945'. In his conclusion, Day notices how numbers marching in support of the annual Boyne parade in Liverpool have fallen from 20,000 in 1980 to around 5,000 in 2009, but the question he seeks an answer to is how we should interpret this, as a sign of a changing world or as a sign that people now believe but don't belong. Stephen Hopkins's essay 'A weapon in the struggle? Loyalist paramilitarism and the politics of auto/biography in contemporary Northern Ireland' contrasts the personalisation of the Irish republican tradition with the absence

---

149 Mervyn Busteed, Frank Neal, and Jonathan Tonge (eds), *Irish Protestant Identities* (Manchester: Manchester University Press, 2008).

of such a tradition among Protestants. However, as Hopkins points out, the list of autobiographical texts included at the end of the essay suggests a different story in the making.

Fintan Vallely's *Tuned Out: Traditional Music and Identity in Northern Ireland* (2008) continues this reassessment of the Protestant contribution to modern Irish culture. He writes well about Jackie Boyce, a Protestant singer from Comber in County Down, and quotes the singer saying 'I must be the only person ever to have been called a Fenian bastard and a Protestant bastard in the one night – in the same pub, all for playin' Traditional music'.[150] Only since the advent of the Troubles has there been an aggression about the music, and we are reminded of the way sectarianism once threatened to overshadow every aspect of the culture in Northern Ireland.

Frank Ferguson's *Ulster-Scots Writing: An Anthology* (2008) deserves to be better known.[151] In a short but generally persuasive introduction, Ferguson provides a justification for his anthology, motivated as it is by two questions: what is meant by the term 'Ulster-Scots' and what texts would constitute an anthology of Ulster-Scots writing? Ferguson is aware of the contentious field he is seeking to map, but in some respects that makes for this book's appeal. I particularly enjoyed seeing again W.R. Rodgers's 'Epilogue to "The Character of Ireland"' surrounded by other Ulster-Scots writing:

> I am Ulster, my people an abrupt people
> Who like the spiky consonants in speech
> And think the soft ones cissy; who dig
> The *k* and *t* in orchestra, detect sin
> In sinfonia, get a kick out of
> Tin cans, fricatives, fornication, staccato talk,
> Anything that gives or takes attack,
> Like Micks, Tagues, tinkers gets, Vatican.

150 Fintan Vallely, *Tuned Out: Traditional Music and Identity in Northern Ireland* (Cork: Cork University Press, 2008), 34.
151 Frank Ferguson (ed.), *Ulster-Scots Writing: An Anthology* (Dublin: Four Courts, 2008).

This is the kind of verse you want to hear someone from Belfast reading out loud. The glossary at the end of the anthology contains more spiky consonants, and I cannot resist quoting some for the letter k. Keckle for cackle, ketched for caught, kilt for clothes well tucked up, kimmer for male companion, kipple for couple, kittle for tickle or irritate, krisnin for christening, kythe for show or display. We might not agree how we define this language, but there's nothing 'cissy' about this anthology.

2009 was also a year for celebrations. The Samuel Beckett Bridge, connecting Sir John Rogerson's Quay on the south side of the river Liffey with Guild Street and North Wall Quay on the north side, was opened by the Lord Mayor of Dublin in December. Brian Friel's eightieth birthday was celebrated in style by both the Gate Theatre and the Abbey Theatre with tributes, new performances of his plays, and a bronze plaque of his handprints to join those of Luciano Pavarotti, John B. Keane, Milo O'Shea, and Niall Tobin. The revival of *Waiting for Godot* at the Haymarket Theatre in London in May 2009, with an all-star cast of Ian McKellen as Estragon, Patrick Stewart as Vladimir, Simon Callow as Pozzo, and Ronald Pickup as Lucky, was also something of a celebration. On display throughout was McKellen's Lancashire accent, a reminder that the Irish writer's play can incorporate so many different accents and yet still be itself. This production, directed by Sean Mathias, also brought out the way Lucky's speech draws attention to words and phrases already introduced earlier in the play. In that respect, it is a play full of connections like beads on a chain.

REVIEWS

CHAPTER 7

JOYCE'S EUROPEAN CITIES

JOYCE IN ROME: *THE GENESIS OF ULYSSES* (ED. GIORGIO MELCHIORI) ROME: BULZONI, 1984

Rome, that 'vast wreck of ambitious ideals', caused profound inner turmoil in Dorothea Casaubon, the newly-wed Protestant from Northern Europe.[152] By contrast, it elicited no such response in the young Joyce, the ex-Catholic from a Northern European Catholic country. 'Rome reminds me of a man who lives by exhibiting to travellers his grandmother's corpse.'[153] He arrived in Rome with Nora and Giorgio on 31 July 1906 to take up a post in the private bank of Nast-Kolb and Schumaster, and stayed for seven months and seven days. This collection of essays, drawn from the Rome Centenary Conference of November 1982, goes a long way to correcting the impression that this was a barren time for Joyce as a writer.

A nicely produced book with an engaging mix of biography, criticism, history and politics, *Joyce in Rome* also includes a range of visual material, much of it informative and new: anti-clerical cartoons from a satirical magazine *L'Asino*, reproductions of newspaper articles,

---

152 See George Eliot, *Middlemarch* (Oxford: Oxford University Press, 2008), chapter 20.
153 James Joyce, *Letters II*, 165.

and photographs of Paul Bompard, the only friend Joyce made there, together with one of Guiglielmo Ferrero, an important influence on his political thinking at this time. The editors have also reproduced the tablet commemorating Shelley's residence in Rome, a memorial which Joyce commented on in one of his first postcards. Produced in Rome under the editorship of Giorgio Melchiori, the collection reflects its Italian origins, so that details which at first intruded were in the end engaging. The Italian inverted commas, for example, are a constant reminder of Joyce's remarks about 'perverted commas'.[154]

In a thoughtful essay Melchiori seeks to underpin the collection's subtitle 'The Genesis of Ulysses'. Joyce referred to the idea and title of *Ulysses* in letters of 30 September and 13 November 1906 respectively. Citing the information (or lack of it) about Alfred Hunter in Richard Ellmann's biography (1959:1982), Melchiori asks why Joyce chose at this particular time a Jew for his central character, and provides at once an unexpected response that Jews were then a focus of attention not only in Roman politics but also in Ferrero's political writings. This is a clever intervention on Melchiori's part for it lifts the discussion onto a wholly different plane away from what might be expected from a book entitled *Joyce in Rome*.

Melchiori's essay needed perhaps a tighter line. I was willing to be persuaded by his overall point that from its very inception, its genesis that is, *Ulysses* is a political novel. However, to my mind it was in the actual writing of the novel that Joyce came to see what he thought. The post-1919 *Ulysses*, much of which was composed in one of Joyce's other European cities, namely Trieste, has the look of a different book to how it might have begun. In what sense therefore was *Ulysses* 'evoked', as the commemorative tablet in Rome now states, in 1906? After the last word of the novel Joyce deliberately added 'Trieste-Zurich-Paris', three cities linked by two hyphens and then, on a separate line, the years '1914–1921'.

Melchiori raises the issue but few of the contributors address the problem of where to locate the politics of Joyce's writings. 'Wandering

---

154 James Joyce, *Letters III*, 39.

Rocks' and 'Cyclops' seem the favourite quarries to illustrate his politics (his attacks on Church and State, on narrow-minded nationalism, his defence of minorities, his pacifism), but in my opinion modernist texts tend not disclose their (political) secrets in this way. The word 'politics' is never easy to define but perhaps it also needs clarification, especially in the area of literature and the arts. Melchiori intriguingly refers to Joyce's discovery in 1906 of 'politics as ideology', of (presumably) seeing how ideas support the interests of a particular class. But the major work in understanding ideology – at least from a Marxist perspective – came later in the century with Antonio Gramsci and Georg Lukács. In this regard, Joyce is hardly a precursor in the field, although he does perhaps anticipate, as Diarmuid Maguire suggests, the 1960s and the extension of the political to include the personal.

According to another contributor, Dominic Manganiello, Joyce is a political writer because he expresses political ideas in his work. Manganiello's Joyce is an anarchist, who seeks to undermine institutional religion, who insists on conscience as the sole guide to action, who feels the need to escape history (but not presumably language). At one point where he claims that Joyce argues 'not so much for a change of politics as for a change of vision which is political nonetheless', Manganiello comes close to Peter Berger's a-political position of the social construction of reality as a kind of do it yourself kit of the universe.[155] Taking his cue from MacCabe, Maguire bravely (im) poses a political reading of *Finnegans Wake,* but he slips back into the Manganiello position of identifying politics with content. The essay can be quickly if baldly summarized: the arch enemies for Maguire are the Church, the State, and Imperialism, while on the opposite hill stand socialism, sexual liberation, and pacifism.

Seamus Deane's stimulating essay offers a more fruitful approach to locating Joyce's politics. At every point in his essay 'History as fiction – Fiction as history' there are moments of rare insight, revelatory both about Joyce and the context for his work. He discusses the wider patterns of significance and signification: the prevalence in texts of

---

155 See Thomas Luckmann and Peter Berger, *The Social Construction of Reality: A Treatise in the Sociology of Knowledge* (London: Allen Lane, 1967).

Revival writers of the linguistically extravagant hero, Joyce's connection with other contemporaries such as Ezra Pound and how both reflected the crisis of consciousness in an atomised world, the modernist melancholy and, within that, the nostalgia of Revival writers. He also comments on the conflict in Ireland between a pastoral Gaelic world and a modern one that links with the conflict inside Joyce, a conflict which Deane identifies as between a nationalism he repudiated and a socialism which he cannot connect with. He then adds that those vestigial and authentic qualities in socialism are enfolded within nationalism, producing yet further conflict for Joyce. The Irish writer is forced to counter an intractable history with fiction; history is fixed, fiction open. Fiction can therefore realize the potential which history fails to achieve. But then comes the question of the inaccessibility of the text. The dilemma is actually, as Deane suggests, insurmountable, although it is negotiated by many Irish writers who make a virtue of linguistic dislocation.

Such a skeletal tracing of this stimulating essay hardly does it justice, but it does provoke some immediate comment. The 'crisis of consciousness in an atomised world' extends beyond the Irish context, so the specifically Irish character of this crisis or of its expression would need attention. It is also unclear how this crisis connects with Ireland's 'intractable history'. If it is 'intractable' the most appropriate mode of writing perhaps ought to be tragic, but the Revival writers, Joyce included, for the most part eschewed tragedy. The contrast between Yeats and Joyce, which Deane makes throughout, is instructive, but he tends to overlook how Yeats, too, was aware of the intractable nature of history. As regards the nostalgia of Revival writers, this needs further inquiry. To take two relevant texts: there are very few traces of nostalgia in Yeats's book of stories *The Celtic Twilight* (1893); there is little if any of Walter Benjamin's revolutionary nostalgia in *Ulysses*.

Conferences of their nature echo with many different voices, and the editors of this collection are to be congratulated for creating a sense of a coherent critical debate. Manganiello's essay is a reminder of a missing paper linking the two great Italian and Irish thinkers of the eighteenth century, Vico and Berkeley. Conversely, I felt the contrasts rather than the similarities between Rome and Dublin should have been emphasised. I also thought the contributors too willing to accept the representative nature of Joyce's view of the Dublin he left behind in 1904. John Eglinton is mentioned by Joan Fitzgerald, but there were others much closer to Joyce's politics who were devoted to freeing Ireland from the Citizen. Fred Ryan and Francis Sheehy-Skeffington are two who spring to mind. Ryan was an untiring advocate for a socialist and secular Ireland (and later for an independent Egypt), and four of his nine articles in *Dana* (of which he was a co-editor with Eglinton) consisted of attacks on the influence of the Church in Ireland. But history seems to have misrepresented and misnamed him: he surfaces in Manganiello's *Joyce's Politics* (1980)[156] for example, as Trial rather than his actual pseudonym Irial, and, cruelly, as 'Fraidrine' in the 'Scylla and Charybdis' episode of *Ulysses* (U 9:1084). Sheehy-Skeffington, who wrote a warm tribute to Ryan on his untimely death in 1913, is another relevant figure, a socialist and an early Irish feminist. Distance enabled Joyce to write about his native city, but it wasn't always – as he himself conceded in a letter written during his stay in Rome – an accurate picture, for it was sometimes 'unnecessarily harsh'.[157] This volume performs a necessary corrective, and in the process goes a considerable way to returning Joyce to the 'quickening power' as George Eliot called Rome.

JOHN MCCOURT, *THE YEARS OF BLOOM: JAMES JOYCE IN TRIESTE 1904–1920* DUBLIN: LILLIPUT, 2000

The two editions of Richard Ellmann's biography, published in 1959 and 1982, are rightly hailed as the authoritative life we have of Joyce, but this does not mean they are error-free or cannot be improved upon. The task of correcting the record or filling in missing parts has fallen to a generation of younger scholars, and in this regard *The Years of Bloom* deserves to occupy the shelves next to Ellmann, for it is

156 Dominic Manganiello, *Joyce's Politics* (London: Routledge and Kegan Paul, 1980).
157 James Joyce, *Letters II*, 166.

indeed essential reading for anyone interested in Joyce's life during his formative years in the decade after leaving Ireland in 1904. Ellmann spent only a short period of time in the 1950s in Trieste and this particular section of his biography suffers as a consequence. John McCourt, who has lived in Trieste for many years, possesses a keen insider's view of the city, and his biography is enhanced accordingly. He is familiar, for example, with the *Triestino* dialect of Italian spoken in Trieste, the racy form of communication that Joyce himself used with friends and examples of which can be found in his letters and throughout *Finnegans Wake*. Indeed, after reading McCourt's book we might with some justification conclude that such familiarity constitutes a prerequisite for a biography of Joyce. Not that McCourt is over-critical of Ellmann. Indeed, the opposite, for he can afford to be generous toward his predecessor, as if he knows instinctively that the story he has to tell is more than a corrective to the master but rather offers itself as a more nuanced account, the one that now matters.

The stance or disposition of biographers toward their subject varies considerably. Some biographers are (fairly) negative about their subject, even hostile, or become so in the writing. Others turn biography into hagiography. Many adopt the principle of following the life year by year, and some combine this with a theme or they highlight significant relationships either inside or outside the family. In Joyce's case, whatever course the biographer might envisage at the outset, the writer manages to put down a personal marker, and it is a marker that resists the biographer's natural inclination to own him. In his favourite photograph in Zurich, Joyce has his back turned in a gesture we might well interpret as a refusal to allow anyone to act as his spokesperson. Ellmann tends to rely on meticulous research to carry him through his biography. McCourt, an established Joyce scholar, accepts that the role assigned the biographer is essentially that of an onlooker. At the same time, with sympathies readily engaged and driving forward the narrative, his biography can be considered to be compensatory, a necessary and a welcome counter to the subject's indifference or silence. In the process, McCourt perhaps gives us more of Joyce than would be the case if Joyce had penned his own autobiography.

However, he sensibly avoids too much psychologising and allows his subject to exist independent of the contexts being defined for us. Thus, Joyce the man and Joyce the writer are allowed sufficient room to be appreciated either separately or together.

In spite of the phrase 'The Years of Bloom' overshadowing McCourt's biography this is not a literary biography. The incident when Joyce threw into the fire the manuscript of *A Portrait* is referred to in passing, but we learn little more about Joyce's composition of his semi-autobiographical fiction in these years in Trieste or indeed about the incident itself. McCourt rightly attends to particular real-life models for Leopold Bloom, but such a focus is a familiar one to readers of Ellmann or Joyce. More importantly, in labelling his biography 'The Years of Bloom', McCourt signals something else, perhaps consciously, perhaps unconsciously. The momentum is forward but the interpretation is backward. It is not 'The Years of *Dubliners*' or 'The Years Writing *A Portrait*' or even, following Giorgio Melchiori in *Joyce in Rome* (1984),[158] 'The Genesis of *Ulysses*', but the years of a fictional character who made his formal entry into the world of modern literature with *Ulysses* in 1922. For one moment Bloom seems to be positioned as the person who influenced Joyce. Elsewhere, McCourt recreates a convincing picture of Joyce's family, friends, his teaching and the climate of opinion surrounding him at this time. But running through his biography is the culture which went into the formation of Bloom, and at the centre of that culture was a city that was 'an Oriental workshop for Joyce' (41).

Trieste was Joyce's 'città immediata' (*FW* 228.23), his immediate city, or home from home as McCourt puts it. When he contemplated returning to the city after his seven-month unrewarding sojourn in Rome in 1906–7, the phrase used by his first biographer, Herbert Gorman, to characterise Trieste is 'an irresistible magnet'. The phrase and the sentence Gorman deploys at this point sound like Joyce himself: 'Trieste, the city he had left in disgust, began to draw him like an irresistible magnet' (see McCourt, 84). According to Nino Frank in

158 This is the subtitle of Giorgio Melchiori's *Joyce in Rome* (Rome: Bulzoni, 1984).

an interview with Ellmann in 1953 Joyce called the city simply 'my second home' (Ellmann, 1982: 389). As it happened, Joyce occupied eight different residences in the first decade of living in the city and he repeatedly struggled to pay the rent, so the irony of such a comment might have escaped him.

As he walked its busy quays and surveyed the scene, with ships loading and unloading produce for the Austro-Hungarian empire, he must have been occasionally reminded of his native city, a city also divided between people and rulers. Inside his family he spoke Italian; outside he had a 'ramshackle' empire to contend with.[159] *Triestino* was the language of the tribe and fostered irredentist talk. Joyce steered clear of trouble in his immediate city but his brother, Stanislaus, did not, and during the Great War was imprisoned for drawing attention to his irredentist attitudes. In McCourt's hands, we sense a city awakening to a new century with excitement as it looked across the deep waters of the Adriatic to the inviting shores of Italy, where for some its future destiny lay. Today much of the old part of the city remains as it was in Joyce's day, but the quayside looks slightly abandoned, its industrial past long faded and only its sunken railway tracks to remind the visitor of a past that once belonged to 'old Auster and Hungrig' (*FW* 464.27–8).

McCourt is as fascinated with the city's diversity as Joyce was. In some insightful remarks on the Eastern atmosphere of Trieste he dwells on its population, culture and architecture as well as on the 'creation and maintenance of standard Western stereotypical visions of the East' (41). He shows how the two sides, the reality and the myth, come together in Joyce's portrait of Bloom. Trieste enabled Joyce to confirm certain stereotypes but at the same time to challenge them. On leaving Dublin in 1904 Joyce, as he tells us in *Finnegans Wake*, 'caught the europicolas and went into the society of jewses' (423.35–6). He abandoned the Society of Jesus, that is, and joined the six-and-a-half thousand Jews then living in Trieste. It was like a disease he caught, the desire to live in continental Europe where he would exchange Jesus for 'jewses'. And inside 'europicolas' can be heard the newspaper for

159 A 'ramshackle affair' is how Joyce described the Austrian empire to Mary Colum. 'I wish to God there were more such empires.' See McCourt, 96.

which Joyce wrote articles from 1907 onwards – *Il Piccolo della Sera*, edited by Teodoro Mayer, who was himself a Jew.

Jews were prominent in the city at this time, and Joyce became close friends with several of them. The pupil-teacher relationship was often reversed, for Joyce was learning all the time from his pupils. Ettore Schmitz (aka Italo Svevo), a secular Jew and manager of a local paint factory, provided Joyce with useful information on Jewish lore and customs. Moses Dlugacz, another student in the years from 1912 to 1915, was a fervent Zionist, whose ideas, as is evident from the 'Calypso' episode of *Ulysses*, were of more than passing interest to Bloom. It is striking what Joyce does with Dlugacz, for the owner of a pork butchers on Lower Dorset Street in Dublin, where Bloom gets his kidneys for breakfast, is rather unceremoniously assigned that name. This may or may not represent Joyce's attitude to Zionism; after all, as McCourt recalls, he gave Dlugacz a presentation copy of *Dubliners*. (235) What we can be sure of is that Joyce enjoyed playing with stereotypes and mixing things. Any acquaintance he may have had with the small number of (mostly Lithuanian) Jews in Dublin was very limited, but in Trieste he was able to juxtapose myth and reality and sometimes to humorous effect. As McCourt convincingly shows, Bloom is a product of both Dublin and Trieste, and the two belong together. We should never forget that without Trieste there would be no *Ulysses*.

For more on the Jewish theme, McCourt's account needs to be supplemented by Ira Nadel's more nuanced view in *Joyce and the Jews* (1989). However, McCourt has a sure touch in conveying the atmosphere of the city in Joyce's day. Moreover, he carefully summarises the tensions between Joyce and his brother, together with the personal support he received from his sisters, who had been sent for from Dublin. Joyce inherited from his father an inability to handle drink or money so that, close-up, unless you happened to be a drinking partner, he was never an easy person to deal with. As he later admitted himself in *Finnegans Wake*, or as he admitted to himself, with a mixture of tenderness, truth and humour, 'trieste, ah trieste ate I my liver' (301.16). McCourt is never censorious, but never, you sense, uncritical. He notices almost in passing that in Pola while there in 1905 both Nora and James 'enjoyed a lifestyle well beyond their means, and once they had established this habit they would (or could) never break it' (18).

Joyce's relationship with Nora is sensitively handled, including the period in 1909 when Joyce was in Ireland and composed some of the so-called 'dirty letters' to her. McCourt alludes in passing to the number of unhappy marriages in *Dubliners* and how Joyce coped with his relationship with Nora by recasting it in his fiction. (37) But he makes the additional, intelligent point that Joyce's writing is also about the future: 'Many of the stories can be seen as commentaries on Joyce's troubled vision of the life ahead with his partner.' (37)

I would have liked McCourt to delay more when he quotes part of a letter from Nora to Joyce in 1909. Joyce is in Dublin in connection with the Volta Theatre and she is in Trieste taking care of the children and feeling abandoned. He sends her some gloves and furs and she replies:

> dear Mr Joyce how can I thank you for your kindness the box of Gloves which you sent me are lovely and a splendid fit it was a great surprise to get such a nice present I hope you are quite well, and will be very pleased to see you I hope you will write to me and let me know when I am to meet you again. (*Letters II* 259)

McCourt continues: 'But the truce did not last long' (148). The passage itself has the potential to provide a sharp insight into their relationship, for it is more than about the truce in their relationship. After five years of living together, Nora addresses him as 'Mr Joyce'. One cannot be sure but the tone seems to be without irony. The passage is full of formulaic phrases, and it is as if Nora feels the need to protect herself from herself and from the master of the household. In a biography that includes other business correspondence addressed to 'Mr Joyce', this has the look of a painful letter calling out for comment by the biographer.

Half way through *The Years of Bloom*, McCourt makes the valuable suggestion that 'Music played a major role in keeping the Joyce household together' (132). It is a good note on which to end and it is one that can be made more of in the light of McCourt's biography as a whole. We learn for example that Joyce enjoyed listening to Nora singing 'My Dark Rosaleen'. This was a song which was a favourite among Irish exiles and which had been translated into English in the nineteenth century by the haunted figure of James Clarence Mangan. In an undelivered lecture on Mangan in 1907, written in Trieste at a time when an intolerant form of nationalism was on the rise, Joyce affirmed that he was 'the most significant poet of the modern Celtic world' and, as he told Stanislaus, he was 'beyond the shadow of doubt the national poet of Ireland' (120). Joyce's championing of Mangan is a reflection of something deeper, which is brought out by a reading of this biography. Mangan, who witnessed the ravages of the Great Famine in the 1840s, represents the Irish tradition as in some sense broken, its language diminished, its people dispersed. It was natural for the Irish exile in Trieste to be reminded of the theme of possession and dispossession. But it was more than this, for, added to possession and dispossession, what we witness in Joyce in Trieste is a process of repossession. As he looked back on his country from his voluntary exile abroad he was realigning, translating, repossessing his world. After reading McCourt's fine biography, we can discern how through the character of Bloom, through his years in Trieste, Joyce came to repossess his country.

IRA B. NADEL *JOYCE AND THE JEWS: CULTURE AND TEXTS* LONDON: MACMILLAN 1989

For an epigraph to his introduction, Ira Nadel quotes a line that he claims constitutes a summary of 'Joyce's longstanding and continual involvement with Jews': 'Then he caught the europicolas and went into the society of jewses' *(FW* 423.35–6). The author sets about his task of delineating this involvement with confidence and conviction, and he ambitiously – and not unsuccessfully – assembles a remarkable range of material and ideas. Underlying his study is the belief that 'integration, or the "coincidence of opposites" (Bruno) was the goal of Joyce, who united myth with naturalism, Christianity with Judaism, Ireland with Europe, and his Catholic past with a "Jewish" or alienated present' (241). But it is precisely here that one might take issue with Nadel's thesis, for it is equally possible to suggest the opposite: that the goal of the 'jewjesuit' (*U* 9:1159), as Mulligan calls Stephen in *Ulysses*, was to sabotage elegant divisions between religions and races, to play with the question of identity, and to mock coincidence even as he draws it.

The epigraph, in other words, is neat; but, one wonders, if it will do. Is it accurate, for example, to say that in the phrase 'society of jewses' Joyce 'unites' Christianity (the Society of Jesuits) with Judaism? In *Ulysses*, Stephen imagines he was 'going to do wonders, what? Missionary to Europe after fiery Columbanus' (*U* 3:192–3). Joyce, it could be argued, seems to be doing something different with the issue of identity. In *Ulysses*, a more cohesive framework of identities is to the fore, especially between Jews and Irish, Jews and Greeks; this is perhaps best expressed in the phrase 'Extremes meet' *(U* 15:2098). In *Finnegans Wake*, on the other hand, the associations seem slacker. Earwicker, for example, is a Protestant, accused of being a 'jewbeggar' *(FW* 70.34–5) (the once-loyal Joseph Biggar turned against Parnell) and, with Moses in mind, he is told to 'Read your Pantajoke' (*FW* 71.18–18). In his last text perhaps only coincidences meet – after all, Joyce had on his side a language which could conflate 'Jesus' and 'jewses'.

The paragraph in *Finnegans Wake* following the epigraph, where the relationship between Joyce and the Jews is described in terms of 'identity' and 'correspondence', is also troubling. One sentence reads: 'Joyce could identify with only one group entrapped by similar contradictions: Jews' (1). This is immediately followed by: 'The reasons for this correspondence make up the content of this study.' Such shifting around with basic concepts makes any study of Joyce and the Jews problematic from the outset. Is the argument that Joyce identified with Jews or that he exhibited similarities with Jews? Is it a strong identity argument or a weak case of similarity? Ironically, the author's thesis would be more persuasive if he had adopted the weak position. Equally, the author might have asked himself why Joyce, the Irish ex-Catholic and consummate non-joiner, should identify or feel the need to identify with any social group? Why is it assumed that he did? Do not his texts explore the territory of difference between himself and Jews? Indeed, one wonders if his background had been Jewish, perhaps Joyce would have been, like his close friend Ettore Schmitz (Italo Svevo), a name-changer, a 'non-Jewish Jew', intent on distancing or on making his past unrecognisable.

One can be over-critical for this is indeed a fine study, and perhaps it is for this reason that it prompts criticism. Nadel arranges his material into five sections: the Jewish exodus (not 'exile', he insists), views of history, Jewish typology, the idea of the Jew, and Joyce's Jewish cities. Such an arrangement has considerable merit even if it risks the occasional repetition: the work of Charles Vallancey, the eighteenth-century Irish antiquarian who developed the Semitic view of Gaelic, is introduced three times; the opening of the Jewish Synagogue on Adelaide Road suffers a similar fate, as does the reference to the Swiss authorities' initial refusal to grant Joyce a visa in 1940. In his chapter on Joyce, Jews and History, the author characterises Joyce's view of history in *Ulysses* as either divine or demonic. Elsewhere in the chapter Nadel betrays an (understandable) uncertainty about whether Joyce subscribed to a chronological or a cyclical view. A few pages later he writes, 'Joyce's historical scepticism can be found as early as "Stephen Hero".' It might be more sensible to admit it from the outset that the antinomian Joyce is never easy to pin down.

There is the occasional problem, therefore, with the disposition of the material, an undue reliance on the assumption that everything contributes to Nadel's overall thesis. For not everything *can* contribute. 'Joyce's texts are Talmudic not only in the sense of the scrupulous attention to detail ... but in their demonstration of what the Talmudic scholar Jacob Neusner has called the "search for the unities hidden by the pluralities of the trivial world"'. (108) The adjective 'scrupulous' recalls Joyce's well-known description of the stories of *Dubliners* and their 'style of scrupulous meanness' (*Letters*

II 134). But this phrase, written in May 1906 about stories he began composing nearly two years previously, shows Joyce to have been 'scrupulous' long before he had composed or had even heard of a Talmudic text. And this is to say nothing of the faulty logic; for not everyone who writes with scrupulous attention to detail writes a Talmudic text.

These reservations notwithstanding, *Joyce and the Jews* provides a richly rewarding and highly stimulating starting-point for those interested in a topic that is central to understanding Joyce's mature writing. The case can be overstated, but Joyce frequently triggers a desire among people from different social groups, cultural backgrounds, or national identities to claim him for their own. Secular and religious Jews have a particular claim in this regard, and we can never forget the role that Paul Leon played in the 1930s as Joyce's secretary nor his death in a Nazi concentration camp around April 1942. The character of Bloom could not have been imagined, or rather the central place accorded to Bloom could not have been made, one suspects, unless Joyce in Trieste and Zurich had mixed with Jews from Eastern Europe. For, as Louis Hyman remarks in *The Jews in Ireland* (1972), 'the mere concept of the Irish Jew raised a laugh in the Ireland of Joyce's day'.[160] Bloom is Joyce's counter to those who sought a narrowing of the ground of Irish identity. As John McCourt shows, *Ulysses* contains cultural stereotypes of the Jews, but Joyce drains such stereotypes of much of their power. At the same time Bloom's Jewishness can only be understood in Irish terms. Here is the dilemma for the critic – the necessity of holding together a complex vision or reality. In this regard it would have been interesting to watch Nadel tackle the conflict of identities in Joyce's portrait of Bloom, the character who is closely identified in 'Sirens', the episode immediately preceding the Citizen's attack on his Jewish identity, with 1798 and the Croppy Boy.

160 Louis Hyman, *Jews in Ireland From Earliest Times to the Year 1910* (Dublin: Irish University Press, 1972), 176.

THOMAS FAERBER AND MARKUS LUCHSINGER, *JOYCE IN ZÜRICH* ZURICH: UNIONSVERLAG, 1988

'What a city!' Joyce exclaimed to Carola Giedion-Welcker about Zurich, no doubt with his native city in mind. 'A lake, a mountain and two rivers are its treasures.' And with its plentiful supply of the 'electric' Swiss white wine Fendant de Sion, it was enough to make Joyce feel at home, the city surrounded by the Alps and forever associated with Dublin's Anna Livia, with *Finnegans Wake*'s ALP that is. One of Joyce's four European cities, Zurich was twice a sanctuary for him from two World Wars, and fittingly for a city that resembles 'zuruck' (the German word 'back') his final resting-place. Zurich, or 'Turricum' (*FW* 228.22) in Latin, the city of steeples and towers, is where Joyce, 'the same zurichschicken' 'swobbing broguen eeriesh myth brockendootsch' (*FW* 70.8,4), swapping that is an Irish brogue for broken German, 'collapsed carefully under a bedtick from Schwitzer's, his face enveloped into a dead warrior's telemac' (*FW* 176.34–6), and wrote *Ulysses*.

Zurich is both/and, both apart from and a part of the course of European history. It is more, for while it is the city of SS Felix and Regula (prosperity and order), it is also the cradle of Dada, the 'white in black arpists' (*FW* 508.33), who anticipated Joyce's own 'warping process' (*FW* 497.3) in 'Work in Progress'. If it were possible, Zurich brought out even more of the opposite in Joyce. When he arrived from Trieste in 1915 he commented, 'Zürich ist so sauber', not just clean that is but also sober. At his last Christmas in 1940, he turned to Giedion-Welcker and said (uncannily as it turned out), 'You have no idea how wonderful dirt is.' Within a month the warrior was interred in the 'dirt' of the city, and it is there that the author of 'Telemachus' now resides.

Like San Francisco, Zurich is a city that knows how, but more so than San Francisco it also knows how to laugh at itself, and this lavishly illustrated book operates in the same dual mode. *Joyce in Zürich* is a rare treat, whose effect is cumulative and persuasive, with nearly everything working to establish the importance of the city in Joyce. For the most part, the authors, Thomas Faerber and Markus Luchsinger, wisely avoid the pressure of ensuring everything dovetails. They do not succumb therefore to the one-dimensional kind of comment frequently observed in biographies, where the text becomes a mirror of or a quarry for some equivalent biographical moment, or vice versa. Zurich breathes here as it did for Joyce, largely because of the book's appearance, its intelligent use of space, attractive layout and right mix of word and image.

Two-thirds of the book is devoted to the crucial period 1915–19, when most of *Ulysses* was written. Here the authors include in their illustrations: contemporary photographs of the Hotel Pfauen; the Augustiner Restaurant; the Kronenhalle, the restaurant where Joyce was taken ill on January 10th 1941 when celebrating Paul Ruggiero's birthday; the various houses and flats rented by the Joyces; the Joyce friends; examples of poems and letters in Joyce's handwriting, a reproduction of the cover to issue no 2 of *Der Dada*, drawings by Frank Budgen and Wyndham Lewis, the game of Labyrinthspiel, which Joyce played with his daughter, Lucia, and which contributed to his depiction of his native city in the 'Wandering Rocks' episode of *Ulysses*. In passing, Bartholomew's street map of Dublin showing Dail Eireann is from the period after 1922, so runs counter to the book's attempt to reconstruct the original historical contexts, where *Ulysses* is described as 'ein historischer Roman'. It's a rare lapse in a book that sets the benchmark for illustrated books on Joyce.

The authors range widely in their discussion of Joyce: Dada and Zurich; Joyce's financial position while in Zurich; Georges Borach on Joyce's singing (in the 1918 *Who's Who* for Zurich Joyce lists singing as one of his recreations); the Martha Fleischmann episode, which includes Budgen's illustration for 'Nausicaa'; Joyce's direction of the English Players at the Pfauen Theatre in June 1918 and the subsequent altercation over 'Private Carr's swank hose', as the incident is described in his satirical poem 'New Tipperary' and which is made much of in Tom Stoppard's sparkling play *Travesties* (1974). Joyce wrote most of *Ulysses* in neutral Zurich but his life outside the novel continued apace – as did the Great War.

The remainder of *Joyce in Zürich* is devoted to the 1930s and Joyce's return to the city in December 1940 from Saint-Gerand-le-Puy in occupied France. Among the illustrations reproduced here are: portraits of Alfred Vogt, the eye surgeon who operated on Joyce in 1930; Othmar Schoeck, the only modern composer, according to Ellmann, besides Antheil for whom Joyce had any taste; C.G. Jung, who briefly acted as Lucia's consultant in 1934; two attractive photographs of Joyce posing with Nora and friends in Lucerne in 1935; the burning of the winter-demon Böög ('Mester Begge' *FW* 58.16) during Sechselauten, the spring festival which is heard throughout *Finnegans Wake* as 'Sexaloitez', 'saxy luters', 'silks alustre' (*FW* 213.19, 492.14–5, 528.19); a photo of Zurich's ugliest building the Sihlpost (the 'sillypost' *FW* 200.22); a group of portraits of Joyce at the Platzpits where the Sihl and the Limmat meet ('Dies ist mein liebstes Portrat' said Joyce about his favourite portrait, the one with his back to the camera, hands on hips, cane in right hand, hat to one side, the railing in front decorated with bird droppings); a series of official documents relating to permission to return to neutral Switzerland in 1940; the death-notice in the *Neue Zurcher Zeitung* for January 14th 1941; the funeral at the Fluntern Cemetery; a photograph of Pound looking at Milton Hebald's statue of Joyce, a remarkable vignette in its own way of the passing of modernism; a useful map of the city with the Joyce sites clearly marked; and, finally, lists of the Joyce addresses and hotels where he stayed and of the episodes of *Ulysses* composed in the city.

It took a considerable amount of effort and money on the part of Joyce's Zurich friends (most notably Giedion-Welcker) to get him across the border. Now the 'lyonine city' (*FW* 155.6–7) claims him for its own. In 1979 Zurich hosted the 7th International James Joyce Symposium. There has been for a long time a James Joyce Pub, which comes complete with the interior mahogany decor that once graced Jury's in Dublin. More importantly for Joyce students there is the James Joyce Foundation on Augustinergasse, a key centre for Joyce studies round the world. It is fitting that *Joyce in Zürich* includes a photo of the Foundation's Director, Fritz Senn, along with the humorous caption 'Finnegan Neckt'.

CONOR FENNELL, *A LITTLE CIRCLE OF KINDRED MINDS: JOYCE IN PARIS* DUBLIN: GREEN LAMP EDITIONS, 2011

Written with verve and enthusiasm, *A Little Circle of Kindred Minds: Joyce in Paris* possesses a certain charm, and I have no doubt it will appeal to a wide range of people interested in learning how Joyce spent his time in Paris in the 1920s. Conversational phrases such as how Lucia 'fancied' Samuel Beckett or how someone 'had no time for such a such a person' or recourse to 'the last straw', phrases which add something to its pages, might provoke some reviewers into mild apoplexy, but, on reflection, these form part of its appeal, a book that is composed by a born raconteur who has a good eye for putting together a story.

The question that often arises when considering Joyce in Paris is whether all his life went into his writing and whether there was anything left over for just living. Perhaps not surprisingly, it is a question that remains after one has finished Fennell's account. Repeatedly, the author suggests that Joyce incorporated details about Dublin and Ireland from conversation with his circle of friends. He quotes the well-rehearsed incident with Beckett during a dictation session and how the phrase 'come in' surfaced in *Finnegans Wake* (without telling the reader where exactly it appears in that text). But the mountain Joyce was drilling into from both sides remains largely a mystery in this account. It is as if Fennell accepts that Joyce lived in two worlds, one concerned with the practice of writing, the other a parallel universe where of an evening he would frequent the best Parisian restaurants and then adjourn to his apartment with friends, where he would sing Irish ballads and slightly off-colour songs such as 'The Brown and Yellow Ale' or show his guests his skill at high-kicking until he collapsed on the sofa or retired to bed, ready for the next day's piece of writing.

According to Fennell, Joyce 'manipulated' or 'exploited' (14–15) his friends, but I am not sure if those are the words I would choose. I think he made good use of his friends; manipulation or exploitation is an unnecessary criticism of Joyce's character – at least at this point.

He got his friends to read books for him, run errands, write positive things about his new work, support him financially, and so on. He apparently told Arthur Power, 'I'm always friends with a person for a purpose' (14), but, again, that is not evidence that he is an exploiter or a manipulator, and, equally, you cannot always trust Power.

Attachment is a related matter, but that is something Fennell only discusses in passing, and often only in relation to the attitude of those in the circle toward Joyce, not the other way round. So there is something one-dimensional about this account. Missing is a general exploration of Joyce's sense of attachment both in regard to his friends and also in regard to how he conceived the relation between attachment and friendship. The falling out with Beckett is described, as is the reconciliation, but perhaps there could have been a wider discussion about the nature of friendship and attachment. In the mid-1930s, when all the exiles return home and Joyce is left on his own, again the reader looks for some reflection on how this affected the Irish exile. Perhaps he didn't need friends, only a wife and family. Perhaps others in the circle were mere acquaintances, who came and went with the seasons and the fortunes of the French economy and exchange rate.

Thomas McGreevy, who was sufficiently inside the circle to become Giorgio Joyce's best man at his wedding, suggests that 'Joyce was not interested in personal friendship or friendships'. And he adds: 'When new acquaintances turned up, I would say that his first and only consideration was whether they could be of use in relation to the still unnamed work' (196). I suspect Fennell takes that phrase 'could be of use' as further proof of his theory of 'manipulation' and 'exploitation'. We don't have the full context, either in McGreevy's unpublished memoir as cited or in Joyce's own life, but the phrase can be interpreted in a less hostile, more ambivalent, way. As for McGreevy's distinction between friends and acquaintances, that deserves more consideration in a book about friendship.

Fennell deals with each of the friends in the circle in turn: Patrick Tuohy, Robert McAlmon, Power, George Moore, Padraic and Mary Colum, Ernest Hemingway, Scott Fitzgerald, Sylvia Beach, Harriet

Shaw Weaver, Beckett, and McGreevy. His description of Power's first
meeting with Joyce is striking, particularly when Power is politely (or
perhaps humorously) asked by Joyce if he is 'a man of letters' (35). In a
comment that is reminiscent of what Yeats said to Synge in Paris in the
1890s, Power is told by Joyce to write in the Irish tradition: 'You must
write what is in your blood not what is in your brain' (35), a remark
that to this reader doesn't sound like Joyce. Fennell also reminds us that
the circle of friends were not slow to voice their opinion about the
great man. McAlmon calls attention to the key role of Nora for Joyce;
Hemingway to how the Blooms saved Joyce; Mary Colum to how
Joyce had 'little time for intelligent women' (140); McGreevy, rather
surprisingly, to how Joyce might not have been a drinking man.

Most readers, I suspect, will find that last remark a little far-
fetched, especially coming in a book which delights in naming all the
restaurants, cafés and bars where Joyce imbibed. On the other hand,
we are indebted to Fennell for exploiting McGreevy's unpublished
papers, and he might have made more of his find. What he doesn't
notice is that, before he became a confidante of Joyce and Beckett,
McGreevy in Dublin in the 1920s had played a similar role with
George Yeats. Through her lively and intimate correspondence with
McGreevy, we gain a sharp insight into Yeats's marriage to a woman
half the poet's age. Later in Paris, he provides a close-up view of
the character of Joyce which also doesn't always accord to what we
might expect. McGreevy represents an important witness and line of
continuity in this period, the shrewd observer at home and abroad,
who introduced Beckett to Joyce, someone who, according to Joyce,
could talk about paintings like Yeats. 'Where did you pick up that
way you have of speaking about painting?... I never had it' (201). And
it is fitting that you can hear the Irish accent coming through the
Kerry poet's memory of that conversation.

A Little Circle of Kindred Minds: Joyce in Paris reminds us of the
enigma that is Joyce. Fennell concentrates on the narrative to the
detriment of analysis. It is surprising to read that Joyce 'had little
time for Irish politics' (50) when, earlier, Fennell had suggested that
Joyce sought to 'redeem his country through his writing' (13). I must

confess I am still no clearer after reading this book to understanding the enigma. How did he write *Finnegans Wake* when he was perhaps surrounded not by friends but by people, like McAlmon, who thought his 'infatuation with words' was 'something all writers go through before they mature' (72)? The clue must lie elsewhere than in his circle of friends.

CHAPTER 8

JOYCE, YEATS AND
THE MATTER OF IRELAND

JOHN KELLY, *A W.B. YEATS CHRONOLOGY*
BASINGSTOKE: MACMILLAN, 2003

ROGER NORBURN, *A JAMES JOYCE CHRONOLOGY*
BASINGSTOKE: MACMILLAN 2004

In the subversive Lessons chapter of *Finnegans Wake*, Joyce 'answers' Yeats's gyres with a sketch of two overlapping circles to represent the female genitalia, and yokes together his own career as a writer with that of his one-time model: 'a daintical pair of accomplasses! You, allus for the kunst and me for omething with a handel to it' (*Finnegans Wake* 295:27–8). The portmanteau words betray a childlike playing with words and cross-gendering: 'daintical' carries both dainty and identical and 'accomplasses' the words accomplice, compass, and lasses. The stress on identity, gender, and transgression is continued in Joyce's schoolboy playing on the German word 'kunsthandel' or art dealer. Yeats was always for the 'kunst' (for Art, for women), Joyce is for music, but, more down-to-earth, he is also for anything with a handle to it (commerce, the male body or friendship, 'omething'). Between them

151

the dreamy Yeats and the wideawake Joyce created and divided a large part of the spoils of modern writing in English, so that without these two Irish accomplasses the look and character of that period would be significantly altered. With two new chronologies of their lives in front of us, it is always worth rehearsing something of their extraordinary imaginative power and their continuing capacity to shock and move us. For even as we seek to account for or to trace their lives, whether singly or together, we cannot ever forget the disjunction between the life and the art, the tantalizing thread that at once separates and joins the person who sits down to breakfast and the individual who creates.

Previous authors in this 'Author Chronologies' series include Milton, Browning, Ruskin, Poe, Lawrence, Waugh, and Orwell. The format is in one sense straightforward: a chronology of the events that constituted the life of the writer, beginning in Yeats's case in 1865 and ending in 1939 and in Joyce's with 1882 and 1941. John Kelly, the chief editor of what will become the twelve-volume edition of the *Collected Letters of W. B. Yeats*, is the natural choice to tackle such a complex subject, while Roger Norburn proved a good choice with regard to Joyce. Kelly's volume forms a handy complement to the two volumes of Roy Foster's *W. B. Yeats: A Life* (1998, 2003), while Norburn's, which is more dependent on the work of others, has much to commend it.

With regard to *A W.B. Yeats Chronology*, the first comment to make concerns the disposition of the material. The *Chronology* itself occupies some 300 pages, with 172 pages devoted to Yeats's life up to the outbreak of the Great War, and 118 to the remainder, or 193 pages up his marriage in 1917 and 107 thereafter. Sixty-one pages are devoted to the 1920s, 42 to the 1930s. So there is an imbalance here, more so since the final two decades were not only Yeats's most creative decades as a poet but also the least well-known in terms of his still-unpublished correspondence. A second issue relates to Kelly's treatment of the gulf between man and writer. According to Kelly, a visit to an art gallery in 1937 'inspires' his poem 'The Municipal Gallery Revisited' – he makes a similar comment about Yeats's inspection of St Otteran's School in 1926 and the ensuing poem 'Among School Children.' Such remarks seem out of place with most writers but especially so with Yeats, who was given to writing occasional verse but who rarely confused occasion with inspiration. Norburn, too, with his constant references to individuals who were the models for particular characters in Joyce's fiction, also falls into a similar trap, but in his case it is less disabling. As genetic scholars of Joyce enthusiastically remind us, the *Irish Times* provided Joyce with a wealth of material when he began composing *Finnegans Wake* in the 1920s, but they might add that Joyce's stature has remained largely untouched by the charge of plagiarism and that arguably the real question concerns not derivation but function, how the 'lifted' material is used by Joyce.

Much is made by Yeatsians of the continuity and the unity of his work. Kelly refers to Yeats's 'ultimately coherent canon' (ix), but this characterization is belied by his *Chronology*. December 1934, for example, begins with the publication of 'Meru' and other poems in the *London Mercury* and ends with an injection by Norman Haire, who in April was responsible for performing the Steinach operation on Yeats. In between come meetings at the Abbey Theatre in Dublin, dinner with Margot Collis, lunch with T. S. Eliot, a meeting with A. P. Watt his literary agent, an encounter in the street with a former mistress Alick Schepeler (whose name he cannot recall), the beginning of an affair with Ethel Mannin, and the first convening of the Group Theatre Committee. If there is a coherence here it is not the coherence of 'Meru' and the 'desolation of reality' that is a consequence of the ravaging human intellect, but more like the coherence noticed by Dorothy Wellesley when she concluded that 'Sex, Philosophy and the Occult preoccupy him.' One could take a different tack, abandon coherence and have recourse to the more reliable trope of juxtaposition, but even here there are problems. In early January 1919 when 'The Second Coming' was being written, George was ill, news came through of his father's accident in New York, and a quarrel with Maud Gonne caused Yeats severe nervous exhaustion and eye trouble. Kelly inserts a full-stop and continues: 'Writes "The Second Coming."' (202) To extract from this entry – and I am sure this is not Kelly's view – that Yeats was a little depressed when he wrote his great poem confirms the importance of retaining the gulf or the idea of discontinuity between man and poet.

To attend to Yeats – and the contrast with the 'pelagiarist' Joyce is instructive – is to be involved in unravelling, so that the construction of Yeats is inevitably also a form of deconstruction.

On the other hand, certain sequences remind us of continuity. The month of July 1922 is utterly gripping in the way it is presented to us in Kelly's *Chronology*, gripping for both the man and poet. On the 4th Yeats hears wild rumours about the Irish Civil War while staying at his tower at Ballylee. But the rumours prove to be more than this when Gregory's neighbours, the Scovells, who the previous month were ordered out of the country by Republicans, are threatened again, and we learn that a fearless Yeats intervenes on their behalf with the Free State forces in Gort. On the 12th Yeats optimistically thinks there has been a settlement in the War. On the 14th he is writing a draft of Part VI of 'Meditations in Time of Civil War.' Missing at this point in Kelly's account is a specific reference to the murder on the 15th of a Free State soldier in Gort – 'that dead young soldier', as he appears in the poem. On the 16th Kelly refers to Yeats discussing with Gregory at Coole the ambush the previous evening near Gort. On the 20th Anne his daughter falls ill and the following day is taken by George to Dublin for treatment. On the 24th while staying at Coole Yeats hears a bomb explosion, and on his return to Ballylee he hears a fire-fight, which lasts an hour. On the 29th, while driving from Ballylee to Coole, he sees a dead man in a car. The following month the bridge outside his tower is blown up in the middle of the night by Republicans. No biography could better capture this moment of danger or indeed the context for Yeats's magnificent poem. Foster concentrates on a reading of the poem itself, but Kelly gives us more by allowing the events to speak for themselves. The one moment of real tension in *A James Joyce Chronology* occurs in the months leading up to Joyce's escape from Vichy France to neutral Switzerland in December 1940. The incident during the Irish Civil War in April 1923, when the train on which Nora and the children are travelling comes under fire, is simply recorded by Norburn in parentheses as: '(On their return journey to Dublin their train is shot at)' (103).

In spite of its general reliability and accuracy – the 54 page Index is a triumph in this regard – it would be worth signalling here other specific qualifications about Kelly's *Chronology* if only to set the record straight. No mention is made of a revealing letter on 1 February 1923, first identified in my own work, when George Yeats, the Civil War all around her in Dublin, pleaded with her husband in London not to abandon his links with Ireland by settling permanently in England.[161] Kelly compounds matters with the entry for 2 February, which refers to Yeats dining with George's mother who 'urges him to move the family to Chester' (225), but this is to misread the tenor and flow of events during this crucial period. At other times Kelly fails to establish the relevant connection. When Yeats travelled to the United States in January 1914, he met Lily Carstairs on board the *Lusitania*, and Kelly informs us in the Index that Carstairs was a 'socialite.' In point of fact, Carstairs, an American, was the daughter of the London representative of Knoedler and Co, the prestigious New York art dealer, who before the Great War acted as an important clearing-house in Europe for old masters and early British painters. On 27 December 1913, with her brother Carroll, she accompanied Lady Gregory on a visit to Yeats at Stone Cottage in Sussex, where they sent a postcard to Gregory's nephew, the art-dealer Hugh Lane, whose disputed bequest, as the *Chronology* suggests, occupied a considerable amount of time for both Gregory and Yeats (details of the postcard and visit can be found in my own work). Lily may have been a 'socialite' but this is hardly the term to apply to her in relation to Yeats, and it also raises the question of whether or not, a month earlier, they had indeed planned to meet on the voyage across the Atlantic.[162]

Other blemishes can be quickly recorded. There is no mention of the Stephen's Green Club in the Index and yet this is repeatedly mentioned in the *Chronology* itself – Kelly also fails to record that Yeats stayed here in early June 1916 when thoughts of 'Easter 1916' (and clubs) were in his mind. The Kildare Street Club, where Yeats had lunch on several occasions, is also missing from the Index. Nothing appears in the *Chronology* itself of the Abdication crisis in

161 See my *Yeats's Worlds*, 219.
162 For more on Lily Carstairs, see my *W.B. Yeats: Critical Assessments* vol 1, 5–7.

1936, an event that affected Yeats and his titled English friends. More
worryingly, we learn that in October 1917 Yeats 'chaffs' George about
Machiavelli. (195) As it stands, this is certainly an enigmatic remark
and, until the full correspondence is actually published, will leave most
readers in the dark. The actual letter reveals a different picture. Yeats
did not mean to chaff her: he wanted to hear her explain her views to
the assembled company and turned the focus on her accordingly. In
contrast to the confident articulation of his friends – this is within a
week of their wedding – she, he notices by way of an apology, is more
modest and given to the service of others. So the chaffing, which can
only be deduced from this letter, is followed by an apology; as for
Machiavelli, he is but a sideshow, and, in fairness to George, Kelly
might have transcribed Yeats's unsuccessful attempt at spelling the
Italian author's name. It would be more accurate if the entry read:
'WBY apologises to GY for embarrassing her among his friends.'
The underplaying of the female presence also appears in Kelly's entry
for 17 July 1924, which derives from Yeats's correspondence with
George. Kelly records Yeats's daytime activities writing verse in the
morning and, later, attending meetings to establish a new political
party, followed by debates in the Senate, but omits the tender note at
the end of the letter, how he is missing her when evening falls.

   In stressing various blemishes with this *Chronology*, my intention
is to suggest how a story can be differently told and to caution
against thinking that reference books, even by established scholars,
are wholly reliable or free from tendentiousness. On a positive
note, while this *Chronology* is not a biography of Yeats, it certainly
provides material for a sharply realized, succinct view of the writer's
extraordinary involvement in the history of his time. It cannot be
praised enough. The most hilarious moment, apart from the reference
to his mistakenly eating two dinners at the Arts Club, occurs on
12 October 1923, when the publisher Werner Laurie, five days after
receiving part of the manuscript, asks Watt if he could 'coax WBY
into writing a description of *A Vision* as no-one has the faintest idea
what it is about' (230). There is a similar moment in the *James Joyce
Chronology* in November 1926 when we read: 'Having received the

whole of Part III of *FW*, Pound can make nothing of it, but wishes JJ well.' (126)[163]

A James Joyce Chronology presents a different set of problems. In general, this is a well-researched and, except for a consistent misuse of restrictive and non-restrictive relative clauses, a largely error-free digest of the day-to-day details that make up the life of James Joyce. The story is for the most part well-known and there is little here that is new, but this is not to say that it is without merit or interest. Norburn acknowledges his debt to Richard Ellmann and at the same times gives examples of factual errors in the latter's 'magisterial' biography. What he doesn't acknowledge is not so much Ellmann's mistakes or indeed misreadings and omissions (which can be quickly corrected) as the construction of a life which has recently been subject to an overhaul by Joyce scholars, partly using Ellmann's own papers deposited at the University of Tulsa. Norburn's excellent, up-to-date bibliography carries some of these changes but not enough of this is reflected in the *Chronology*. It still comes as a shock, for example, to recall that Ellmann delayed but weeks in Trieste in the 1950s when he was researching the ten formative years Joyce spent there between 1905 and 1915.

Among the valuable material gathered at the end of Norburn's *Chronology*, there is an appendix listing monetary equivalents for the various occasions in Joyce's life when he received money, so that we can judge that his father's gift of £7 on his departure for the continent in October 1904, worth £440 in today's money, was very generous, and that Harriet Shaw Weaver's gift of £5000 in May 1919, equivalent to £137,522, was princely. In other appendices, the stories of *Dubliners* and the episodes of *Ulysses* are listed, though without the dates of composition or first printing. Although it would fill several pages, a list of Joyce's various addresses would also have proved enlightening for anyone under the misapprehension that his ordered mind was underpinned by an ordered life. A Who's Who, designed to furnish other information on major players in the Joyce story,

---

163 I assume the reference to *Finnegans Wake* is a mistake. In 1926 it was still known as 'Work in Progress'.

comprises potted biographies of thirty-one individuals including family, friends, publishers, writers, musicians, and promoters of his work, but the list is not without its problems. Missing from the Sylvia Beach section is an account of her stormy relationship with Joyce; the enigmatic entry for 15 November 1922 in the *Chronology* – 'Has a hard talk with Beach' (107) – gives a flavour of this but more needs adding. In a Headnote to the Who's Who appendix, Norburn tells the reader he will 'deal with the subjects' lives away from the context of James Joyce', (202) but the Frank Budgen entry is confined to his friendship with Joyce, while Mary Colum is portrayed simply an adjunct to Padraic Colum when she was a contemporary of Joyce's at university and, later, a shrewd critic of Irish writing. The author is right to stress Weaver's left-wing affiliations but to mention that she supported the Soviet invasion of Hungary in 1956 perhaps detracts from her role as Joyce's chief benefactress. As for Oliver St John Gogarty, Norburn suggests that he 'may well go down in history as the "Buck" Mulligan of the first sentence of *U*' (204), a remark that does injustice not only to Gogarty, who has a following in his own right, but also to the figure of Mulligan, who is arguably a more attractive character at the beginning of the novel than Stephen Dedalus. We might also recall that in the very centre of John Ryan's 'Bloomsday, 1904', which I reproduce on my frontispiece, is the figure of Mulligan in his dressing-gown greeting the day.

As for the disposition of Norburn's *Chronology*, the balance here is evenly distributed with 40 pages devoted to the 1900s, 43 to the 1910s, 51 to the 1920s, 40 to the 1930s, and 7 to the final 13 months. Blanks are still well-represented in the life of Joyce, and the chronologist has nothing to record for example for November 1908, January 1909, May 1909, March-June 1911, January 1912, March 1912, June 1912. If any month stands out in this account as pivotal it is December 1913, for with Pound's interest in getting Joyce published in *The Egoist* (at that time the *New Freewoman*) his hoped-for breakthrough in terms of money, success, and fame had arrived, and in one sense Joyce never looked back, especially when, six months later, Weaver took over as principal editor. A decade later in June 1925, he tells her not that he has written 60,000 words but that he has 60,000 words to sell.

Yeats, who was also active on Joyce's behalf, believed all our ideas are in place by our twentieth birthday. In Norburn's account the years from Joyce's birth in 1882 and his eighteenth birthday merit only some three pages (Kelly has one more for Yeats). So what the chronologist or indeed biographer select as significant always needs to be tempered by what the subject might have been experiencing away from the glare of publicity. All his life went into Joyce's writing. Remove problems with his eyes, difficulties with securing employment, getting his work published, threats of litigation (and actual court cases), and moving house, what does a *Chronology* of Joyce's life amount to? The answer must be – and again the contrast with Yeats is instructive – disappointingly thin and unremarkable. When sitting for a portrait by Patrick Tuohy, Joyce is reported to have said: 'Never mind my soul. Just be sure you have my tie right.'[164] And we learn from this *Chronology* that the self-regarding artist, who sought publicity but only on his own terms, asked Carola Giedeon-Welcker for copies of the photograph she took of him overlooking the Limmat in Zurich with back to camera since he liked it so much. (182) Joyce reserves the confessional mode for his imagination, and when he steps outside the church as it were he leaves behind that mode. Unsurprisingly, his correspondence with Weaver, for example, is filled, as he admits in October 1918, with 'problems and delays' (84), that is with problems not about his private life but about his writing. Interestingly, and not without a grain of truth, in January 1915, during the Great War, the Citizen is recommended to the Austrian authorities as 'quiet and only wanting to make a living' (63). So there is something external about the Artist's life, a life that is closer in some respects to the chronicling of the chronologist than to the imaginative grasp of the biographer. The entry for 24 April 1916, a day that changed the course of Irish history as Yeats reminds us, merely records: 'The Easter Rising breaks out in Dublin.

164 Richard Ellmann, *James Joyce* (Oxford and New York: Oxford University Press, 1982), 577.

Sheehy Skeffington, attempting to stop the looting which follows the uprising, is arrested and shot without trial.' (70)

The importance of some issues such as Joyce's concern in the 1930s for the mental health of his daughter Lucia can be registered simply by counting the number of entries, but, in general, this *Chronology* has little to say about some of the underlying themes and patterns. Unsurprisingly, the Index carries no entries on Joyce's sense of betrayal, the mixed attitudes toward his native country, or his use of language as a discourse on freedom. If his departure with Nora Barnacle for the continent in 1904 was poetry – the start of a modern love story outside the Church and a heroic life guided by conscience and the ambition to be a writer – then all the *Chronology* gives us is prose, a reference in this case to John Joyce's £7 and a curious phrase which hovers between an additional comment, an innuendo, and a qualification: 'not realizing JJ will be accompanied on his journey' (223). Elsewhere, the significance of some entries can only be guessed at. In September 1926 Vincent Cosgrave's body is dragged from the Thames after his committing suicide. Cosgrave had appeared earlier in the *Chronology* in August 1909 when he told Joyce he too 'had been walking out with NBJ [Nora Barnacle] during the summer of 1904' (42). Joyce's jealousy was aroused and he wrote at once to Nora, but, in spite of J.F. Byrne's reassurances given him at 7 Eccles Street (where Byrne was staying) that Cosgrave was lying, Joyce continued to entertain fears and doubts about her faithfulness (not for nothing does the scene of Molly's unfaithfulness in *Ulysses* take place in the same house). So what are we to make of the 1926 notice or Byrne's informing him about this in November 1927 when he came to stay with him in Paris? The entries suggest a continuing torment or even a modern case of nemesis, but neither of these seems probable or indeed intended by Norburn. The information would have provided the two friends, who hadn't seen each other since 1909, with a common topic of conversation, but by itself it can only confuse the reader. Ellmann is the source but he records that Joyce was 'excited' by the news, and in the same paragraph includes a comment by Byrne that Joyce and Nora should consider raising their common law marriage to a civil one (which they duly did in July 1931).[165] So the suicide seems to belong to a story that also ended in London, but this time at Kensington Register Office.

ALISTAIR CORMACK, *YEATS AND JOYCE: CYCLICAL HISTORY AND THE REPROBATE TRADITION* ALDERSHOT: ASHGATE, 2008

This is an ambitious and challenging study, which attempts to link the two writers under the aegis of Blake's figure of the Reprobate and within the Irish comic tradition, a tradition characterised by 'heretical idealism' (20). It is an impressive undertaking, marked by a Yeatsian endeavour, not least in the commitment by the author to hammer his thoughts into unity while simultaneously insisting on holding opposites in tension and doggedly refusing to resolve them. In this way Ireland, as Alistair Cormack suggests in his closing moments, 'may be allowed to continue its contrary existence' (188), where 'contrary' is given an unexpectedly nuanced inflection depending on where the stress falls.

Doing justice to the 'daintical pair of accomplasses' (*FW* 295.27) has never been easy; even the biographical details remain slightly obscure. In a chapter entitled 'The Punch and Judy Show of Irish Modernism', Cormack, who is intent on avoiding a biographical reading, concedes too much in the act of raising it to the meeting in 1902 which ended with Joyce inferring the poet was too old for him. He might have delayed more on their other meetings and exchange of correspondence, for, while there were comic elements, it was rarely a Punch and Judy show. Their attitudes toward each other remained mixed. Cormack concentrates almost exclusively on the 1937 edition of *A Vision*, but he could have usefully discussed how and why Yeats's attitude to Joyce changed after voicing criticism in the 1925 version. Joyce, on the other hand, who repeatedly acknowledged Yeats in his writings, knew that their differences needed asserting, sometimes in

165 Ellmann, 598.

striking fashion. Hence, in spite of 'daintical', they were never identical, and if Yeats was all for 'Kunst', for Art or women, the Shem-like Joyce was for 'omething with a handel to it'.

Cormack assumes a playground game constitutes the focus at this point in the Lessons chapter, whereas for many readers it is this but it is also full of innuendo. While erudite, his discussion seems occasionally off-key or fails to address the relentless movement downward. He reads 'All's fair on all fours' as about their enmity as writers (all's fair in love and war), and continues the numbers game by noticing the sets of four in the *Wake* and *A Vision*. Compasses are rightly identified in 'accomplasses', but the portmanteau word is then accorded his own kind of twist, the two being accomplices in their discovery of a cyclical idealist history. Not everything fits, and Cormack is silent on the distinctly heretical exclamation mark accompanying the phrase 'Gyre O, gyre O, gyrotundo!'

The task Cormack sets himself is, therefore, quite daunting, made more so by developments in modern critical theory. Thomas Whitaker's *Swan and Shadow: Yeats's Dialogue with History* (1964), an under-acknowledged account which informs Cormack's study, appeared before the emergence of post-structuralism, deconstruction, and postcolonialism. The assurance in Whitaker has been replaced by something more nervous and less convincing, by something which occasionally resembles special pleading. Thus, as if he were first in the field, Cormack emphasises the ubiquitous presence of irony in the second version of *A Vision*, but Whitaker had already drawn attention to how Yeats's 'prose is constantly shaped by the pressure of ironic qualifications' and did not need all the apparatus erected by Cormack.[166]

However, whether as a trellis or an argument against materialism there is an extensive and frequently insightful discussion of the ideas of Bruno and Vico in the work of Yeats and Joyce. Vico was a reminder that all cultures are dialogic and that history was not a form of teleology. There is a nice moment when Cormack draws attention to mediums and 'mediated', and in the process recalls Beckett's phrase 'a history

---

166 Thomas Whitaker, *Swan and Shadow: Yeats's Dialogue with History* (Chapel Hill, NC: University of Carolina Press, 1964), 88.

of representations'. More contentious is his claim that both writers constructed their idealist histories from esoteric sources. All the while, another thesis is being advanced, for the complementary side to this study, indeed its rationale, is the attempt to yoke together their interest in the philosophy of history with modern Irish history.

Repeatedly, Cormack finds support in the work of Emer Nolan and the qualifications entered by nationalist critics he identifies as 'Irish Ireland'. 'Cyclops' is read not in terms of the conventional opposition between the Citizen and Bloom but as indicative of the culture's creativity. *Finnegans Wake* and *A Vision* were composed after political independence, but the issue of Irishness, linked by Cormack with the Reprobate tradition and the long view of history, continued for both authors. In a move that is surprising, given their life-long interest in the occult, it leads Cormack, after some remarks about the 1930s providing a high point between decolonisation and modernism, to speculate that the meaning of national consciousness 'must have been so problematical that an esoteric response became an attractive…step' (70). However, when he confines himself to what he knows, Cormack is on solider ground.

FRANK SHOVLIN, *JOURNEY WESTWARD: JOYCE, DUBLINERS AND THE LITERARY REVIVAL* LIVERPOOL: LIVERPOOL UNIVERSITY PRESS, 2012

Taking its cue from the work of critics such as Cóilín Owens, Kevin Whelan and John V. Kelleher, *Journey Westward* focuses on the Irish contexts, whether historical or geographical, which informed Joyce's writing. With particular attention to the allusive quality inhering in street names, names of characters, titles of songs and even brands of whiskey, Frank Shovlin offers a reading of *Dubliners* that insists on Irish history almost to the exclusion of all else. While his study is thought-provoking and often rewarding, accompanying it from the outset, even for readers sympathetic to such an approach, is a certain doubt as to whether or not the information uncovered is noteworthy, more or less relevant, or, indeed, what Joyce intended. The masterly accumulation of detail in evidence here issues, then, in the mischievous thought that, if those who are familiar with Irish history are at an advantage when tackling Joyce, they are not necessarily the best or only readers.

Frequently, as in his discussion of the statue of King William in 'The Dead', Shovlin can be genuinely insightful. The same is true of the blind stripling's 'tap' heard in the 'Sirens' episode of *Ulysses*, which he convincingly links to 1798 and William Rooney's 1902 commemorative poem, 'The Priest of Adergool'. (146) Rooney's poem also emerges in Gabriel's surname in 'The Dead', for the priest in question, who wakened his parishioners to the news of the French landing at Killala in County Mayo, is a Fr Conroy. Equally, a line from the poem resurfaces in Gretta Conroy's account of Michael Furey trying to contact her: 'There's someone at the window. Tap! Tap! Tap, anew.'

Shovlin also focuses on an earlier defeat in Irish history with the extinguishing of the Jacobite cause at the battle of Aughrim in County Galway on 12 July 1691. The deliberate repetition of 'Poor James' in 'The Sisters' he reads as a Jacobite echo, and detects in the phrase 'their friends, the French' in 'After the Race' Joyce 'tapping into the Aisling tradition' (71), a view supported by a possible reference to the French General, Ruth, in the figure of 'Routh', the Englishman who wins at cards. This is less convincing, but it is not impossible to imagine Joyce, in a series of revengeful acts, peppering his stories with concealed allusions still to be uncovered. The subsequent issue is not so much belief as how such details contribute to the story or collection as a whole.

If 'Poor James' begins the collection, 'The Lass of Aughrim' rounds out the Jacobite theme. (91) Shovlin follows Paul Muldoon in his suggestion that Lord Gregory's name is omitted because that might remind readers of Lady Gregory and lessen the impact of the historical reference. But Shovlin, who detects in Joyce's insertion of 'Nuns' Island' an allusion to the Protestant Persse distillery, wants more from his discovery, and he is unable to temper his criticism of Lady Gregory (née Persse) and her husband, who was the author of the 'Gregory Clause', which prevented anyone during the Great Famine with more than a quarter-acre of land from claiming famine relief. (104)

In 'Clay', Maria, as if paralysed by the thought of her own fate, repeats a stanza when reciting 'I Dreamt that I Dwelt'. Unless it belongs to his suppressed lyricism, why Joyce omits lines from 'The Lass of Aughrim' seems uncertain. The song, after all, is a Child Ballad and Scottish in origin, so, in one respect, it has nothing to do with the battle. Equally, Lady Gregory's husband was a 'Sir' not a Lord. When he made *The Dead*, John Huston, as if he sought some kind of ownership over the story, was in no doubt about the power of the song, which needed to be rendered in full. The film is missing from Shovlin's account, as is something else. The reference to 'the dark mutinous Shannon waves' strays beyond history to show us perhaps how gender intrudes and disrupts things, including all kinds of ownership and all kinds of cut-and-dry history, whether linear or tragic. Dispossession, as much as possession, hovers over Joyce's story.

Allusiveness, an under-theorised concept in Joyce studies, works in various ways. In a revealing slip, Shovlin claims that the ballad of 'Finnegan's Wake' is 'not mentioned directly in the novel' (33). Leaving aside the reference to *Finnegans Wake* being a novel, we should not forget that in *The James Joyce Songbook* (1982) Ruth Bauerle references more than fifty pages where the ballad appears, which is probably an under-estimate.[167] But what intrigues me is the phrase 'mentioned directly' (33), for this cuts across the drift of his argument, which is intent on stressing indirectness, the power of allusion and the fine line between what is mentioned directly and indirectly. The heart sinks but Shovlin surmises that in future we might read *Dubliners* with a set of notes 'the size of a telephone book' (155). In fact, he has already begun the task with a spirited journey that delights in showing what should be included in an annotated edition.

---

167 Ruth Bauerle, *The James Joyce Songbook* (New York: Garland, 1982), 553.

DUBLIN JAMES JOYCE JOURNAL ISSUE 1 DUBLIN: UNIVERSITY COLLEGE DUBLIN AND THE NATIONAL LIBRARY OF IRELAND, 2008

The first issue of a new journal in Joyce studies is always a cause for celebration. Because of its association with University College Dublin and the National Library of Ireland, this journal, edited by Luca Crispi and Anne Fogarty and to be published on an annual basis, possesses the right pedigree to enhance the cause of Joyce studies round the world. The wealth of manuscript and research material held by the Library and the series of annual lectures by visiting scholars at the Joyce Summer School will furnish a ready supply of articles and submissions for future issues, and if Issue 1 is anything to go by we are at the beginning of a highly successful venture.

The confident cover design is by Design HQ, a company with an appropriately pointed address 1 James Joyce Street at Liberty Corner in the centre of Dublin. Standing proud on the cover there is the classic image of Joyce in waistcoat with hands in pockets in front of Constantine Curran's greenhouse, head to one side, wondering if he could ask the photographer for some change. Joyce's image (minus the greenhouse) is set against an attractive mid-blue, a blue that recalls the cover on the Shakespeare and Company early editions of *Ulysses*, and it comes complete with a decorative magenta band at the bottom and white banner at the top proclaiming the journal's title with James Joyce picked out in blue. Listed on the back cover are the seven essays which make up the first issue.

There is a down-to-earth quality about this new journal. All but one of the essays boasts a business-like, helpful colon in the title. There are no flyleaves or reviews or correspondence and margins are kept to a minimum. Each page carries around forty lines and around twelve words per line, so the eye confronts a manageable 400–480 words per page. Ten black-and-white illustrations accompany the essays, nine of which could perhaps be sharper, the one exception being the route of the Robert Emmet 1898 centenary procession, which Cóilín Owens skilfully incorporates into an essay on 'After the Race'. The

1894 period photos from *The Illustrograph*, reproduced in Stephanie Rains's essay on 'Araby', are a real find, but I am sure the originals, especially those by Chancellor, yield more pixel information than are reproduced here in this journal. This might seem heresy to some but at times when the paper quality is not sufficiently photographic it is better to lose the wide-angle view and crop an image down to size, that is to forgo the Victorian posed shot for something which has more immediacy for a modern reader.

Dublin James Joyce Journal provides a back-to-Dublin view of Joyce, a view which has much to commend it. Christine O'Neill recalls Niall Montgomery's lively contribution a generation ago to Joyce studies. The striking thing, however, about force of personality – and Montgomery by all accounts had this in abundance – is that it evaporates into thin air with the passage of time. Moreover, as we move further away from Joyce's period, we are forced to rely less on personal knowledge and insider information and more on the anonymous historical record. According to Montgomery writing in 1968 to the German translator of *Dubliners*, 'In Joyce's time, most of the business in the city was Protestant. I have heard my old friend, Mr Jack Yeats, the painter, say that in his youth there was no Irish name to be seen on a shop fascia in the city' (5). No doubt there's some truth in this remark but *Thom's Business Directory of Dublin and Suburbs for the Year 1906* (when Yeats would have been 35) is full of Irish names and suggests otherwise. As Terence Killeen's essay also reminds us, correcting the exaggerations of one generation is often the task of the next, and not infrequently the individual reminiscence gets in the way of the record. I was particularly intrigued by Montgomery's gloss on 'country cute', the cutting remark about Gretta Conroy that appears in 'The Dead': 'In Dublin we look on ourselves as simple, easy-going people, terrified of the clever rustics who run our city and state – "country cute", though an old-fashioned phrase, mirrors precisely the Dublin attitude to the Irish' (6). This is the kind of gloss to delight the cognoscenti but it must have slightly perplexed the German translator. And what precisely does such a phrase tell us about the Dublin attitude to the Irish? That Dubliners are not Irish? In Joyce's story of course the movement is the other way round, for it is the female West – the 'dark mutinous Shannon waves' – which subverts the patriarchal power of Dublin and the state.

'Araby', a story about eastern promise and desire, is brought down to earth in Rains's essay. 'Those who examine the archives…are likely to conclude that Joyce was basing his story very loosely indeed upon the real event' (17), the Araby Bazaar of 1894 that is. I wonder if 'basing' is the right word. If she had written 'drawing on' or 'making use of', she would not need the qualification 'very loosely'. Returning Joyce to any base whether in social history or genetic criticism is not without risk. I admire the historical excavation on display in this essay, but sometimes after all the hard work something remains tentative and unresolved. In this essay the aporia or conundrum focuses on 'English accents' – for, according to Rains, the volunteers at the Araby Bazaar were Irish. There's clearly a problem here, and Rains addresses it by having recourse, on the one hand, to Joyce's 'creative adaptation' or, on the other hand, to how such voices might have sounded to the 'inexperienced ear' of the lower-middle-class narrator (21). It's a neat move but not terribly satisfactory.

The snatch of conversation is difficult to resolve either way. It would support Rains's case if 'fib', one of words the narrator alights upon, was used only by speakers of Hiberno-English, but one suspects it was fairly common among speakers of English on both sides of the Irish Sea. To my mind that passage serves to illustrate the restricted speech of shop assistants and further evidence of the theme of the harp of romance and the impossibility or inanity of its setting. Some things in Joyce cannot be straightened out. The volunteers could have come across from Britain for the week to help out their aunts or cousins; in mockery the volunteers could have been imitating English accents; Joyce could have been obliquely suggesting such bazaars were part of the Crown's putative hegemony, part of what Owens calls the 'viceregally sponsored bazaars' (33); perhaps the boy was collapsing two such memories of visits to bazaars and market stalls. Certainly, with the single exception of a woman's head with accompanying scarf or coverlet and entitled simply 'Araby', the series of photographs of various amateur groups attending the bazaar and originally published in the July issue of *The Illustrograph* in 1894 convey almost nothing of the exoticism or excitement of the East, or, indeed, the excitement among the huge crowds attending. This artificial aspect Joyce has captured particularly well in 'Araby', where passion and desire are confined to the boy visiting the bazaar and not to be found in the bazaar itself. In this regard the story provides a striking contrast with the Oriental theme on display in Bloom's imagination when we first meet him in the 'Calypso' episode of *Ulysses*.

Owens's essay is more convincing than Rains's partly because the history is woven into the narrative. According to Owens, 'After the Race' constitutes an 'oblique memorial to a famous Dubliner', namely Robert Emmet. The various landmarks in Dublin associated with Emmet not only form the background to the story but they are also essential to understanding Joyce's 'exercise in poetic justice' (40). That movement from background to foreground is expertly handled, for this is a remarkable essay and offers further insight into Joyce's characteristic methods and use of understatement. I particularly liked Owens's alertness to the vain hopes that inform the story.

Terence Killeen's essay on Alfred H. Hunter makes effective use of the 1911 Census of Ireland to counter the myths that have grown up around the model for Bloom in the Joyce community. Here the historical record reveals a potentially more intriguing figure than we encounter in the second-hand conjectures of Richard Ellmann and Hugh Kenner. The advertising agent wasn't Jewish but he had a wife who was born Margaret only to become a Marian by 1911. Killeen wisely holds back from adding that the Census reveals Hunter's middle name was Henry.

Every essay is worth the delay. In his essay on Joyce's Orientalism, Malcolm Sen offers some valuable comments on 'the unstable topography of Joyce's Orient in *Ulysses*' (60), and how his Orient is a 'mixture compiled of previous learning' (63), some of it, as with the name ALP, derived from Samuel Taylor Coleridge. He is particularly good at showing the postmodern way Orientalism functions in Joyce and how its inheritance is always 'a symbol of a symbol, a "copy of a copy", and an approximation of the real' (65). Anne Fogarty's essay on Dublin statues in Joyce's writing is a model of its kind. Throughout she is alive to Joyce's working method where statues are 'both casually observed, inert objects and also redolent and evocative symbols that act as co-ordinates for buried but vital cultural and historical memories' (70). With his eye on a Chinese audience, Fintan O'Toole completes this fine volume with an equally impressive take on Joyce, the city and globalisation. His essay includes a provocative re-evaluation of the central place of Mina Purefoy in *Ulysses*.

VOICES ON JOYCE, EDITED BY ANNE FOGARTY AND FRAN O'ROURKE. DUBLIN: UNIVERSITY COLLEGE DUBLIN PRESS, 2015

This collection of twenty essays has its origins in a lecture series given at University College Dublin (UCD) in the centenary year of 2004, with most of the essays dating from that period. All the contributors have some connection with UCD whether in the past or present. Indeed, in its own way this book is a celebration of a leading international centre not only for Irish Studies but also, increasingly, for Joyce studies. Appropriately, it includes a characteristically close reading by Fritz Senn of the sleepy figure of Morpheus in the 'Eumaeus' episode of *Ulysses*, but it should not be assumed that because five of the other twenty contributors have acquired the title 'Emeritus' that this is a backward-looking volume or full of nostalgia. On the contrary there is something refreshing about leading figures in the fields of history, philosophy, anatomy, geography, Italian, music, drama and cultural studies taking up the challenge presented by one of UCD's most remarkable students.

The collection is enhanced by a series of thirty black-and-white photographs which were taken by Lee Miller in 1946 and published the following year in *Vogue*. Much is made of this visual material by the editors and by Terence Killeen, who provides a six-page essay on the American photographer. A book on Joyce accompanied by illustrations has much to recommend it, especially when the illustrations formed part of a recent exhibition at UCD. The original photographs, which can be accessed online at leemiller.org, are something special – sharp and intelligent, never dull, occasionally humorous, always evocative – and they rightly convey something of post-war Dublin awaiting the appreciation of later generations. We are reliably informed that the captions in the *Vogue* issue are 'tremendously spirited, independent, sometimes feisty comments that are a joy to read' (135). Unfortunately, they are missing from this volume, which is a shame for I am sure they would have added something to the reader's enjoyment. Most of the photos extend into the gutter and off the page, so they are framed by the edges of the oblong page itself. Bleeding has a special place in page design, but it needs careful handling and should be used perhaps sparingly. After all, there is nothing inherently wrong with margins of white paper space, especially when the originals are not oblong. As for cropping, this also requires more than a little care, and I refer to just one example of what can happen, that of the flower-seller on Grafton Street on page 200. Juxtapose this image with the one available online and it is clear that the class opposition is missing, for, presumably, Lee Miller has intended that we do not neglect the well-dressed mannequin in the fashionable shop behind the woman in a shawl selling flowers.

The essays open with a densely written introduction by Anne Fogarty summarising the book as a whole and how it all fits together. Her own discussion of Joyce and Parnell offers itself as a model, in this case of memory, whether conceived, as Paul Ricoeur has suggested, in terms of collective memory or an official history, for memory also has a future. Hence the significance in *Ulysses* of the unrealised statue of Parnell at the top of what is now O'Connell Street. Fogarty includes a useful survey of how critics have interpreted the relationship between Joyce and Parnell, before injecting something new into the discussion. She shows how the tragic story of Joyce's youth gave way to his view that Parnell occupied the site of contradictory impulses. Joyce, therefore, moves away from the shadow of the Chief, and comes to understand how the different guises of his literary Parnellism served 'the unrealised promise of nationalist ideals' (40).

Fogarty's stress on 'unrealised' affords a helpful way of thinking about the volume as a whole. Historians are in the habit of policing the borders of their subject; literary critics and others regularly overstep the mark. In a well-researched essay on Leopold Bloom and Irish Jewry, the economic historian, Cormac Ó Gráda, excoriates Joyce for his ignorance of Jewish life in turn-of-the-century Dublin, particularly Jews from Lithuania, the dominant group. Thus, Joyce's portrait of Bloom 'owed much more to information garnered during his time in Trieste (1904–15) than to first-hand contacts with Irish Jews before leaving Dublin at the age of 22' (22). Arguably, there are few readers who look to *Ulysses* for an authentic portrait of Jewish life in Dublin. For that you would have to go to a social historian or Ó Gráda himself. Where history ends and literature begins is invariably an intriguing question especially when the antinomian Joyce is in focus, and Ó Gráda seems to acknowledge this in closing: 'None of this, of course, takes away from the genius of James Joyce or *Ulysses*' (23). But such an admission cannot seriously challenge the settled view that there is something outrageous and comic about Joyce's decision to insert a Jew into the heart of Catholic Ireland.

The urban geographer, Joseph Brady, in 'Dublin: A City of Contrasts', also emphasises something that is unrealised in *Ulysses*, namely that, in spite of Joyce's famous remark to Frank Budgen, the novel 'does not offer the possibility of reconstructing a complete picture of Dublin as it was in 1904'.[168] Most readers, one suspects, recognise Joyce's claim as an exaggeration. We have enough of the realistic texture of the city to feel we know the city and to know that, for Joyce, Dublin was an already built city, always there, and, consequently, he felt no pressure as a wordsmith to invent something that existed long before he came along. In an essay on Ireland in 1904, the historian, Michael Laffan, emphasizes the changing nature of Ireland: 'To some people Ireland seemed calm, while others viewed it as moribund.' Then he adds: 'Yet Joyce and Barnacle left Ireland at a time when old patterns had begun

---

168 Frank Budgen, *James Joyce and the Making of 'Ulysses' and Other Writings* (Oxford and New York: Oxford University Press, 1972), 69.

to fracture and (with the benefit of hindsight) new patterns could be discerned' (35). The implication of 'Yet' is that Joyce could not discern the changes; otherwise, he might have stayed. Either way, Laffan leaves open, or unrealised, the extent to which those changes made their way into the novel.

Running through this book alongside 'unrealised' there is the sense of tradition or the line of continuity. In his essay on Joyce and Vico, Darragh O'Connell concentrates on the idea of the providential. James Pribek argues for the importance of analogy in an essay connecting Joyce and UCD's founder, John Henry Newman. In a wide-ranging philosophical discussion on epiphanies, Richard Kearney takes us back to Thomas Aquinas and Duns Scotus and forward to Molly Bloom's humorous rewriting of Homer's Penelope. According to Adrian Hardiman, the three legal cases of unnatural death in *Ulysses* have something unresolved about them, largely on account of circumstantial evidence. Doubt is the keyword here, and the Justice of the Supreme Court of Ireland provides an always timely reminder that 'Many characters in *Ulysses* jump to conclusions' (52). Terence Dolan reminds us of the linguistic canvas that Joyce drew on, not least Irish-English, and he shows how Joyce belongs to a longer tradition dating back to the seventh-century Hiberno-Latin text known as 'The Hisperica Famina'.[169] Indeed, Dolan goes further and wickedly suggests that Joyce was 'something of an impostor' (103), a remark with which the author of the 'last word in stolen telling' (*FW* 424.35) would possibly concur. As for jumping to conclusions, this is also true of Conal Hooper's claim that 'hat trick' (*U* 15:195) is primarily a reference to cricket when it looks as if it is something to do with Bloom having luckily survived three misadventures.

There is merit in thinking the 'us' in Declan Kiberd's '*Ulysses* and Us' derives from the first and last letters of Joyce's novel, but that might be unintended. However, there is a problem with his line of continuity, for some things need distinguishing rather than joining, and Us is one of these. Us can refer to everyone and no-one. Some of Us recoil

169 F.J.H.Jenkinson (ed.), *The Hisperica Famina* (Cambridge: Cambridge University Press, 1908).

from assuming we belong to the word even if we use it rhetorically in writing. Joyce may have followed Newman as Pribek suggests, but he wrote a grammar of dissent not assent.[170] In Tony Harrison's poem 'Them and [uz]' the schoolmaster's voiceless [ʌs] is contrasted with the voiced [uz], which is a mark of solidarity among the working class in the north of England.[171] There is nothing of this here. Us is distinguished by Kiberd from 'experts', from the 'technocratic readings of experts' (229), from those who participate in the cult of Bloomsday, who may not have even read the book (223), from 'French' readings of Joyce (222), from the 'specialists who emerged in the middle decades of the twentieth century, when the idea of a common culture was lost' (226). Anyone reading this might have already decided they have been excluded from Us. As for 'a common culture' no gloss is forthcoming. Kiberd is right to suggest that *Ulysses* belongs to wisdom literature, but his chosen examples – 'how to cope with grief, how to be frank about death in an age of its denial, how women have their own sexual desires which are not always compatible with those of men' (232) – could be more incisive.

Gerardine Meaney's lively essay on Joyce's place in contemporary Irish culture and criticism completes the volume, a volume that begins with a woman and ends with one, the only two. In a central section on 'The Dead' she takes to task largely male critics such as Luke Gibbons, Kevin Whelan, and Joe Cleary (and John Huston in his film of the story) who misread the lines from the song as from 'The Lass of Aughrim'. Meaney returns to the folk song tradition and the various versions that belong to Scotland, England and North America, where it often appears as it does in the Child Ballads under the title 'The Lass of Loch Royal' or, more often, 'Lord Gregory'.[172] In these versions the lines are not about a country with a post-Famine national trauma but remind us of 'a history of the women who hid 'their downfall' in the sea or were

---

170 John Henry Newman, *An Essay in Aid of a Grammar of Assent* (ed. Ian T. Ker) (Oxford: Oxford University Press, 1988).

171 Tony Harrison, *Selected Poems* (London: Penguin, 1987), 122.

172 Frank James Child (ed.), *English and Scottish Popular Ballads* vol 2 (Mineola, NY: Dover, 2003), 213. Ballad number 76.

themselves hidden in mother and baby homes and Magdalene asylums' (293). Her argument may not be entirely convincing but Meaney's provocative comments are telling, and it is appropriate that she has been allowed the final say over this fine volume of essays: 'Joyce's most useful legacy is, after all, a national epic which re-wrote Ireland from the point of view of an ethnic outsider and a ferocious parody of the one-eyed monster of national certainty' (296).

CHAPTER 9

JOYCE AND MODERNISM

MARGOT NORRIS, *JOYCE'S WEB: THE SOCIAL UNRAVELING OF MODERNISM* AUSTIN, TX: UNIVERSITY OF TEXAS PRESS 1992

In Ethel Mannin's little-known novel of the jazz age *Sounding Brass* (1926), Florence Pringle, a Manchester builder's daughter, is determined to change her newly married husband. They had spent their honeymoon abroad watching everybody enjoy themselves: 'Look at the good times they could have if they danced! You were never too old to dance nowadays; in fact *nobody* was old nowadays.' James Rickard, who runs the largest publicity agency in London, is taken aback for he 'had no idea that his wife was capable of such modernism'.[173] The use of the word modernism in this context recalls an original meaning now increasingly forgotten by critics: modernism as a forward attitude, a marker of youthful self-expression, in this case on the dance-floor and so part of popular culture, closer to the *nouveaux riches* of the twenties than to T.S. Eliot's version of modernism.

In this admirable feminist study Margot Norris attempts to distance herself from the ahistoricism of her *Decentered Universe of*

---

173 Ethel Mannin, *Sounding Brass* (London: Jarrolds, 1937), 220.

'Finnegans Wake' (1976) and return modernism and Joyce to history and social practice.[174] As its title suggests, *Joyce's Web* is concerned with raveling and unraveling. Joyce is a modern Penelope unraveling 'the modernistic formalism that consolidates his power as an artist of the dominant culture'; his texts possess 'an ideological self-correction aimed specifically at the socially empowering features of its own aesthetic modernism' (7). Her overall argument is both powerful and clear, but Norris's choice of title and subtitle is slightly puzzling. The title evokes the realism of George Eliot's *Middlemarch* (1871) and the extended imagery of the web with its strong sense of the interdependence of social groups. Unraveling suggests an original raveling, but I couldn't quite resolve its meaning or its effect. The question arises: would the raveling need unraveling if a non-modernist such as Mannin rather than the high modernist Eliot were brought into the frame with Joyce? Equally, the image of a seamless web hovering over the title is also perhaps an unnecessary distraction. Few critics are better at revisiting Joyce's texts than Norris, but I wonder whether her argument could have sheltered under a weaker title.

Norris writes particularly well about the submerged female figures of Joyce's texts such as the 'old maids' in 'Clay', 'The Dead', 'Nausicaa', the washerwomen in 'Anna Livia Plurabelle', the children in 'The Mime of Mick, Nick, and the Maggies'. Norris takes care in the process to distinguish Joyce from Henrik Ibsen, the Norwegian dramatist much admired by the writer as a young man. As a consequence of the 1903 Papal announcement banning women from singing in Church, Julia Morkan is effectively silenced. According to Norris, 'The Dead' is Joyce's *Doll's House,* but what Joyce provides is a critique not so much of social oppression as of art's oppressive practices. In this regard, Norris forcefully defends Julia's singing against its representation in John Huston's film of the short story.

Less convincingly, in some comments on 'Clay', Norris castigates us as readers who create the pressures that necessitate Maria's defensive manoeuvres in inventing her story. As for 'Nausicaa', she reads this as

---

174 Margot Norris, *The Decentered Universe of 'Finnegans Wake': A Structuralist Analysis* (Baltimore, MD: Johns Hopkins, University Press, 1976).

pulp fiction 'tricked out' as a classic, its prose riven by the gulf between its poetic reach and its poetic grasp. 'The Mime of Mick, Nick, and Maggies' in *Finnegans Wake* provides a view of childhood not divorced from culture, as is the case with the myth of the sensitive child in Joyce's earlier prose, but part of it, suffering but no longer subject to martyrdom. Such a brief summarizing does not do justice to Norris's richly persuasive handling of her material.

Running through her thesis is the helpful suggestion that Joyce's later texts rewrite earlier ones, as in the way 'Shem the Penman' desublimates the artist as apotheosised in Stephen Dedalus. Norris also attends to the issue of labour and the right of those who labour to be remembered. The washerwomen in 'Anna Livia Plurabelle' carry within their voices not only the mountain streams but also their social conditions of poverty, isolation and derision. This is a valuable corrective, but it could be argued that missing from her analysis is any reference to William Morris. The Victorian social reformer also understood that News from Nowhere was indeed News from Somewhere, but he made a crucial distinction, missing from Joyce, between useful work and useless toil.

Joyce's Web is an impressive achievement and remains so. Norris's dispute is essentially with Eliot and his characterisation of Joyce's use of Homeric myth in *Ulysses* as 'a step toward making the modern world possible for art'.[175] We might add that a 'poor-joist' (*FW* 113.36) had no difficulty disentangling himself from 'tag for ildiot' (*FW* 37.14), and Norris might have spent time tackling Joyce's utopianism, his 'wastobe land' (*FW* 62.11), his was-to-be-land that is, with its play on Eliot's *The Waste Land* (1922). *Sounding Brass* is more straightforward in this regard and for that reason less interesting, but it does offer a reminder of a different twist to the relation between art and life: 'What chance had beauty in an age obsessed with commercial values?.... If it were true...that when the people forget the poets and the poets forget the people it shall go ill with a nation, then of a verity was the jazz generation doomed.'(315–6)

---

175 T.S.Eliot, '*Ulysses*, Order and Myth' in *Selected Prose of T.S.Eliot* selected by Frank Kermode (London: Faber, 1975), 178.

REVIEW OF *JOHN NASH, JAMES JOYCE AND THE ACT OF RECEPTION: READING, IRELAND, MODERNISM* CAMBRIDGE: CAMBRIDGE UNIVERSITY PRESS, 2006

As editor of *Joyce's Audiences* (2002), John Nash was responsible for one of the liveliest collections of critical essays on Joyce in recent years.[176] Now in his new book, *James Joyce and the Act of Reception*, he has tackled a theme that has become his own, and he does so with considerable success. His thesis is that throughout his career Joyce was not only responding to his audiences but also incorporating those responses into his creative work. This is especially true of early responses to *Ulysses*, as *Finnegans Wake* Notebook VI.B.6 reminds us. That is well-known, but Nash wants to show how Joyce's work rewrites such responses seen now in broader political terms. In this sense his argument with reader-response theory, which as he notes 'remains profoundly troubled by reading as a historical act' (18), and with Derrida, who 'favours the textuality of deconstruction over its historical formulation' (167). Derrida anticipates a possible 'new enlightenment', but, according to Nash, Joyce, ever alert to the importance of 'reception as a political and material activity' (167), is always sceptical toward a future audience.

The thesis is advanced in the various Irish contexts of revivalism, religion and the university question, and the new State that emerged in Ireland in the 1920s. Boredom, surveillance, exhaustion, and hypocrisy — these are the cultural or ethical indices attached to these particular contexts. According to Nash, *Dubliners* is characterised by boredom, Dublin being in Seamus Deane's phrase 'the world capital of boredom' (41). In stories such as 'An Encounter', 'A Painful Case', and 'Eveline' a 'thwarted journey is associated not just with monotony, but with a language of monotony' (31). Gabriel in 'The Dead' is a participant in his own demise, and his anxieties constitute a reflection of Catholic middle-class attitudes to cultural nationalism. In the 'Scylla and Charybdis' episode of *Ulysses*, Edward Dowden is juxtaposed with

---

176 John Nash, *Joyce's Audiences* (Amsterdam: Rodopi, 2002).

Stephen Dedalus, Protestant versus Catholic, Trinity College versus the Royal University, Shakespeare as exponent of an integrated society versus Shakespeare as exponent of fissured society. In a third chapter on exhaustion (as in sales of a book being exhausted), Nash draws attention to the Irish readers of the first edition of *Ulysses*. He also provides some valuable comments on the kinds of readers at the *Wake* and whether or not, for example, it is possible to be a bad reader of Joyce's last book. His fourth chapter, which includes a discussion of the stamps in circulation at the inception of the Irish Free State and Yeats's emblematic status, focuses on the Civil War context of the *Wake*. In an Afterword, Nash discusses his differences with Derrida.

This is a valuable book, but not as valuable as I was hoping it was going to be. I have never been terribly convinced by the argument that *Dubliners* is about paralysis or boredom. Joyce's discourse is invariably polysemic, and what intrigues me perhaps most is that his mind appears to be constantly elsewhere. 'Eveline' is an emigration story with a difference, and I find its poignancy draining and utterly persuasive. The passivity Eveline adopts in the face of her fate is very special, so special that we never hear one of her own sentences or indeed catch a flavour of her spoken voice. Until its closing moments, the plot is nicely balanced and could be resolved either way.

As for the 'thwarted journey' in say 'An Encounter', isn't this what happens in boyhood? As for 'The Dead', I am reminded of Joyce's comment in March 1907 to an Italian audience which is reproduced in the notes to Nash's book: 'The Irish...never fail to show a great reverence for the dead' (179). This is a very different voice to the one we hear in the story he began working on in the ensuing months. The audience is inscribed in the tone of this observation. So to say he is unable to address an audience in *Dubliners* isn't quite true. In his imaginative texts Joyce's mind seems to be elsewhere, and I would have liked more on this sort of cross-over. But these are only quibbles in what remains a fine achievement by a critic steeped in the resistance of Irish history. Derrida worried that 'everything we can say...has already been anticipated'. Nash shows us that it hasn't, and, what's more, he includes such an anxiety in his own recasting of the question of Joyce's reception.

PAUL STASI, *MODERNISM, IMPERIALISM, AND THE HISTORICAL SENSE* CAMBRIDGE/NEW YORK: CAMBRIDGE UNIVERSITY PRESS, 2012

This handsomely produced book follows a conventional format for a modern thesis in the humanities: two theoretical chapters followed by four illustrative chapters in which the theory is operationalised. In terms of length, there are some 140 pages of text followed by over 30 pages of notes and a standard bibliography of over 170 titles. *Modernism, Imperialism, and the Historical Sense* is an ambitious under-taking and its focus is larger than the more traditional thesis, but for all that it manages in the space provided to succeed as a book and a thesis.

If I had briefly to summarise what the book is about I would pose it as a question, one taken from Patrick McGee and cited by Paul Stasi himself: 'How does one formulate a counter-hegemonic vision within the framework of a hegemonic culture?' (89) Or, to give it a sharper edge, modernist writers such as T.S. Eliot, Ezra Pound, James Joyce, and Virginia Woolf not only emerged alongside imperialism, they forged something new from their own grounding in it. We are right to hear in this the famous declaration by Marx about people making history but making it not of their own choosing but in 'present circumstances, given and inherited'. For what Stasi is claiming is something about the centrality of agency to the Marxist tradition: determination yes, but also agency. So the focus here is Marx supplemented by Georg Lukács, not the Lukács who derided modernism as lacking a hierarchy of significance but the Lukács who in *History and Class Consciousness* (1923) emphasised the idea of totality and who distinguished between the empirical and the imputed consciousness of the working class and consequently made the future available even if the deformed present was not.

Stasi, therefore, sees in the high modernists not so much a group of elitists or reactionaries as writers steeped in their time. Pound's fascism is relegated in favour of the poet who in *The Cantos* attempted to produce 'a language adequate to the globalized world in which [he] lived, a language that would both represent and respond to the increased contact across cultures he observed' (80). When imperialism was seeking to homogenise the world and turn things into (consumer) commodities, Pound sought a public poetry and the persistence of values which capitalism imagined it had effectively destroyed.

Stasi is at his best writing on Pound, in part because he is working directly with the poetry. His chapter on Eliot and *The Waste Land* yields fewer insights although the phrase 'Unreal city' triggers a promising line of inquiry into the unreal centre of capitalist modernity. His interest in Woolf is confined to the passage from the voyage out in the 1915 novel of that name to the voyage in where his focus is on Mrs Dalloway and forms of national subjectivity. The canvas here perhaps needs broadening to include her later works such as *Three Guineas* and *Between the Acts*, a novel that Stasi might well have used especially since in the previous chapter he refers to 'Wandering Rocks' as 'entr'acte' (103). And in turn this might have made room for *A Passage to India* (1924), E.M. Forster's 'imperial' novel, which includes a reference to Mrs Moore leaving, 'between the acts', a performance of a play at the Club to see the local mosque. Other opportunities are declined. In focussing on the reified traditions and atavistic primitivism of 'imperial time', Stasi stresses the way the past is repeatedly invoked by Woolf; what he misses is that she was always aware of living on borrowed time, between the acts that is.

The chapter on Joyce's *Ulysses* begins by challenging the view that the nightmare view of history is the whole story. For Stasi, 'the task of the periphery is to locate some form of agency within an omnipresent relationship of dependence' (90). The agency he has in mind is tied in part to Stephen's consciousness, which leads at one point to what many readers will find odd. For Stasi claims that in his critique of Stephen's aesthetic theories Joyce 'demonstrates the path by which Stephen can ultimately become the writer of *Ulysses* itself' (94). Stephen's familiar fate as a colonial subject is well-combed by Stasi but there will be few readers who think the flâneur (as he is described by Stasi) could have written the novel or created the characters of Leopold and Molly Bloom.

Stasi's psychologising tendency is continued into his discussion of 'Eumaeus' and cliché. Thus the opening sentence is read as an oscillation between Stephen and Bloom, how the attribution of need to Bloom is at first a mistake but how we then realise that 'Bloom's need to play the Samaritan is stronger than Stephen's need for his help' (105). What Stasi is looking for is some anchor, some origin, to this kind of sentence. We are back to his overriding theme of determination/agency but here the search lacks sophistication. Indeed, as I suggest in my essay 'Preparatory to Anything Else: The Opening to "Eumaeus"', there's something peculiar about trying to straighten out the grammatical and other errors in this episode, a move which translators have to guard against. For this is an episode which, surprisingly, contains few actual clichés but which includes a host of phrases to caution us or make us laugh. There is nothing orthodox about 'Eumaeus'.

LUKE GIBBONS, *JOYCE'S GHOSTS: IRELAND, MODERNISM, AND MEMORY* CHICAGO AND LONDON: UNIVERSITY OF CHICAGO PRESS, 2015

This is a commendably ambitious study by the influential Irish critic, Luke Gibbons. At its core lies the thesis that Joyce's Irishness is intrinsic to his modernism. In a series of closely-argued and thought-provoking essays, in which he draws on the full panoply of contemporary critical theory, Gibbons shows how Joyce belongs to his country of origins, now defined not as provincial or parochial but as central to the emergence of modernism and to our understanding of modernity. There are few critics able to handle such a range of complex material, or to incorporate so many different voices, and at the same time provide a richly rewarding commentary on his chosen selection of texts.

In an opening section Gibbons reminds us in passing of all the words and concepts we might associate with ghosts including: phantoms, shadows, uncanny, fantastic, apparition, hallucination, traces, vestiges, spectre, hauntings, absence, silences, revenant, and trans-subjective. He dismisses any thought of W.B. Yeats with a single remark in which he contrasts the 'grounded' Joyce with the poet who was 'away with the faeries in the Celtic Twilight' (1). It is a level-headed introduction, made in the interests of not losing his audience, for 'ghosts' conjures up initially not the vocabulary of modern theory but the paranormal and séances and the occult movement that emerged alongside modernism in the period from the 1870s to the 1920s. Of course, linking such a movement with modernism is in part what Gibbons seeks to unravel, but at first he is right to co-opt modern theory to his enterprise. Later in his study, he makes room in an epigraph for the voice of Yeats's English wife, George, who took a leading role in automatic writing sessions with her husband in the years after their marriage in 1917, but who was never away with the fairies: 'All spirits in fact are not, as far as psychic communications are concerned, spirits at all, are only memory' (144). This is used by Gibbons in connection with Mr Duffy in 'A Painful Case' being excluded from life's feast. The full letter, however, written in November 1931, is more nuanced for she was trying to keep spiritual matters separate from psychological explanations.[177]

Stephen Dedalus is asked by his pupils to tell them a 'ghoststory' (*U* 2:50). Joyce himself, on the day of his mother's funeral, attempted with his sister, Margaret, to call up her spirit, and it is recorded that Margaret did indeed have an apparition of her in a brown habit, a scene Joyce perhaps has in mind in the opening episode of *Ulysses*. So, Joyce was no stranger to the world of faeries, and Gibbons might have spent more time on the world to which he was subject. I am thinking here of the occult stories composed by Yeats which Joyce is supposed to have memorised in part, or of his possible contacts with occult circles in Dublin at the turn of the twentieth century, which included George Russell (AE), the practical visionary and editor the *Irish Homestead*. We know he was superstitious and, into adulthood, was afraid of thunder, but perhaps there is more to the 'ghoststory' Joyce did not tell, unless it materialises whole, as Gibbons seemingly would want to claim, in *Ulysses* itself.

There is a natural reluctance to spend too much time on context and background when the focus lies elsewhere or, as Gibbons remarks at one stage, 'pointing to something beyond' (214), but a concern with

---

177 For more on George Yeats and the letter from which this sentence is taken, see my *Yeats's Worlds*, 61. The letter is to Yeats and dated 24 November (1931).

historical particulars is in many ways also at the heart of this study. In some original research into the 'Bible wars' in Dublin, Gibbons shows how the phrase 'U.p: up' (*U* 8:258), which was sent on a postcard to Denis Breen, should be interpreted not so much as innuendo (or underproofed or approaching death or whatever) as the initials of 'United Presbyterian'. This was a Scottish religious faction committed to proselytism in Dublin in the 1880s, who, according to a report written by Michael Cusack in the *Celtic Times* on 18 June 1887, insisted on keeping *up* appearances 'while carrying on…sectarian anti-Irishness under the guise of a picnic in a park'. The implication is that Josie and Denis Breen would have been incensed at being identified with such a group.

Gibbons might be correct that this is the primary reference Joyce had in mind, but it is not clear how this advances his overall argument about ghosts, unless it is that Joyce wants us not to forget the religious tensions which had a long history in nineteenth-century Ireland as a whole. Such tensions surfaced, for example, in Evangelical proselytism in Dublin in the 1820s and 1830s, to which the novelist William Carleton was subjected, or in the fate of 'Soupers' during the Great Famine when the rural poor were enticed to betray their faith for a bowl of soup handed out by Protestant charities, and the sectarianism continued. Indeed, he might well have underscored his point by quoting from comments made by the anti-Catholic polemicist Michael McCarthy in *Irish Land and Liberty* (1911) about the Catholic Irishman having 'little self-reliance', 'inflated self-esteem', 'his nerves sensitive and raw', 'crafty', 'unstable character' (62), but Gibbons employs McCarthy to illustrate (uncritically) a different claim about interiority and Irish culture.[178]

Gibbons is particularly alert to the workings of the police surveillance system and how control over daily life was exercised on the streets and in the pubs of Dublin. He also attends to how that system works in *Ulysses* especially in overheard conversation. In some insightful remarks on the glance between Bloom and Stephen in

---

178 Michael McCarthy in *Irish Land and Liberty: A Study of the New Lords of the Soil* (London: R. Scott, 1911).

'Eumaeus', when Skin-the-Goat is mentioned in the context of the murder of Lord Cavendish in the Phoenix Park in 1882, he reflects on how things could be known and acknowledged but, with informers ever-present, not publicly discussed. Even the unspoken was policed. In characteristic fashion, Gibbons takes his insight to another level: 'It is mainly out of a determination to obstruct the panoptical gaze or its fictional equivalent, the omniscient narrator, that Joyce sought to *implicate* the reader, calling for the kind of active, heterogeneous interpretations that rule out any controlling vision' (47–8). As he trenchantly remarks, in a colonial setting the glance speaks volumes.

A very valuable discussion of Lily and ghosts in 'The Dead' and John Huston's film of the story is to some extent marred by a misinterpretation of the song 'The Lass of Aughrim'.[179] In Francis Child's *The English and Scottish Popular Ballads* (1882–98) there is a ballad called 'Lord Gregory', which is perhaps Scottish in origin or has Scottish links. Hence, presumably, the line 'For he's gone to bonny Scotland to bring home his new queen', a line that suggests the song we have is more a fragment than the finished article. The ballads collected by Child are notoriously difficult to date or pin down, and one suspects that the author of 'Lord Gregory' had never seen the 'dark mutinous Shannon waves' (*D* 223) as they are described by Joyce in his story. In *The Songs of Elizabeth Cronin* (2000), who was among the finest sean-nós or old syle singers of her generation and recorded by Alan Lomax and Peter Kennedy in 1952 for *The Folk Songs of Britain* (1961), the song is given as 'Lord Gregory'.[180] A variant, which was widely available in Ireland but which Child learned from an Irish emigrant to the United States, is entitled 'The Lass of Aughrim'.

Gibbons follows other critics such as Frank Shovlin in *Journey Westward* (2012) in assuming that 'Lord Gregory' is the husband of Lady Gregory. He even assigns him a separate entry in the Index and takes him to task for introducing legislation during the Great Famine to make it harder for the rural poor to receive relief. This last piece of

---

179 See also remarks on Gerardine Meaney in my review of *Voices on Joyce*, above.
180 Dáibhí Ó Cróinín (ed.), *The Songs of Elizabeth Cronin: Irish Traditional Singer* (Dublin: Four Courts Press, 2000), 138–9.

information is accurate but the superior title he acquired is not. Sir William Gregory (1816–92), a Liberal MP at Westminster, has, almost certainly, no connection with the song called 'Lord Gregory'. In a note written in 1822, two decades before the Great Famine, the wife of Richard Trench, who was a family relative of the model for Haines in *Ulysses*, speculated that the song was 'the recasting of a ballad in the Irish language', adding that there are 'several Scotch variations of the same'. [181] A longer version of the ballad, reproduced following the note, includes reference to the night being 'far too murky', which sounds too literary for the folksong tradition, and a question: 'who will shoe my little foot?', which sounds like a line from a different song.[182] In addition we learn of 'Lord Gregory's castle gate' and his 'cruel eyes'. Some lines, such as the beautiful one about 'My babe lies cold within my arms; Lord Gregory let me in', surface intact through different versions, which in turn serves to remind us of how memory works among singers in the oral tradition. Instead of pursuing the historical figure behind 'Lord Gregory', therefore, Gibbons might have been better advised to explore the ghosts inside the ballad itself. Nothing in his life suggests William Gregory was a Lord. When the Right Hon. Sir William married Augusta, youngest daughter of the late Dudley Persse, Esq., D.L. of Roxborough, County Galway in 1880, she acquired the title 'Lady'. [183] His estate at Coole in County Galway was a park or in his own words a 'demesne' but not a castle. As a footnote, after William Gregory died, his young wife, born in 1852, dedicated herself

---

181 Richard Chevenix Trench, *The Remains of the Late Mrs Richard Trench* (London: Parker, Son and Bourn, 1862), 481. Haines, we might recall, is also interested in Irish 'remains', in cultural sayings and *ghostly* remains that is. Although he is cast as an Englishman in the opening episode of 'Telemachus', Joyce knew all about the antiquarian interests of his model's Irish ancestors, one of whom, his grandfather, was a philologist and the Archbishop of Dublin.
182 The adjective 'murky' in fact sounds as if it is indebted to Robert Burns and the Scottish folksong tradition. One of the songs about Lord Gregory, sung by Karine Polwart on her album 'Floo'ers of the Forest', is entitled 'Mirk Mirk Is This Midnight Hour'.
183 For more information, see Lady Gregory (ed.), *Sir William Gregory: An Autobiography* (London: John Murray, 1894), 368 fn.

to her tenants and to the Literary Revival, and the house at Coole was damaged but survived largely intact during the Irish Civil War in 1922–23. This was not the case at Moore Hall, the ancestral home of George Moore in the neighbouring county of Mayo.

Unless it reflects his suppressed lyricism, why Joyce omits lines from 'The Lass of Aughrim' seems less clear-cut, as I suggest in my review of Shovlin. Perhaps it belongs to what Derek Attridge elsewhere has observed about extratextual factual details and how Joyce's texts '*allow* meaning to arise…by the operation of chance' rather than to stabilize meaning (198). In this way we might then discern the relevance of the variant to the story. If he had wanted to include Gregory in the story Joyce would presumably have done so by continuing the extract into the following line 'Lord Gregory, let me in', but one suspects he knew the song as simply 'The Lass of Aughrim' from hearing it sung by Nora's mother in the Barnacle kitchen in Galway. Whatever the case, the ballad resonates for Gretta Conroy not for its evocation of a bad landlord but because it draws into it a memory of a former lover. When he made his film, John Huston, as if he sought some kind of ownership over the story, was in no doubt about the power of the song, which needed to be rendered in full, even if it is different from the melody we hear in Cronin and the one perhaps Joyce heard in Galway.

The strongest cluster of ideas that appears in *Joyce's Ghosts*, and the one that commands our attention, belongs to vernacular idiom and free indirect discourse, inner speech, and the associated theme of interiority. With regard to the first, Gibbons provides a useful sketch of the evolution of nineteenth-century fiction from Maria Edgeworth's *Castle Rackrent* (1800) through Emily Lawless's *Grania* (1886) to *The Untilled Field* (1902) of George Moore. Joyce is then situated in a line that is inherently Irish, out of whose form he emerges and develops. Unlike his predecessors, however, Joyce breaks free entirely from the reader over his shoulder or the gaze of the outsider, whether that is interpreted in the guise of a metropolitan audience or the presence of the coloniser. Now, the Irish novelist could turn the tables, and, in Joyce's case with 'Ithaca' in mind, persuade us that 'it is Standard English itself that is regional and idiosyncratic' (100). Free indirect discourse has a long history dating back to Geoffrey Chaucer, and it can be analysed from several different directions including the psychology of character, narrative technique, the use of irony, or, as Ann Banfield suggests in *Unspeakable Sentences* (1982), language in need of a theory, but, reading Gibbons, we can begin to recognise that it has a special place in the struggles of a colonial country to find expression.[184]

With the help of the art installation *For Dublin* (1997), in which Frances Hegarty and Andrew Stones projected onto buildings and quaysides illuminated phrases from Molly Bloom's soliloquy, Gibbons argues that on display was exemplified what Lev Vygotsky might call 'the inner speech' of the city. (55) As they encountered the various installations, Dubliners had the possibility of discovering new meanings from the disconnectedness of Molly's speech. In line with others, Gibbons emphasises that Molly's soliloquy is not so much private speech or univocal as a dialogic discourse. More broadly, as Terence Killeen suggests elsewhere in *Joyce's Ghosts*, *Ulysses* might be best understood as 'the collective voice of Dublin' (41). Words in Joyce are at the service of others, but, if we needed a proviso, they do not always float free of their base.

In another development, Gibbons seeks to extend his argument with the claim that Joyce is involved in questioning interiority, but this is perhaps more opaque. To take a different example from the beginning of *A Portrait*, Gibbons assumes that politics frames 'the child's emerging conscious life' (107), but a more sceptical reading might propose that a known history never supplants the story Joyce is telling, and, moreover, that Joyce's primary concern is with an interior consciousness *before* history intervenes. This is something Gibbons might have explored in the light of his overall theme regarding ghosts. The problem with consciousness and with interiority, therefore, is that we are not sure what we are handling. Consciousness (and unconsciousness) is normally followed by 'of' but interiority arguably takes us back to the region of the soul. Equally, the consciousness of some people does not merit projection, only explanation. Thus Mr Duffy, according to

---

184 Ann Banfield, *Unspeakble Sentences: Narration and Representation in the Language of Fiction* (Boston: Routledge and Kegan Paul, 1982).

Gibbons, belongs to 'a dislocated post-Famine culture in which the individual has no recourse to a permeable inner life' and 'has only his conscience to chew on' (149).

For the epigraph to 'Pale Phantoms of Desire' Gibbons quotes a line from Joyce's essay 'Ireland, Island of Saints and Sages': 'The economic and intellectual condition of his homeland do not permit the individual to develop'. This is followed by Gibbons contending that the absence of individualism constitutes 'a driving force in the Cultural Revival' (138). Joyce seems to be offering a general observation; Gibbons turns this into a comment on literature and culture. The slippage is noticeable, but missing from *Joyce's Ghosts* is any reference to J.M. Synge, whose hero in *The Playboy of the Western World* is strikingly individual and who arguably belongs in the front rank of Gibbons's 'vernacular modernism'. This is a way of saying that *Joyce's Ghosts*, already a considerable achievement, could be expanded to include other Irish writers.

CHAPTER 10

ULYSSES IN PERSPECTIVE

REVIEW OF TERENCE KILLEEN, *ULYSSES UNBOUND: A READER'S COMPANION TO JAMES JOYCE'S 'ULYSSES'* BRAY, CO. WICKLOW: WORDWELL, 2004

Bound, unbound, disbound, rebound − every book title sets its own expectations and its own boundaries, and this book is no different. Bound to the mast, Odysseus listened to the Sirens while his men stopped up their ears. In Terence Killeen's companion, 'Sirens' too, in conjunction with 'Wandering Rocks', assumes significance as the episode in which *Ulysses* changes direction. While the earlier episodes embody Michael Groden's 'initial style', thereafter the novel becomes increasingly detached from its moorings, and the question Killeeen eventually asks is also a mast one but now given a (misplaced) Yeatsian inflection 'Can the centre hold?' Or in Killeen's own words: 'What makes this book hang together?' (252)

   With the student in mind, Killeen tackles each episode in turn, gathering his material under various headings: plot summary, Homeric correspondences, style, commentary, biographical / historical information and glossary. What Joyce, through long years of writing and revising, had bound together the commentator unbinds, but in this case with a lightness of touch frequently missing from other student guides. Summarising the plot of *Ulysses* is no mean achievement and Killeen handles this with confidence. The Homeric correspondences are also foregrounded in a way that is enabling for students, who will see what Joyce at each point is doing with his great teacher. The various bits of information about the characters and events of *Ulysses*, even if they are occasionally repeated, are provided with an insider's view of his subject. The entries he is forced to notice in the glossary remind us that *Ulysses* never stops resembling a book of foreign phrases for use in the classroom.

The section on style, however, is the least satisfactory as if the author was unsure of his ground. At times Killeen treats style as what Joyce in the 1921 Schema calls 'technic'. With 'Nausicaa' this works, with Killeen, at his most literal, enjoying the tumescence, detumescence idea. Elsewhere, as in 'Lotus-Eaters', Killeen notices how the technic of narcissism belongs more to the tone rather than to the style of an episode. *Le style, c'est l'homme*, but style we are quite certain — at least in one sense — is not the man in *Ulysses*, the man that is who in T.S. Eliot's words 'showed up the futility of all the English styles'. However, there is still considerable merit in describing changes in the style of each episode, and here, I believe, we have something different from Hugh Kenner's 'Uncle Charles Principle', or Karen Lawrence's odyssey of style, or the movement away from the 'initial style'.[185] We are informed, for example, that the opening sentence of *Ulysses*, with its 'carefully chosen adjectives', 'leaves nothing in shade or unclear' (18). But Johnson's *Dictionary* (1755) lists 'stately' as both an adjective and an adverb, and there is no room for 'statelily', that clumsy word which

---

185 'The Uncle Charles Principle' Kenner defined thus: 'the narrative idiom need not be the narrator's.' See Hugh Kenner, *Joyce's Voices* (Berkeley, CA and London: University of California Press, 1978), 18.   For the 'initial style', see, in particular, Michael Groden, *Ulysses in Progress* (1977; Princeton, NJ: Princeton University Press, 2014), and Karen Lawrence, *The Odyssey of Style in Ulysses* (1981; Princeton, NJ: Princeton University Press, 2014). Killeen acknowledges his debt to this discussion of the initial style.

later appears in *Ulysses* as if to confirm the dual status of 'stately'. With the presence of more than 82 adverbs ending in -ly, 'Telemachus' is an overwhelmingly adverbial episode, closer therefore to manner as to quality, and as much about *how* as *is*, about attitudes towards the world as about the world itself. In this respect, it is an episode that is at once bright and dark, bathed in clear Mediterranean blue but restrained by a mother's brown graveclothes.

Little disagreements can be quickly identified and glossed over. Bloom uses one of Beaufoy's stories as toilet paper but we would be wrong to imagine, as Killeen implies, that such action represents Joyce's opinion of the *Tit-Bits*' litterateur. The claim that there is 'no precise source text' (151) for 'Nausicaa' needs at least to discuss, if only to discount, Maria Cummins' novel *The Lamplighter* (1854).[186] 'As you are now so once were we' in 'Hades' is not so much spoken by the dead themselves – 'obviously' (62) is how Killeen puts it – as a conventional phrase on tombstones which is filtered through Bloom's consciousness. John Eglinton is rightly glossed in the 'Scylla and Charybdis' episode, Killeen observing that he was 'the prototype of revisionist intellectuals such as F.S.L. Lyons and Conor Cruise O'Brien' (97). This is not an uninteresting point but it would have been more relevant to mention Eglinton's 1932 essay 'The Beginnings of Joyce', where Eglinton recalls Joyce's determination to succeed at a time when 'no one took him at his own valuation'.[187] In the Conclusion there are some tendentious remarks about literary Modernism where Killeen sets Joyce apart from those who believed in hierarchy and order, in the will to power, or in 'a return to mythical roots for a renewal of a degenerate society' (25). I also think the figure of the Arranger, the presiding spirit of this book too, could have been introduced at the beginning instead of delaying until 'Oxen of the Sun'.[188] The period postcards that launch each chapter add a nice touch to this very enjoyable companion.

---

186 Maria Cummins, *The Lamplighter* (London: G. Routledge, 1854).

187 John Eglinton, 'The Beginnings of Joyce' in *Life and Letters* 8:47 December 1932, 404.

188 For more on The Arranger, see footnote in my essay above on 'Eumaeus'.

PATRICK MCGEE, *PAPERSPACE: STYLE AS IDEOLOGY IN JOYCE'S ULYSSES* LINCOLN AND LONDON: UNIVERSITY OF NEBRASKA PRESS, 1988.

This book, with its engaging and enigmatic title, 'conducts a dialogue with the positions of Lacanian psychoanalysis, deconstruction, feminism, and contemporary Marxism' (1). Its five central chapters are framed by an introduction and an epilogue. In the introduction, Patrick McGee outlines his intention and seeks to place his work in the context of complementary and competing contemporary theories. A deconstructive critic, the author is keen also to assert a political dimension to his account, and thus distances himself – though less than his study in fact warrants – from, among others, the editors of *Post-structuralist Joyce* (1984), whom he accuses of a fetishism of the text; from Wolfgang Iser, who stresses the gaps in reading but not in the reader; and from Colin MacCabe, whom he links with a contemporary critical bias against interpretation.[189] For McGee, 'interpreting Joyce is not *politically* negligible' (8).

The author aligns himself, firstly, with Jacques Lacan, especially in view of the latter's treatment of the relation between the reading subject and the text and of seeing Joyce as 'symptom'; secondly, with Jacques Derrida and the need for the critic's own position to be deconstructed; and, thirdly, with Fredric Jameson and the Marxist obligation to bridge psychoanalysis and history.[190] He might have added Julia Kristeva to this list, because she is in many ways the

---

189 Derek Attridge and Daniel Ferrer (eds), *Post-structuralist Joyce* (Cambridge: Cambridge University Press, 1984). Wolfgang Iser, *The Implied Reader: Patterns of Communication in Prose Fiction from Bunyan to Beckett* (Baltimore: Johns Hopkins University Press, 1974). Colin MacCabe, *James Joyce and the Revolution of the Word (London: Macmillan, 1978)*.

190 Jacques Lacan, 'Joyce le Symptóme' in *Joyce & Paris 1902–1920 – 1940–1975*, 2 vols. (eds Jacques Aubert and Maria Jolas) (Paris: Editions du C.N.R.S., 1979. Jacques Derrida, 'Two Words for Joyce' in *Post-structuralist Joyce*. Fredric Jameson, 'Ulysses in History' in W.J. McCormack and Alistair Stead (eds), *James Joyce and Modern Literature* (London: Routledge and Kegan Paul, 1982.

presiding presence here. [191] McGee has written a properly ambitious book, which attempts to pull together under a single umbrella a range of positions within modern critical theory. Illustrating how Joyce's *Ulysses* can be glossed or given a makeover using one particular theory is ambitious enough, but McGee has drafted in almost a full complement of the most advanced contemporary European thinkers, and he has done so with some panache and not a little success. Throughout the book there are special insights which come precisely from his reading outside of Joyce.

The first chapter on 'Gesture: The Letter of the Word' stresses the gnomic, gestural, resistant qualities that run through the opening eight episodes of *Ulysses*. In 'Telemachus', McGee concentrates on Mulligan's parodic gestures, on the image of the cracked mirror and on the wider issue of power evident in Stephen's relation with Mulligan and Haines, and on 'that word known to all men' *(U* 3:435). He insightfully interprets the nature of Stephen's double bind in relation to his mother thus: if he had obeyed his mother's dying wish 'he would have betrayed her, though in not obeying her he still betrays her by depriving her life of its meaning and its justification' (15). With the Poor Old Woman and his mother still in his mind, Stephen in 'Nestor' taxes his pupils (and the reader) with a riddle about the fox burying his grandmother under a hollybush. This is followed in 'Proteus' with Stephen's meditation on Eve, the first woman with no navel, on her being 'whiteheaped corn' (*U* 3:43), an image lifted from *Song of Solomon*. McGee discerns in this image the phallic mother, and he continues with reflections on motherhood and patriarchy and how meaning and reality are forever sundered, and how meaning therefore is always other. Such an 'excentric' feminine reading is traced through to the Parable of the Plums, to the story of two middle-aged women spitting out the plumstones from the top of the 'cultural erection' (24) of Nelson's pillar. Their refusal to act as mirrors and instead to face

---

191 Julia Kristeva, *Revolution in Poetic Language* (trans Margaret Waller) (New York: Colombia University Press, 1984). On her concept of the abject, see *Powers of Horror: An Essay on Abjection* (trans Leon S.Roudiez) (New York: Columbia University Press, 1982).

down as it were the phallic monument is, perhaps over-optimistically, interpreted by McGee as an example of the subversion of patriarchy by pleasure, by *jouissance* to invoke Kristeva.

Juxtaposed with the female line McGee discusses Bloom's path, and here the author concentrates on letters (both as correspondence and as words) and on their significance. With Derrida's *La Carte postale* (1980) in mind, he suggestively refers to Bloom as 'the Ulysses of the postal era' (25).[192] Martha's letter, paradigmatic of *Ulysses* as a whole, shows how every style 'betokens a relation of value determined by the relations of power that frame it' (28). According to McGee, her desire is for 'a world of finalized meanings in which the secrets of desire in words are revealed' (28). Bloom is Henry Flower and aware therefore of the conscious limits of names; what he desires is 'somewhere between "will" and "would not"' (36). In another insightful move (the debt to Freud and Kristeva needs little insisting on) McGee picks up the significance of the transitions from one episode to the next, how in this particular case Bloom's 'floating flower' and his 'limp father of thousands' (*U* 5:571–2), which he observes in the bath, point the way to 'Hades' and death. He does the same with the transition from 'Hades' to 'Aeolus', bringing out how the old rusty pumps of one episode reappear at the very beginning of the next in the HEART of the Hibernian metropolis. McGee might have made more of this outrageous moment, for it stands out for the reader even as its outrageousness is suppressed by the text. Bloom listens to what he imagines is the language of the printing presses – 'Sllt' (*U* 7:174). The environment is noisy but Bloom is not overwhelmed by the mechanical and material forces at work in modern mass culture. He would certainly not have agreed with Filippo Thommaso Marinetti's hymn to machines and progress – even though 'Sllt' might have echoes of the Futurists Joyce encountered in Trieste in the years when *Ulysses* was gestating.[193] When made to feel an outsider, he

---

192 Jacques Derrida, *La Carte postale: De Socrate á Freud et au-delá* (Paris: Flammarion, 1980).

193 For more on Futurism see the comments by John McCourt in *The Years of Bloom: James Joyce in Trieste 1904–1920* (Dublin: Lilliput, 2000), 159–167.

retreats into the self. McGee goes further and at one point, though this is perhaps too blunt a formulation with its echoes of Karl Marx on history, he claims that Bloom 'takes life as a sort of farce' (32). In such ways – and in this, he is both similar to and different from Stephen – Bloom reveals a strategy of resisting power and finds a use therefore for '[u]seless words' (*U* 8:477).

'Between: A Name of the Mother', the second chapter, focuses on 'Scylla and Charybdis' and on the relationship between Stephen Dedalus, Stephen Daedalus, and James Joyce. Taking care not to identify Stephen Dedalus with Joyce, McGee underlines the need for seeing a dialectical play between the two, how in fact, to cite Mulligan's earlier quotation from Hamlet, 'the play's the thing' (*U* 9:876–7). He begins with Shakespeare, whose presence or otherwise in his plays provokes a similar question that can be asked about Joyce. It is a topic that is particularly germane to a study that centers on *deconstruction*, absence, gaps, notes, and the 'between.' Tellingly, McGee contrasts Literature as an institution with literature as writing. Ann Hathaway has no place in the former but John Eglinton's claim that 'she died, for literature at least, before she was born' (*U* 9:216) points to a more complex set of relationships between author, the writing subject, and writing, one that anticipates therefore an important strand in contemporary critical theory. In dwelling on the space between Shakespeare and Hamlet, between Hamlet's ghost and Hamlet, between Shakespeare and Ann Hathaway, between Stephen and Joyce, between Joyce and his mother, between Joyce and his father, between speech and act, between reason and madness, between *The Egoist*, the London little magazine which serialized episodes from *Ulysses*, and 'Egomen', the Greek word meaning 'I on the one hand' where there is nothing on the other hand, between 1904 and the year of the episode's composition – in all these examples of 'between' McGee convincingly underlines how Stephen confronts the Scylla and Charybdis of Western discourse, namely the violent opposition between subject and object.

In Chapter 3, 'Arch: The Genealogy of Styles', which examines the five episodes from 'Wandering Rocks' to 'Oxen of the Sun', McGee traces how style subverts narrative consistency and liberates the word from meaning. To David Hayman's concept of the Arranger, a figure who is neither a straightforward third-person narrator nor Joyce himself, he adds the figure of the Deranger, 'the always imminent possibility of disorder in the order of signifiers' (74). [194] He considers the break-up of what he terms the 'classical narrator' and how from this point on the author is 'disseminated' in the text. Bloom's various strategies for dealing with power come into play at this juncture – the power of song and the female body in 'Sirens', and the will to power in 'Cyclops.' In 'Nausicaa' he traces how sexual difference is explored through style and how in this episode there is reproduced not so much a young woman's consciousness as the literary man's nausea. In 'Oxen of the Sun' he offers a suggestive comparison between medicine and art, how both are founded on patriarchal theology. Thus, while Mina Purefoy 'labours' off-stage, the medical and literary men are center-stage aggressively gossiping about the women who 'labour.' In this way the episode articulates 'what literature historically has always excluded from itself: the violent ground of its production in the maternal / material space of symbolic representation and process.'

Chapter 4, 'Circe Weaves: The Unconscious Text', examines 'Circe' as *Ulysses*'s unconscious or the representation of the Other. The narrative context is now wholly uncertain and writing takes the form of hallucination (which he identifies with Kristeva's 'Semiotic'). This is a particularly dense chapter on McGee's part, but worth the struggle. It circles around a number of themes, some which are new, others of which we have met before: Bloom's ambivalence and how this is articulated through feminine figures, the position of the reader reading this reading-play, the shifting nature of sexual identity, the mastery and inhibition of desire, the gaze, the dance of death, the meaning of *'Nothung'* (*U* 15:4242) (a gesture 'not of power but of futility'), the writer and the state, economic and sexual domination, and the significance of the panther. Chapter 5, 'A Curtain Falls: The Unnamable', stresses how the *Nostos*, the last three episodes of *Ulysses*, is not so much a return as an anticlimax and how 'Penelope' is neither a

---

194 David Hayman, *'Ulysses': The Mechanics of Meaning*, revised edition (Madison, WI: University of Wisconsin Press, 1982).

conclusion nor a completion, but an opening. In a complex argument, deploying Kristeva's concept of the 'abject', the author suggests that Molly's soliloquy is not Joyce writing the feminine, but his symbolic loss of innocence. Behind her mask stands not masculine desire or feminine style but 'the place where the truth lies', the symbolic, behind which there is the unnamable (an allusion, presumably, to Beckett).

The epilogue provides a recapitulation of the argument of each of the chapters. Here the author ranges more widely over the historical and political contexts for an interpretation of *Ulysses*. He suggests, for example, that 'no single social fact fully accounts for the eccentricity of Joyce's vision' (190); that Joyce's work is not reducible to Joyce the subject; that Jameson's categories of a political, social, and historical horizon to a writer's work can be usefully applied to *Ulysses*; that *Ulysses* contains a Utopia of desire which finds its hopes for a feminist future displayed also in *Finnegans Wake;* that Joyce is a Luddite deconstructing the Symbolic Order and revealing the space for the collective subject; and − returning to Kristeva − that his writing exposes the historical 'abject' underlying the illusions of style.

Clearly, *Paperspace* is a challenging book, one which invites a considered response and one whose effect tends to accumulate with each re-reading. In the remaining space let me register, though, one or two misgivings I have about it. The organisation of the material into a narrative sequence where each episode is traced in turn is not perhaps the best for conveying a deconstructive reading of *Ulysses.* Certain themes recur and could be better handled together. The Index for example, which includes no heading for 'Paperspace' and a limited set of subheadings under 'style', could be fuller. In my own notes I listed under 'Paperspace' (including other references to space): neither author nor text (3); political and social space (6); 'paperspace' in *Finnegans Wake* (12); Joyce's play in paperspace (39); middle space between reason and madness (59); truth lies in middle space (64); space of a genealogy of styles (70); paperspace and the female body (77–8); Joyce in the space between styles (85); space and suspended desire (93); and so on.

As for the 'feminine figures', I think this should read 'female figures', the biological as opposed to the positional. He is right to notice how figures such as Stephen's mother, the Poor Old Woman, Martha, Milly, Molly as Calypso, Gerty, Bella Cohen, Molly as Penelope, or the place of desire or the occurrence of *jouissance* constantly puncture the surface of *Ulysses*. Yet it is not altogether clear what is to be gained by confining a discussion to the framework of separate episodes, for what he unwittingly implies, which I don't think he would want to argue, is that, in a deconstructive reading of *Ulysses,* story should be foregrounded at the expense of discourse. If his thesis had been the crisis of narrativity and how this manifests itself in *Ulysses,* then I could understand the attention to linear sequence. That *Ulysses* 'deconstructs' the autonomous subject, or that its style subverts narrative consistency are cognate issues, but a more far-reaching deconstructive account would argue that the former issue is to be located not in the middle part or second half of the novel, but is there from the start. Joyce's refusal of a psychoanalysis, as Lacan puts it, or the fact that he is a 'symptom' (the articulation of a contradiction between the constitutive subject and the subject-in-process), or the way he illustrates Kristeva's 'semiotic' or 'desire' or 'the abject', or his use of Derrida's 'dissemination', are questions that apply to the text as a (w)hole (and in part perhaps to every text).

Conversely − and here perhaps I am backtracking by invoking a need to distinguish philosophy from criticism − the status assigned to the philosophical discourse in 'Scylla and Charybdis' is perhaps forever trapped in the realm of necessity, precisely because of the narrative frame that surrounds it. Stephen's thoughts on Eve and her body without a navel 'standing from everlasting to everlasting' (*U* 3:43–4) are particularly appropriate in an episode about change and permanence, but they remain part of an unfolding drama and perhaps can be wrested and appropriated only by force. McGee refers at one point to Bloom's 'complicated social mask as an Irish Jew, a womanly man, and a cuckolded Ulysses' (165), but no one in *Ulysses* knows that Bloom is Ulysses.

Related to this is another area of contention. McGee refers to 'the classical narrator of the first half of *Ulysses*' (74) and how this figure is subverted in the middle sections onwards. There seems to be some confusion here, and by 'classical' I think McGee means 'classic realist'. According to S.L Goldberg in his 1961 book on *Ulysses*, a book cited by

McGee in his bibliography, Joyce has a 'classical temper', but Goldberg is not primarily concerned with how Joyce constructs his narrative.[195] In 1978, Colin MacCabe proposed a 'classic realist text', a text which 'functions simply as a window on reality'.[196] As for 'retrospective arrangement' (*U* 10:783), a phrase McGee is fond of quoting, I doubt whether anyone reading this review would detect a so-called classical narrator at work in *Ulysses,* and after reading the various 'styles' of *Ulysses* I doubt whether the term can be used retrospectively at all. It is convenient to have foils like George Eliot (and McGee's debt to MacCabe is acknowledged), or Flaubert, or 'the first half of the novel', but it can be misleading: the case gets overstated, the foil slips and becomes something else, and in the process insufficient attention is paid to seeing how one's subject rewrites, rearranges the past to include the foil – even if ironically.

His remarks on Flaubert have an uneven quality. On the one hand he claims that 'most of the critical discussion of *Madame Bovary* focuses on the truth of Flaubert's representation' (88), a generalization that must be left to stand as it is, for Flaubert has prompted a whole line of criticism and discussion, some of which has issued in the appeal to deconstruction, which McGee espouses. A page later, however, he quite brilliantly shows how in 'Nausicaa' Joyce 'discloses literature as ideology by forcing into it…the genre it excludes, and he disrupts the ideological naïveté of sentimental romance by reinvesting it with uncoded desire' (89). Interestingly, the parallels between Molly Bloom and Madame Bovary, their initials most obviously, for example, or the clever use of the white hand in 'Wandering Rocks' to remind us of the *fiacre* scene, or the conscious debt of 'Ithaca' to *Bouvard and Pécuchet,* should have been the cue for a wider discussion of the texts of the two writers in terms of their *intertextuality,* Kristeva's concept, which is at one level missing from this study.

195 S.L. Goldberg, *The Classical Temper: A Study of James Joyce's 'Ulysses'* (New York: Barnes and Noble, 1961). For more on Joyce's classical temper, see my essay above on *A Portrait.* The phrase appears in *Stephen Hero.*
196 Colin MacCabe, *James Joyce and the Revolution of the Word* (London: Macmillan, 1979), 178.

To return to the opening passage of 'Telemachus', we might agree that this is not the work of a traditional narrator, for no such narrator would open a novel with the word 'Stately' or with a first sentence that seems to scan as two hexameters. Note, Joyce seems to be saying, the contrasts and comparisons between a Greek epic and a modern novel written in English. Here is Joyce announcing the political theme of his opening episode – the (British) state and the English language – and he forces us to be suspicious even in the very structure and rhythm of the opening awkward sentence. He also reminds us in the opening passage of how one discourse speaks to another. McGee insists on the parodic nature of Mulligan's gestures, but he might have drawn even more attention to the (self-)conscious *intratextual* qualities of *Ulysses* (the obtruding signifiers as opposed to the latent themes).

Ulysses emerges out of the years Joyce spent teaching English as a foreign language in Trieste. Complete with substitution exercises and illustrations, the novel is not unlike a manual of English syntax, grammar, and, especially evident in this context, adverbs of place. 'Patience and Perseverance are the parents of success' was one of the inane proverbs students at a Berlitz School were asked to follow, as was 'Rome was not built in a day'.[197] *Ulysses*, too, was not built in a day, and, moreover, it delights in dwelling both in the world of a modern city and in the world of the ancient Greeks, both here and there. But it is not stationary, for its characteristic quality is a never-ending movement between two worlds, defined by such terms as physical and metaphorical, language and reality, art and life, modern and classical, Bloom and Ulysses. However, these opposing terms are not mutually exclusive; rather, they co-exist in the in-between world that constitutes *Ulysses*. McGee is wrong therefore to claim that the novel 'depicts a world without essence' (114), for even the idea of 'between' also has an ontological status, an example in its own way of the 'paperspace' at the heart of this book. That the novel is set on one day in June 1904, whose date is casually referred to half way through *Ulysses* by a secretary in an office typing it, serves to remind us that conventions are there to

---

197 *Berlitz Idioms and Grammar* (London: Berlitz Holdings, 1939), 5.

be subverted. Indeed, from the very beginning the text is not unlike a machine that, started up, works and does things, sometimes twice, sometimes with two in mind. Mulligan's parodic gesture of the Mass is already enclosed in the first sentence within a parody of Mulligan's own gesture, so that he who is 'plump' yet tries to walk 'stately', and he who berates Stephen for living in the past yet seeks to hellenise Ireland. The 'double writing' begins 'in the beginning' (wherever that is). In *Finnegans Wake* the play on the name Dublin never stops.

The author could perhaps have explored even more this intratextual aspect of 'between' in *Ulysses*, for when Bloom hears the 'Sllt' of the printing press and notices how 'everything speaks in its own way' (*U* 7:177), the reader also hears Stephen's solipsistic musings in 'Proteus' on the nature of reality. Stephen's answer to the epistemological doubt, arrived at only after mental struggle, is that the visible affords him '[s] ignatures of all things I am here to read' (*U* 3:2). Thankfully, there is something invitingly down-to-earth about 'Ulysses of the postal era', but beyond a certain point we find ourselves in a world of signs where language, metaphor and interpretation therefore, are brought into play. Indeed, what such intratextual correspondences and parallels bring out is *Ulysses*'s textuality, how the Arranger is at work throughout *Ulysses,* deconstructing representation even in the act of 'presenting' it.

Both in the introduction and in the epilogue, the author claims that his study engages with Marxism and history, citing Jameson's work, especially *The Political Unconscious* (1981).[198] His remarks on deconstruction, feminism, and psychoanalysis are frequently insightful and suggestive, but the same cannot be said for his remarks on history. To my mind one phrase in *The Political Unconscious* (1981) resonates above all others, and that is the opening one: 'Always historicise!' Yet on turning to McGee's study I find the historical context to *Ulysses* either missing, or unexamined, or unremarkable. It is as if the deconstructive critic pulls back from full engagement with a discourse that might prove threatening or, indeed, overwhelming. According to McGee, Joyce forms a bridge between the modern and the postmodern, which

---

198 Fredric Jameson, *The Political Unconscious: Narrative as a Socially Symbolic Act* (Ithaca, NY: Cornell University Press, 1981).

is an unexceptional observation. Elsewhere, he writes that Joyce's work 'responds to the failure of his father, the early death of his mother, and the general breakdown of the Irish family; to his ambivalent passion for the language and literature of his conqueror and his hatred of English imperialism in general' (189). Such a comment, it could well be argued, is not very different from an account informed by nineteenth-century positivism, from Hippolyte Taine's theory, for example, of 'race, milieu, and moment'.[199] Let me conclude, however, by highlighting something of the weakness of the author's grasp of *Irish* history.

His remarks on Joyce just cited could apply equally to Yeats, but Joyce isn't Yeats. Elsewhere in the study he refers to Mulligan as a member of the Anglo-Irish elite, when in fact Gogarty's family was Catholic middle-class. He confuses George Russell with Mr. Deasy in asserting that the former symbolizes Northern Ireland (he presumably means the North of Ireland), England, the English language. Stephen and Joyce's creditors, such as W.K. Magee (aka John Eglinton), Fred Ryan, or Russell himself, were Irish freethinkers, socialists, journalists, editors, organizers, or mystics, and all were involved in anti-imperialist propaganda, not for Northern Ireland or England but for (a non-Catholic) Ireland. He assumes that the fall of Parnell was equivalent to the break-up of the Irish nationalist movement, which not even Joyce, whose work was produced under Parnell's star, would support. After all, *Ulysses* in more senses than one tracks by a 'retrospective arrangement' the history of the emergence of the Irish State from the ideas of Arthur Griffith and the formation of Sinn Fein in 1904–05 through to the establishment of the new state on the eve of *Ulysses*'s publication in 1922. As for 'the Irish vision in English literature…that periodically drives the writers of that tradition to the brink of madness and death' (14), the heritage that is from Swift to Wilde, this may resonate with some readers, but for others it is a reminder of the studied clear-sightedness that comes from political dispossession. To my mind, in what remains a brilliant study which throughout stresses gaps, breaks, (w)holes, the other,

---

199 See Hippolyte Taine, *History of English Literature* (trans H. van Laun) (New York: Worthington, 1873).

such a reading also needs deconstructing, for if Joyce is credited with rewriting the way we read texts, then we should perhaps ask if he is not also involved in rewriting the way we read history.

ANDRAS UNGAR, *JOYCE'S 'ULYSSES' AS NATIONAL EPIC: EPIC MIMESIS AND THE POLITICAL HISTORY OF THE NATION STATE* MIAMI, FL: UNIVERSITY PRESS OF FLORIDA, 2002.

This is one of those rare books which is easier to read backward than forward. But, given that its focus is 1904 through the lens of 1922, such a comment is not as perverse as it sounds. The subject is intriguing: how to connect the date on which the Irish epic *Ulysses* is set with the year when the Irish Free State came into existence. Part of Andras Ungar's argument is that *Ulysses* 'locates the fortunes of Irish national renewal in the conjunction of its characterization of Stephen Dedalus and its incorporation of the historical argument...of Arthur Griffith's *The Resurrection of Hungary: A Parallel for Ireland* (1904)' (19), that 'the fable [fabula/histoire/story] of Stephen and Bloom enacts the drama of nation and hope' (13). No-one before Ungar has devoted so much attention to how this might be the case, and what he brings to the topic is his Hungarian family background and an emphasis not on Homer but on Virgil (and Camões) as the epic creators and exemplars behind *Ulysses*.

Each of the major characters is discussed in terms of their part in Joyce's epic and how they are 'emblematic of Ireland's self-awareness' (25). In *A Portrait*, Stephen is set on forging the conscience of his race; in *Ulysses*, his ironic depiction means that he is seen from the outside, subordinated to the epic medium, confined to 'ecphrastic surfaces' (28). With Griffith and the principle of nationality in mind, Ungar next examines the encounter between Stephen and Bloom, dwelling on the sense of continuity where biography and history meet. From Lipoti Virag of Szombathely to Rudolph Virag to Rudy, from grandfather to father to son, Bloom's vulnerable sense of continuity connects with what happened to the Hapsburg dynasty with the deaths of Maximilian in front of a Mexican firing-squad and the mysterious death of the imperial heir Crown Prince Rudolf in 1889. The issue of closure in *Ulysses* as an epic is analysed by Ungar in what he takes to be the conception of Milly on Howth Head and how she links with photography and serial replication. A fifth chapter explores other ways in which *Ulysses* provides an inquiry into collective identities and how its epic mimesis 'accommodates a fluctuating composite identity through a range of particulars' such as Bloom's forebears wandering in Eastern Europe and Ulysses Brown, the one Irish Ulysses to appear in *A Portrait* and *Ulysses*. (38) In a final chapter devoted to the limits of the epic mode of synthesis, he illustrates his argument by reference to the characterisation of Milly, Bloom's inadvertent self-historicisation when he confuses operas by Meyerbeer and Mercadante, and the overlap between Lipoti Virag and Dublin's 'Endymion' Cashel…Farrell.

All this is covered in the space of just 109 pages. Some twenty pages are devoted to notes and to a series of arguments with Joyce scholars, which are worth turning to when one is wrestling with the main body of the text. This is not then a light read but it remains a valuable contribution to Joyce studies. Whether approaching his material or drawing conclusions from it, he refuses what he calls elsewhere 'easy sentiment' (32). And yet the sentiment is there, for you only dig around in this area if something real is at stake. Design in history, nationality, nationalism, *Ulysses* and the foundation of modern Ireland, continuity in family life, continuity between the self and community, self and history – all this suggests something of the ambitious nature of this project. And all the time we are reminded that when Joyce left for Zurich in 1915 he had spent a third of his life under the Austro-Hungarian Empire.

The one issue I would want to raise here at the end is this. To follow Joyce in identifying 1904 as a key date in the making of modern Ireland must be if not wilful then another example of 'retrospective arrangement'. You could argue – not that I do – that modern Ireland was born with the establishment of the Abbey Theatre in December 1904, but there's no mention of this in Ungar or *Ulysses*. 1916 would be a more legitimate date, one sanctioned by tradition with the General Post Office, where the monarch's head was daily stamped on, offering itself as the nation's navel. On several occasions, Ungar invokes 'Easter 1916' as if Yeats's poem were one of his controls. In his recreation of 1904 Joyce insisted on topographical accuracy and believed the city of Dublin, if it were ever destroyed, could be rebuilt from the portrait contained in *Ulysses*. But whatever Joyce was up to, after 1916, as 'Easter 1916' reminds us, Ireland would never be the same again. So, unless everything can be made to contribute – including the conscription of Sinn Fein into 1904 or the irony that Joyce got the date wrong – I remain sceptical that *Ulysses* constitutes a reliable epic on the nation state.

LUCA CRISPI, JOYCE'S CREATIVE PROCESS AND THE CONSTRUCTION OF CHARACTERS IN ULYSSES: BECOMING THE BLOOMS OXFORD: OXFORD UNIVERSITY PRESS, 2015

In 1977–8 *The James Joyce Archive*, containing sixty-three volumes and twenty-five thousand pages, was published by Garland Press. The *Archive* provides a facsimile of Joyce's 'workshop' containing virtually everything he wrote including notes, drafts, manuscripts, typescripts, and proofs. The so-called Rosenbach manuscript, which had been published in 1975 and which contained a fair copy of *Ulysses* manuscripts in Joyce's own hand, was the one major resource omitted, although there are problems about how this copy might be used.[200] Just assembling all the material from so many different research libraries was a labour of love. Since then, the *Archive* has proved indispensable for scholars round the world examining the process of composition in *Ulysses* and *Finnegans Wake*. Today everything, or nearly everything,

200 *James Joyce Ulysses A Facsimile of the Manuscript* (New York: Octagon Books; Philadelphia: Rosenbach Foundation, 1975). Like other Joyce scholars, Crispi makes good use of this manuscript. The Rosenbach manuscript is not wholly dependable, but it remains of interest for those examining the process of composition.

apart from the manuscripts themselves, is in one place and available to libraries internationally. But, then, in the first decade of the new century, things changed again when the National Library of Ireland purchased a previously unknown cache of manuscripts, which in the words of Luca Crispi 'contained the earliest known *Ulysses* notebook and draft, as well as two manuscripts that chronicle a crucial, relatively late phase of Joyce's work on *Ulysses* in 1921' (6). Now, a decade or so later, we have *Joyce's Creative Process and the Construction of Characters in Ulysses: Becoming the Blooms*, a delightful book that draws on the new material in such a way as to make sense of it. It does more, for it encourages us to perceive how the 'text of *Ulysses* has its origins and foundations in all of its manuscripts' (36).

In the field of Nietzsche studies, a distinction has sometimes been drawn between gentle and fierce (or harsh) Nietzscheans. Conor Cruise O'Brien in *The Suspecting Glance* (1972) takes issue with gentle Nietzscheans, who seek to underline the spiritual side to Nietzsche's writings as if he were a stern but benign school teacher concerned with mastering the self. At the same time O'Brien emphasises Nietzsche's fierceness, extending his critique by linking the philosopher with Hitler and how, for example, Nietzschean anti-semitism was an 'anti-semitism without inhibitions'.[201] If we leave aside the politics and concentrate on the formal aspects in this distinction, we can perhaps observe among genetic critics something similar, though I hasten to add I am not linking any of them to Hitler.

In general, Crispi is a gentle genetic critic, as the following passages suggest:

> By design, *Ulysses* provides a sufficient variety of perspectives on certain character traits to allow readers to reconstruct a relatively coherent understanding of its characters. (30)
>
> What a critically-interpretative genetic approach to [the lives of the Blooms] reveals is that trying to re-

---

201 Conor Cruise O'Brien, *The Suspecting Glance* (1972; London: Faber, 2015), 60.

read the stories in the book in a linear chronological
mode—that is, reconstructing their biographies
as best we can—is a much more confounding
endeavour, especially when one also tries to take into
account the piecemeal manner in which Joyce wrote
and re-wrote what purport to be the same stories,
often in different episodes, over several years, and on
different manuscripts. (20–1)

As is apparent below, attending to manuscript sources can, firstly, enrich
our understanding of characters and the various stories threading their
way through *Ulysses*; secondly, it can help to prevent misinterpretation,
something which is common enough in Joyce studies; and, thirdly,
it can provide a context not so much outside the work in history or
biography but within the process of composition itself. In this way
the relationship between text and context has been redrawn to reveal
something more internal, local and intense. Crispi, rightly, tends to
pull back from overstating his case, so the phrase 'relatively coherent' is
important to notice, for it constitutes an acceptance that not everything
can be known about Joyce's characters or indeed his intentions. Given
the minimalist way Joyce constructed his characters we should be
content with 'relatively coherent'.

But there is a fierce side, for occasionally the author wants to claim
for genetic criticism something more than an ancillary role. This is
forcefully expressed in the following passage:

Most critical readings of Leopold and Molly (especially
the more ideologically charged positions, whether
mythical or archetypal, formalist or structuralist,
Marxist or post-Marxist, postcolonial or materialist,
gender or queer, historicist or psychoanalytic, post-
structuralist or otherwise) have tended to treat them
and the narrative in which they are embedded as
more or less fixed and stable. Based on the characters'
presentation in *Ulysses*, these readings presume that

> it is possible to make singular over-arching claims
> about what they think, feel, and do, and, therefore,
> critics can argue about what they 'stand for'. This
> book emphasizes a different trajectory. It focuses
> on the more general fluidity of their composition
> (that is, most fundamentally, their conception and
> constitution) until the juncture when *Ulysses* was
> published as a book. (18)

Such a large, unsubstantiated claim about most critical readings
represents something unappealing about genetic criticism. Critics
discussed in the reviews in this book provide ample proof that Crispi's
claim is wide of the mark. The books by Norris and McGee, for
example, emphasise uncertainty or suspicion in our reading of the
novel (which includes characters). Such readings are almost the norm
in Joyce criticism, as the work of Clive Hart, Hugh Kenner or Fritz
Senn indicates.[202] We might also recall that the so-called Joyce wars in
the 1980s over the text of *Ulysses* were in part about how we read the
fictional characters. To my mind, one of the joys of Joyce criticism lies
in its resistance to anything which might be considered a definitive
account. The following statement by Crispi again looks like special
pleading on behalf of genetic criticism:

> One of the strengths of genetic readings as a form
> of critical interpretation is their ability to destabilize
> categorical interpretative accounts about the work
> that are based solely on the evidence of a seemingly
> singular, unitary, published work. Genetic readings,
> therefore, contest the sometimes-monolithic inter-
> pretations that the more traditional approach pro-
> motes. (38)

Crispi did not need to stress so categorically his viewpoint or belief.

---

202 See Select Bibliography for titles by these critics.

Perhaps a lighter or more gentle tone would have been more persuasive, an acceptance that genetic criticism occupies a site somewhere between scepticism and positivism. The material at his disposal is thoroughly engaging and provides many suggestive pointers to our reading of *Ulysses*, but they are pointers and not conclusions. There will always be a gap between a text and its interpretation, and genetic criticism helps us narrow that gap. What it doesn't do is negate or undermine many intelligent, previous readings which do not take account of the process of composition. Indeed, the frequent use Crispi makes of the insights in *Surface and Symbol* (1962) by Robert M. Adams, written at a time when genetic criticism was still in its infancy, suggests otherwise.[203]

Crispi's stress on fluidity in the depiction of the Blooms leads to another general observation. While it may share aspects of deconstruction, the process of composition (or construction) occupies a generally supportive role in Joyce studies. As Crispi underscores, many revisions (mostly additions) by Joyce, are afterthoughts:

> In fact, many of the details that readers may consider basic and fundamental to the Blooms' lives as characters in *Ulysses* were afterthoughts – or at least were included in the text as afterthoughts – that were added to give texture to what was otherwise a quite skeletal narrative that was focused primarily on the events of 16 June 1904, the most significant of which is Boylan's arrival at 7 Eccles Street, as well as the thoughts and memories that occur to Leopold and Molly Bloom throughout the day. (8)

Afterthoughts should not be construed as a criticism of Joyce. He alighted on details as he was correcting or improving his text. This is a perfectly normal process for authors, for not everything can be known in advance or kept in the conscious mind before embarking on a piece of writing. That Joyce took seven years to complete *Ulysses* is a

---

203 Robert M Adams, *Surface and Symbol: The Consistency of James Joyce's Ulysses* (New York: Oxford University Press, 1962).

reflection of his commitment to a process which, inevitably, changed course or, indeed on occasion, got out of hand. And he did not have a computer to sort things out for him. Equally, as Crispi emphasises, the book was not written in a linear fashion. One consequence of all this is that the reader is forced into reconstructing the lives of the Blooms often through fleeting moments, bits of conversation, or memories which are distilled or distorted. The Bloom episodes begin definitively with 'Mr Leopold Bloom', an opening passage which remained largely the same from first draft to publication, but precious little else about his character was so definitive from the outset. Even at the last, as Crispi reminds us, Bloom (or Boylan) was not the only man in Molly's life who would look for almost any pretext to 'put his hand anear' her (*U* 18:304), for in one of his notes Joyce had written: 'For any excuse to touch her (Mulvey)'. (163) *Ulysses*, we might well agree, contains a biography of the Blooms, but it is entirely different to an actual biography such as *Leopold Bloom: A Biography* (1981) by Peter Costello.[204]

We now know from the newly acquired manuscripts that Joyce probably started with the bar-room scene in 'Sirens' and then moved back to compose the early Bloom episodes. So when we first meet the character in 'Calypso', his interior monologue has already been established by Joyce from a later episode. Unlike Molly, who acquired her proper (or improper) name 'Mrs Marion Tweedy' among bar-room gossip in the 'Sirens' episode, Bloom himself has a title from the outset as if he were a real person deserving respect and whose thoughts are his own. As Crispi underlines, there is more to it than this, for, constantly, Joyce moved back and forth regularising dates, shifting dialogue from one character to another, lessening or increasing a favourable response to a character, arranging things. Indeed, to my way of thinking, only with time and only after he had written so much could the thought 'As said before' (*U* 11:519) pop into Joyce's mind as something that might find its way into Bloom's thought processes. The brilliance of this phrase is for all readers to admire, and its virtuosity is because

204 Peter Costello, *Leopold Bloom: A Biography* (Dublin: Gill and Macmillan, 1981).

it occurs in a finished text, not because it belongs to the process of composition. When David Hayman hit upon the term 'The Arranger' in 1970, nearly half a century after the novel was published, we know that the process of composition needs readers to interpret or extend the text.[205] I would have liked Crispi to have spent more time discussing such distinctions and effects.

Crispi's use of the new manuscript material purchased by the National Library of Ireland lends a certain, perhaps natural, bias to his study. The new material on 'Penelope' provides the basis for a revision in our account of the Blooms, but it tends to steer the whole novel in a different direction. Presumably, if a text carried no changes in the drafts, genetic critics would have no large claims to make. Crispi insists that the two major plot-lines are now revealed as adultery and the love-making scene between Molly and Leopold in 1888 on Howth Head. In the newly discovered manuscript we learn of Joyce's change at the last minute of the tentative 'would' to the positive 'will' in Molly's soliloquy. This has the potential to affect the whole way we read the novel. As Crispi suggests:

> [Joyce] transformed the narrative voice of the ending of *Ulysses* by using a future tense verb, thereby making it a representation of direct speech. It is no longer just a moment recalled sixteen years after the event; with the change of tense, the reader participates in the mode in which Molly relives that moment for all time. In its new formulation, Joyce represents Molly's acceptance of her life-mate on that memorable day on Howth in the summer of 1888, as well as again at the end of Bloomsday, and for all eternity. (175)

Apart from the faulty phrase 'future tense verb', this is persuasive, for 'would' looks less committed than 'will' and it is one step removed from direct speech. Joyce's substitution is completely unexpected,

205 See David Hayman, '*Ulysses*': *The Mechanics of Meaning* revised edition (Madison, WI: University of Wisconsin Press, 1982).

215

unexpected, of course, largely because we did not know about it. Of course, without a sighting of an alteration at the last stage we are or would be reading a different novel, but the scale of the difference is open to question. Part of the problem lies in our having to reimagine a novel we have read over the years in a certain way. But I am happy to go along with Crispi's realignment. It makes sense to see and not to see 'would'. After all, Joyce kept adding 'yes' to each revision until we now have ninety-one, so 'will' must at some stage have forced its way into the mind of the creator.

Crispi insists on the theme of adultery as the other main theme of the novel. Indeed, his second chapter is entitled 'Boylansday', and he argues throughout for its importance alongside 'Bloomsday'. Again, it makes sense to give so much prominence to Boylan if the newly acquired manuscript is an early draft of 'Sirens' and the last stage of 'Penelope'. As Crispi draws out, in the early draft of 'Sirens', Boylan had a stronger presence, while Joyce had not settled on how to integrate Bloom into the bar-room scene or how to get right the structure of the episode. In 'Penelope' Boylan slaps Molly on the bottom, which we think of as is typical of the man and disrespectful to the woman, but the draft reveals something else:

> Joyce only provided Molly with the reason why Boylan slapped her bottom on the final proof level: it seems it was 'because I didnt call him Hugh' (*U* 18:1369–71). The addition of this specific bit of information is transformative. (278)

Throughout *Ulysses* Boylan is nearly always referred to by his nickname, which is another example of how synecdoche attaches to him like his fancy socks and shoes, but it is only at the end that we realise his true feelings about his moniker. Joyce's late addition we might agree is a nice embellishment but not terribly significant. It might be, if the deleted middle initial, which appears between Blazes and Boylan on the 'Calypso' typescript from the Buffalo manuscript in the *Archive*, was deleted for a purpose or is simply a typo.[206] This was a manuscript dating from March or April 1918 when Joyce was still in the middle of writing *Ulysses* and when perhaps he had decided not to reveal Boylan's other names until much later in the book.

Joyce's Creative Process and the Construction of Characters in Ulysses is such an interesting and enlightening book that any quibbles on my part are in essence just that. I have seldom read a book on *Ulysses* with so much pleasure, and part of me wants everything to be perfect. In settling on the twin themes of adultery and lovemaking on Howth Head, Crispi has in his possession a powerful way of handling manuscript material. Character and stories come together with a purpose, and in turn a line is advanced, arguments developed, crossovers explored, and the rational mind given time to reflect. Some material never made it into the text, and Crispi is alive to these kinds of issues and implications. Very minor figures, such as Lieutenant Stanley Gardner, suddenly become more important or have a higher profile because of the process of composition. And in the rush to get the novel published on his fortieth birthday in February 1922 things got missed out or inserted at the last minute. In turn, Joyce did not have time for a second look, so details could not be inserted into an earlier part of the text as a consequence of a late addition to 'Penelope', and this, we might recall, was his characteristic way of working.

A small point can be mentioned here which is not specifically about the process of composition but related to it. Lunita Laredo, a name that Crispi finds 'beautiful' (110), is to my mind an example of Joyce's characteristic humour. Lunita or little moon fits in with the menstrual theme of 'Penelope'. Laredo sounds like a Mexican town in Texas where they sing about cowboys who know they've done wrong. The reference to 'whoever she was' *(U* 18:846–7) captures something precise about the ambivalent Molly in her attitude toward her mother and also something about the humour of the person who invented the little moon of Laredo. So much Bloom does not know about his wife, and, equally we might say, so much we do not know about *Ulysses*.

---

206 *James Joyce Archive* Volume 12: 267 Buffalo V.B.3.a

Lack of knowledge in the first case allows Molly to retain a sense of a self outside the marriage, but because the addition about 'Lunita' is inserted so late Bloom doesn't have an opportunity to have his say on his mother-in-law. No doubt he would have commented on her name. Perhaps it doesn't matter. Perhaps if Joyce had delayed publication he may have done something about it. Crispi is alert to what is missing in the text, but, inevitably, for the most part such discussion will come to an inconclusive end.

The process of composition is a sifting process. Some things are completely inconsequential and some things the opposite. Equally, some readers will find significance where others find nothing. The role of Stephen Dedalus in *Ulysses* is downplayed in this study. Crispi quotes the well-known remark of Joyce to Frank Budgen in 1918 how 'Stephen no longer interests me to the same extent. He has a shape that can't be changed.'[207] But there is more to the novel than adultery and a kiss. The father-son relationship, the *Hamlet* theme that is, is also central, as is the mind of the would-be artist in contrast with the down-to-earth citizen. The newly acquired manuscripts in the National Library of Ireland tell an important part of the new story, but this cannot be at the expense of all that went before. The twenty-four pages of notes on Shakespeare's dates, which can be found in volume 12 of the *Archive* in connection with 'Scylla and Charybdis', are a reminder that Stephen once seriously interested Joyce. This is to say nothing about the first three episodes of the novel or some wonderfully pithy remarks which deserve never to be forgotten. 'Signatures of all things I am here to read' (*U* 3:2) at a stroke suggests an answer to epistemological doubt and at the same time brilliantly captures humanity's place in the universe. No, whatever about his unpopularity among some critics today, there will be always the potential for future readers to revive Stephen's fortunes. Heaney's *Station Island* (1984) has shown the way.

Linked to this is something else that is missing from Crispi's account. Again in the process of composition, though this is not so apparent in the final stages, Homer's classical world loomed large. In

---

207 Frank Budgen, *James Joyce and the Making of 'Ulysses' and Other Writings* (1934; Oxford: Oxford University Press, 1972), 107.

the 1918 Zurich Notebook (Buffalo VIII A.5) Joyce writes out in Greek the names of some of these figures including Odysseus. It is as if he is trying to get a flavour of the classical world through the transcription of names. Beneath the name of Penelope, who is not as pretty as Artemis, we read another word in Greek and beside it in brackets the equivalent of a wedding gift. Mention of this word recalls the references in *Ulysses* to wedding garments, wedding rings, wedding cake, wedding bells, but nothing about the wedding day between the Blooms, the one that matters. *Ulysses* is such a richly layered text that we forget what's missing, and sometimes that belongs to the classical background. After all, if Telemachus sent his mother away with one of her suitors, he would be forced to pay back her dowry and risk retribution from her father. Interestingly, as Crispi notices, there is a mention of wedding gifts, but this is an oblique reference in the unromantic question-and-answer episode of 'Ithaca': 'On the mantelpiece, he ponders the several frozen and dead symbols of their marriage: a stopped marble clock, an encased tree, and a stuffed owl, each of which we are told were wedding gifts from their friends.' (181) In the same Notebook, we might also notice possibly the Greek word that appears at the beginning of *The Odyssey* 'polytropon'.[208] Odysseus is many sided, can turn his hand to many things, is wily. So is Bloom. In the process of composition in Zurich in 1918 Joyce consciously returned to one of his central sources for the novel, and, while too much can be made of the Homeric correspondences, they cannot afford to be written out or downplayed.

Wherever Joyce is studied, *Joyce's Creative Process and the Construction of Characters in Ulysses: Becoming the Blooms* is a book that will win friends and admirers. Long acquaintanceship with drafts and manuscripts has given the author not just knowledge and expertise but also confidence in his judgements. And his study is full of judgements,

---

208 See for example the word in the middle of page 132, which is possibly the word Joyce is trying to transcribe. In 1923 he drew a caricature of Bloom with the first line in Greek from Homer's *Odyssey*. For a reproduction of the image, see my *James Joyce's Ireland* (London and New Haven: Yale University Press, 1992), 134. The reference to Penelope and Artemis is on page 137.

most of which command assent. Here can be found an answer to the question as whether or not the phrase in the Gabler edition 'Who said four?' (*U* 11:352) should read 'All said four', as it does in texts before Gabler. (See 57ff). Drafts reveal that Bloom's father committed suicide not because of financial difficulties but on account of the loss of his wife. Crispi also adds something from his own research into the suicide in 1917 of Isaac Marshall, proprietor of the Queen's Hotel in Ennis, and how Joyce used this historical connection to prevail over 'the fictional implausibility that a relatively impecunious recent immigrant to Ireland could have acquired such an establishment' (74). Finally, we might also notice how Crispi intervenes in the much-discussed list of Molly's lovers and how Molly thinks Bloom does not have the courage to commit adultery. The kiss, therefore, in the words of the author of this fine book, is 'timeless' (279).

CHAPTER 11

ON COLLECTIONS OF ESSAYS

THE CAMBRIDGE COMPANION TO JAMES JOYCE (ED. DEREK ATTRIDGE) CAMBRIDGE: CAMBRIDGE UNIVERSITY PRESS, 1990

This is an intelligently constructed book, and most of the essays can be warmly recommended and some exhibit a classic quality. The attempt to situate Joyce in the differing contexts of Ireland, Europe, modernism, reading, and his own texts is commendable, and even for seasoned readers of Joyce there is something of interest throughout. The opening essay by Derek Attridge on 'Reading Joyce' consists of an enjoyable and illuminating discussion of two passages, one from 'Eveline', the other from Book II of *Finnegans Wake* (359.31–360.06). He writes well about the instability of the relationship between form and content in 'Eveline', the uncertainty arising from a careful reading of the story especially in the light of Joyce's use of free indirect discourse, and the tension between the demands of naturalism and the progress of the narrative. As for *Finnegans Wake*, it is impossible to separate form and content or indeed ever to enjoy a sense of mastery over the text, for *Finnegans Wake* 'explodes the belief that language, to be meaningful, must be subservient to the singleness of intention or subjectivity' (13).

The next two essays by Seamus Deane on 'Joyce the Irishman' and Klaus Reichert on 'The European Background of Joyce's Writing' belong to a more advanced book on Joyce. Deane attempts to situate Joyce in the nineteenth-century Irish tradition or, rather, the lack of one. He underlines the language conflict in the development of cultural nationalism, the importance of James Clarence Mangan's work on translation, and how, like Mangan, Joyce came to consciousness in a world 'dominated by the same linguistic anxieties' (34) with no alternative to imperialism and nationalism 'other than an attitude of fierce repudiation' (35). Unlike Attridge, Deane is concerned with sources and origins and eventually finds one – or one that is cognate to origin, namely pattern – in the theme of betrayal. The lost language of Ireland is also 'the lost language of the Irish soul, that entity which had not been articulated into existence before Joyce' (51). The path from lost soul to conscious mind is the narrative of 'an Edenic Ireland which, through sin, became postlapsarian and British' (51). Missing from Deane's account is a real sense of his audience. We are told for example that 'Irish history is world history *in parvo*' (5), that Joyce is 'an author without native predecessors' (41), that 'Dublin had not been represented before in literature' (41), and that *Finnegans Wake* is 'Joyce's Irish answer to an Irish problem' (5). Such enigmatic remarks can only be deployed in a situation where the reader already possesses considerable background knowledge.

How much weight we attach to Joyce's ability to construct his own heterodox tradition is an issue that also underlies Reichert's essay. Reichert's wide-ranging survey of the European figures whom Joyce had absorbed before leaving Ireland includes Dante, Bruno. Freud, Flaubert, Tolstoy, Ibsen, Hauptmann, Nietzsche, and Wagner. Even as the listing is unfolded, certain prior questions cannot be ignored. Are we dealing with debt (acknowledged or otherwise), influence (formative or otherwise), parallels, *clinamen* (swerves away), cultural or historical contexts and whether or not these are determining or simply reflective of the spirit of the age? It is in keeping that, because Reichert attempts something more ambitious than a straightforward enumeration of these European figures, his essay raises more doubts than might otherwise be the case. As to what makes Joyce unique, it is presumably not his predecessors. Reichert claims for example that Wagner 'had the most fundamental and the most lasting influence on the writing of Joyce' (77), but that must be an overstatement; it is certainly impossible to verify.

Jean-Michel Rabaté's essay on Joyce and Paris, reminding us that Joyce invented the French heritage he modestly claimed for himself, affords a welcome reply to the two previous essays. This is an intelligent, informative, judicious, exciting, humorous account of the 'paleoparisien' (*FW* 151.9), the arch-Parisian, who felt a primordial calling to live in the French capital. Rabaté tackles the reception of Joyce in Paris, the significance of the city in his work, his understanding of other French writers, and even whether or not Paris spoilt him. He writes well about *Finnegans Wake* as the work of an Irish Parisian, and he manages to shed light on Joyce out of range for English-speaking readers. According to Rabaté, for example, Joyce's understanding of the French language shows awareness of both the spoken voice and tradition: 'This mixture of sophisticated historical knowledge and lack of sophistication in the direct enjoyment of the medium's materiality is typical of the effect *Finnegans Wake* was meant to achieve.' (95)

The other contributions can be more summarily indicated. John Paul Riquelme's essay on *Stephen Hero*, *Dubliners* and *A Portrait* traces the realistic and visionary elements in Joyce's style and the part memory and parody play in this development. Jennifer Levine's essay on *Ulysses* asks if it is a poem, novel, or text (whether as play or in play). As a poem, 'See, it all works out' (*U* 8:122); as a novel, there is character and 'that voyeuristic pleasure in overheard conversation' (146); as a text, it is playful and aligns itself as it were with the reader in motion. By way of illustration she comments perceptively on the opening to *Ulysses* being like a foreigner's language, the subtle portrayal of J.J. O'Molloy in 'Aeolus', and the playfulness of 'Oxen of the Sun'. In her introduction to Joyce's shorter works Vicki Mahaffey offers the useful observation that we perhaps need a 'less consistent, and more Joycean, sense of the continuity and discontinuity of relation' (190) between the earlier and the later works. Hans Walter Gabler's essay on

'Joyce's Text in Progress' is concerned with the 'retextualisation of pre-text' (218), how the November 12–13th 1913 Notebooks surface in *Exiles*, how *Giacomo Joyce* is a reworking of a narrative epiphany, how *Stephen Hero* afforded a notebook and quarry for *A Portrait,* how Joyce is a reader of his own text, 'Penelope' being a 'final rewriting from a re-reading of the pre-text of *Ulysses* itself' (232).

In her essay on 'Joyce and Feminism', Karen Lawrence defends Joyce against the charge of Sandra Gilbert and Susan Gubar that his language represents the triumph of a patriarchal literary heritage. (251) She makes the valuable corrective that the female figures represent the comic potential in language that escapes patriarchal control. Thus, Penelope is a weaver, the hen is a gatherer and scavenger, Anna Livia is a thief, 'a retriever and interpreter of other people's language', a 'figure for an illegality' (244). In a concluding essay, Christopher Butler outlines Joyce's relationship with modernism and post-modernism. Butler is alive to the recalcitrant Joyce, the early modernist who wrote no manifestos, the modern writer who resisted contemporary ideas. Joyce appropriated modernist techniques but remained for the most part uninterested in contemporaries such as Pound and Eliot. Unlike George Gissing and Joseph Conrad, he celebrates the city. Unlike Eliot, he is concerned not with the contrast but with the synthesis between past and present.

The idea of 'Ur-texts' runs through this volume, and I wondered if there was a rubric to the contributors asking them to focus on Joyce's recycling of his material. Nearly all the essays touch on this topic, none with more fluency than Margot Norris in her discussion of *Finnegans Wake*. Her point is that Joyce intended *Finnegans Wake* to be 'the dream' of his earlier texts. In reply to the question where Joyce got the idea to write the 'Anna Livia Plurabelle' chapter, she plays down Joyce's anecdote about Signora Svevo's tresses, the dye-houses along the Liffey, or the visit to Chartres, and instead suggests the chapter dramatises the hidden wishes and fears of Maria in 'Clay'. This is certainly an intriguing thought, the foregrounding of previously background material, but in this particular case it may be Joyce is indebted to his Anglo-Irish predecessor Sheridan Le Fanu. In *The House by the*

Churchyard (1863), Captain Devereux woos Lily by the banks of the Liffey with a song. 'I like the river', says he; 'it has a soul, Miss Lily, and a character. There are no river gods but nymphs. Look at that river, Miss Lilias; what a girlish spirit. I wish she would reveal herself... Look at the river – is it not feminine?...Always changing, yet still the same....It tells everything, and yet nothing.'[209] The whole passage deserves to be better known. Nevertheless, Norris' originality could well be extended to include other kinds of textual material. In a move that could be described as 'Sound seemetery' (*FW* 17.35–60), where Joyce plays on cemetery and symmetry, Norris suggests that chapter one of *Finnegans Wake* is an 'imaginative recreation of poor paralytic Father Flynn lying in his coffin' (178). She also suggests that the last chapter of the *Wake* is 'Telemachus' reversed.

THE CAMBRIDGE COMPANION TO JAMES JOYCE (ED. DEREK ATTRIDGE) SECOND EDITION CAMBRIDGE UNIVERSITY PRESS, 2004

Comparing this edition with the first edition published in 1990 reveals something about the relationship between the academy and the publishing world. Three of the original essays have been dropped – Klaus Reichert's 'The European Background of Joyce's Writing', Hans Walter Gabler's 'Joyce's Text in Progress', and Karen Lawrence's 'Joyce and Feminism' – and five have been added or substituted – Garry Leonard on *Dubliners*, Joseph Valente on Joyce and Sexuality, Jennifer Wicke on Joyce and Consumer Culture, Majorie Howes on Joyce, Colonialism, and Nationalism, and Jeri Johnson on Joyce and Feminism. With the exception of John Paul Riquelme's essay on *Stephen Hero* and *A Portrait*, where the emphasis shifts from 'styles of realism and fantasy' to 'transforming the nightmare of history', the remaining essays are more or less as they appeared in 1990 with some minor updating largely in terms of bibliographical material. There is

209 Sheridan Le Fanu, *The House by the Churchyard* (1863; London: Anthony Blond, 1968), 126.

a brief introduction by the editor to this new edition in which he regrets the loss of the three essays 'for space considerations'. With Reichert and Gabler removed, nearly all the contributors now are North American or, as with Seamus Deane and Jean-Michel Rabaté, based in North America.

Do the old essays merit a re-packaging? Does the new material justify a second edition? If I was less than generous, I would be tempted to say that the original essays feel slightly dated and that the new essays lack power or conviction. Hovering over the first edition was the theme of recirculation, finely illustrated in Margot Norris's essay on *Finnegans Wake*, a work which constitutes 'the dream of his earlier texts'. A decade and a half later, with the waning of deconstruction and post-structuralism, it is more difficult to feel the force behind this insight. In terms of new work, Valente's essay stands out for the energy with which he discusses Joyce in the light of queer theory, and I would add Wicke's essay, which provides a fresh inquiry into consumerism and Joyce. Johnson's essay is a reminder of feminism in retreat, hesitant just when it ought to be gathering strength. Howes marches under the postcolonial banner, the banner that continues to command critical attention. She writes well about Joyce's *Dubliners* possessing a diasporic imagination, but when she suggests, with Mr Deasy in mind, that Britain's economic motives were 'central to Joyce's view of colonialism' (268) she is, perhaps, less reliable.

RENASCENT JOYCE (EDS DANIEL FERRER, SAM SLOTE AND ANDRÉ TOPIA) GAINSVILLE, FL: UNIVERSITY PRESS OF FLORIDA, 2013

'No single perspective can do justice to such a multifaceted writer: next to the medieval Joyce, the modernist Joyce, the Irish Joyce, the European Joyce…we must learn to make room for a Renaissance Joyce' (2). In their attempt at a re-branding exercise, the editors of this elegant, slim volume in The Florida James Joyce Series are nothing if not ambitious. By deliberately switching between 'Renascent' and 'Renaissance', the editors have fashioned a book that eschews comprehensive coverage in favour of 'even further rebirths within the Joycean realm' (6). In turn, what emerges is a study full of suggestive insights into what a thesis on 'Joyce and the Renaissance' might uncover rather than what it should include. Eyebrows might be raised, therefore, that there is no essay for example on '*Chamber Music* and Elizabethan English verse', but, perhaps, on reflection, when it comes to Joyce, difference or a degree of quirkiness can be allowed for. This is not, then, the last word on Joyce and the Renaissance.

'Renaissance' is a nineteenth-century label, which has been the subject of criticism in recent years, in part because of the implied condescension toward the Middle Ages. If Jules Michelet and Jacob Burkhardt had coined the term 'early modern' instead of 'Renaissance' to describe the period from the fourteenth to the seventeenth centuries, the editors of this volume would have been forced into a different kind of book. On the other hand, informing these essays is the traditional idea of rebirth, an idea now conceived in terms other than historical parallels, origins or simple chronology. Thus, to take the most obvious example, two essays on translating Joyce into French conclude this French-inspired volume and reveal a kind of 'rebirth' in another language. Related to this overriding theme is an attention to what Joyce made of his sources and influences, and this is supplemented by excursions into defining Joyce's achievement whether that is set in the past, present, or, in the case of Paul Saint-Amour's essay, the future. Just as there is something problematic about the prefix 're' before 'naissance' so, too, there is something problematic or resistant when the word 'and' is inserted after Joyce. This book, which wisely shelters under the phrase 'Renascent Joyce', is an attempt to shine new light on this complex field of prefixes and suffixes, and, while the volume as a whole might lack a certain, reassuring reservoir of interconnectedness, each of the eleven essays has something distinctive to say.

The essay which opens the volume focuses on the Greek spirit in modernism. With 'Telemachus' and the Renaissance in mind, the big question Philippe Birgy asks is: 'How can a contemporary society start anew or enjoy a second lease of life?' (12). Joyce, he concludes,

rehearses a number of alternatives including Mulligan's conflation of
Nietzsche and Arnold, the tension between sensualism and materialism,
aestheticism and vitalism, mysticism and heresy, interruption and flow
(as in the subheadings in 'Aeolus'). Through it all, Birgy wants to argue,
is the dialectic, the pull, the continuity between these various positions.
Bloom is confident that 'Once you are dead you are dead' (U 6:677),
but then in 'Circe' figures from the past return to haunt him. If there is
a criticism, it is not that Birgy makes no room for gender and Molly's
rejoinder to everything that went before but that his spirited survey
stands in marked contrast to a somewhat lame 'resolution'.

Jonathan Pollock's essay is a more straightforward account of
historical defiance, and how Epicurean atomistic philosophy provided
Renaissance thinkers with a means of challenging the medieval world
picture. Indeed, according to Pollock, *Finnegans Wake* is 'an experiment
in atomist aesthetics', filtered through the work of Joyce's beloved
Giordano Bruno. Lucretius himself is referred to only once or twice
in the *Wake* but this does not deter the author from his thesis. If
he needed further support, Pollock might have made something of
the use of 'swerve' in Joyce's opening sentence, swerve being a core
concept in *De Rerum Natura* and one that has recently been given
a new lease of life by Stephen Greenblatt in *The Swerve: How the
Renaissance Began* (2011).[210] The *Wake*'s opening sentence lends itself to
all kinds of interpretations and processions of one sort or another: from
Heraclitus's 'riverrun' past 'Eve and Adam's' to the 'swerve' or *clinamen*
in Lucretius and onto the Viconian cycle of 'recirculation' (*FW* 3.1–3).
A lively essay by Frederico Sabatini follows, and this, too, is devoted
to Bruno, where he explores the 'coincidence of contraries' (27) and
Joyce's 'intertextual pantomime' (33).

With the help of some beautiful illustrations from *Hypnerotomachia
Poliphili* (1499), Tracey Eve Winton outlines a case for reading
Finnegans Wake in the light of an erotic vision poem that inspired
François Rabelais. 'Ultimately, both books are cosmogonic dreams,
journeys through an underworld tracing the restoration of order in

210 Stephen Greenblatt, *The Swerve: How the Renaissance Began* (London:
Bodley Head, 2011).

228

the absence of the sun, and culminating in the sunrise' (53). While there is some merit in such a comparison, there is too much material in the *Wake* for it to be secured inside the head of a dreamer. To my mind, it is indicative that Joyce's title contains a plural, not the possessive apostrophe.

Two essays on Shakespeare and *Finnegans Wake* traverse a more familiar terrain. It was Adaline Glasheen who declared a generation ago in her *Third Census of 'Finnegans Wake'* (1977) that '*FW* is about Shakespeare', a view subsequently confirmed by Vincent Cheng in *Shakespeare and Joyce* (1984).[211] François Laroque considers Joyce's insight into the name game in Shakespeare and his constant play on the 'Great Shapesphere' (*FW* 295.4). He finds corroboration for Shakespeare's invisibility in Richard Wilson's account in *Secret Shakespeare* (2004), even though Wilson seeks to underline a different reason for his invisibility, namely his 'dual residence' as a recusant in Protestant England.[212] That said, like Shakespeare, Joyce places language centre stage, and Laroque includes some pertinent remarks on the issue of plagiarism in their work and on Joyce's defence of Shakespeare against Robert Greene, the 'faketotem' (*FW* 516.24), '*Iohannes fac totum*' being part of Greene's charge against his young rival.

Renascent Joyce also highlights the active role of juxtaposition in different ideas of rebirth. Jim LeBlanc's polished and helpful essay on 'The Ass Dreams of Shaun's Bottomless Heart' focuses on the parallels between the opening to Book III in *Finnegans Wake* and Nick Bottom's dream vision in *A Midsummer Night's Dream*. Bottom wakes to announce that his dream was 'past the wit of man to say what dream it was', adding that 'man is but an ass, if he go about to expound this dream' (4.1.205–7). Initially, LeBlanc, who continues by invoking Freud's *The Interpretation of Dreams*, has fun with a text which seems to

211 Adaline Glasheen, *Third Census of 'Finnegans Wake': An Index of Characters and Their Roles* (Berkeley, CA: University of California Press, 1977), 260. Vincent Cheng, *Shakespeare and Joyce: A Study of Finnegans Wake* (Gerrards Cross; Colin Smythe, 1984).
212 Richard Wilson, *Secret Shakespeare: Studies in Theatre, Religion and Resistance* (Manchester: Manchester University Press, 2004), 22.

have no bottom and how 'one feels like an ass when trying to interpret it' (82). Maria-Daniella Dick offers a Derridean reading of Joyce's missing *Hamlet* lectures in the 'Scylla and Charybdis' episode of *Ulysses*. In a carefully researched and beautifully written essay, Christine Froula explores the links between 'Proteus', 'that most Parisian of episodes' (107), and Marcel Proust's first book, *Les plaisirs et les jours* (1896).

Sealed from each other, the two essays on French translation offer contrasting views. Liliane Rodriguez outlines Joyce's close involvement in the first French translation of *Ulysses*. It was so close that it leads her to claim that the '1929 translation can be seen as the English original reborn' (123). In a letter to Valery Larbaud in October 1928, Joyce, who had just suffered a collapse, wonders if he cannot get back his sight whether 'it is all U-P up' (*Letters III* 182). Rodriguez continues: 'In *Ulysses*, as we know, "U-P up" is used metaphorically to depict Denis Breen as having less than the standard amount of something (sanity, mental illness)' (128). She assumes that the letter signifies 'underproofed', not fully proofread, and there seems to be some suggestion on Rodriguez's part that this should inform our reading of the postcard. Indeed, citing this example, the editors claim that such an 'authorized translation…may help us solve some of the unsolved puzzles of the original (such as the enigmatic U.p: up)' (6). At this point, to my mind, the errors seem to mount. Josie Breen is pretty sure she knows what the letters in upper case mean (which are quite large in the Shakespeare and Company editions from the 1920s). Just five hundred lines earlier, Bloom is asked by Nosey Flynn, 'Who's getting it up?' (*U* 8:773), so the reader, too, is alert to any suggestive use of the word 'up'. Spaced-out madness, on the other hand, governs *Ulysse*: 'Fou. Tu. : foutu' (*Ulysse*, 177).[213]

Innuendo belongs to the world of winks and nudges, and in this instance there's something to be said for trusting the tale not the teller. Some things are spoilt when clarified. As for Joyce's remark to Larbaud, he might have intended nothing about proof reading but something much more distressing: a momentary realisation or genuine fear that

213 See my review of *Joyce's Ghosts* for Luke Gibbons's alternative explanation of U-P.

the game might be up (he's just referred to a line from Gilbert and Sullivan's *Trial by Jury* (1875)) and that his writing days might be over. In his essay on 'Eumaeus', Robert Byrnes shows himself more alive to the deficiencies in the first French translation, even if he does assume that 'Bloom's idiom infuses the narrator's throughout the episode' (150). Invoking Flaubert in his title, 'Joyce's Dictionnaire des Idiotismes Reçus: Comparing the 1929 and 2004 Translations of 'Eumaeus'', Byrnes cannot be faulted for identifying 2,923 clichés in 'Eumaeus'. However, to lift one of its clichés, I wish it wasn't the case that the episode invites analysis but beggars description.

Let me conclude with Saint-Amour's stimulating essay on the depiction of the future in *Ulysses* and on the idea of Joyce our contemporary, a renascent Joyce that is. According to Saint-Amour, the 'true locus of untimeliness in the text' is not prophecy but hope. Prophecy is one of the novel's great subjects but repeatedly, as in the carnivalesque interruption to Robert Emmet's speech from the dock or in the reference to Mother Shipton's doubly false apocalyptic prediction, Joyce seeks to open a space toward a view of the future which is unforeseeable, one concerned with its 'imprevidibility' (*U* 17:980). Making effective use of Ernst Bloch on political hope, Saint-Amour reminds us that, in spite of its historical grounding, *Ulysses* cannot be confined to that imagined 'national epic' which is 'yet to be written' (*U* 9:309). Indeed, its depiction of the future in the past is also a reminder that a 'well-founded hope', in Bloch's words, 'must be unconditionally disappointable' (Bloch, 341).

'JAMES JOYCE QUARTERLY 50 YEARS VOL 50 NO 1–2 FALL 2012–WINTER 2013'

Since its inception in 1963, the *James Joyce Quarterly* has established itself as a flagship journal. Selecting twenty articles from a formidable inventory must have been quite an undertaking. Sensibly, the current editor, Sean Latham, adopted a managerial approach and asked current members of the board to each choose two or three articles they considered 'influential, enduring, or significant' (12). This resulted in fifty or so nominations, which were subsequently reduced to twenty. The editor then weighted those which had received most votes, at the same time ensuring a spread across the three periods of editorship: Tom Staley (1963–1989), Robert Spoo (1989–1999), and then Latham himself. Inevitably, the coherence of a single view will be lost by such a method and it almost certainly will not end in the satisfaction arising from resolving differences of opinion, but in some respects this has been the strength of the *James Joyce Quarterly*, which Spoo characterises as a 'single-author journal with an anti-cyclopean soul' (181).

When Tom Staley celebrated twenty-five years of the journal in 1987, he did so in his unassuming way not by reprinting selected essays but simply by calling attention in editorial remarks to the 'wide variety of views and approaches' (25:1, p.7) and to how many submissions were now coming from authors who had less affinity with Joyce's works and a greater interest in theoretical issues. The present volume, which includes not only the selected articles but also introductions by the three editors, comments by William Brockman and Jolanta Wawrzycka on the history of checklists, together with reflections by the managing editor Carol Kealiher on her twenty years at the helm, not forgetting nine new book reviews, is much more deliberate in scope, and it constitutes a fine tribute to a remarkable journal and to the people who have sustained it. It may have started out as a project in a garage but bookcases around the world are now sagging under its (continuing) weight.

The three sections each contain, respectively, six, five, and nine articles. The first section includes two articles by Hugh Kenner, the only critic so honoured, one by Fritz Senn, and the longest piece in the whole volume by Florence L. Walzl on 'The Sisters'. The middle section, the period of the Joyce wars, copyright issues, and the emergence of 'theory', has essays by Derek Attridge, Jennifer Levine, Joseph Valente, and Vicki Mahaffey. The final section, which spans some two hundred pages, or over a third of the volume, covers a range of essays from Patrick W. Moran on hoarding and Margot Norris on Possible Worlds theory to a final biographical piece on Joyce's drinking by Austin Briggs.

Selection and arrangement are a matter of impossible choices and any criticism needs to be tempered accordingly. It doesn't really matter that the first section contains five articles on *Ulysses* and one on *Dubliners*, or that the middle section has one on *Finnegans Wake*, two on *Ulysses* and two on *A Portrait of the Artist as a Young Man*, while the final section consists of three articles on *Finnegans Wake*, two on *Dubliners*, one on *Ulysses* and one on *A Portrait*. One can live with such an uneven distribution. For my part, I would have liked to have seen, for example, Robert Adams Day's polished essay in the traditional mode 'The Villanelle Perspex: Reading Joyce' (25:1) or one of Bernard Benstock's nine essays. His '*Ulysses* Without Dublin' contains, conceivably, the most heretical sentence ever published in the journal: '*Ulysses* is no more about Dublin than *Moby Dick* is about a whale', which he then qualifies as if he knows the remark might upset people '-although no less' (10:1, 100–1). I suspect, however, he would have expressed concern at the relatively few, if any, Irish contributors to the volume.

Reading the reprint of an article is not the same as seeing it for the first time. So the reader cannot help but notice a shadow across the page, the trace of a design or pattern imposed elsewhere. While perhaps not intended, the sections and the articles themselves tend to acquire a representative or honorific status. This is more so with the first two sections where we can now discern what is worth preserving. At least three of the six articles from the Staley period, those by Kenner and Senn, retain their freshness and appeal. Michael Groden's essay on 'Cyclops in Progress, 1919' reminds us of his crucial role in interpreting the manuscripts of *Ulysses* as they have become available in the last forty years or so.

Walzl's influential essay on 'The Sisters', first published in 1973, has much to recommend it, not least in showing how a single story of *Dubliners* can yield so much to the keen-eyed observer. On every page there are insights or moments to make us pause. Indeed, there is something impressive, if slightly wilful, about devoting forty-five pages and around twenty thousand words to such a short story. But, as later critics never cease confirming, the irony is that more can be said about a story with a gnomon in it. Indeed, as the first readers of the *Irish Homestead* version presumably half-recognised, there is something suspicious about it, something not quite right. According to Walzl, the title holds the key to the story, and throughout she assumes it must refer to the priest's sisters and not also perhaps to the priest and the boy. Conversely, simony could also apply to the sisters, who looked to their brother, with his special, privileged training in Rome, to lift them out of their hard-pressed circumstances. In this regard it could be argued they were not so much 'piously sentimental' (79) about their brother, as Walzl suggests, as resentful about their fate. Equally, while too much literalism is to be avoided, the stress she places on 'typal' comes at the expense of not looking closely enough at the family's social class, who as it happens are not members of the bourgeoisie but of the (down-at-heel) lower middle class.

For all its qualities, then, and in spite of the way it set in train a whole way of ambitiously tackling the stories in *Dubliners* through comprehensive treatment, I find myself looking elsewhere to, arguably, the finest issue of the journal (10:1), published in 1972, the previous year. Here can be found: Senn's 'Book of Many Turns', the Jesuit Robert Boyle's 'Miracle in Black Ink', Leo Knuth's 'Joyce's Verbal Acupuncture', Morton Levitt's 'A Hero of Our Time', A. Walton Litz's 'Pound and Eliot in *Ulysses*', Robert Scholes's '*Ulysses*: A Structuralist Perspective', Maurice Beebe's '*Ulysses* and the Age of Modernism', and Kenner's 'Molly's Masterstroke', the one essay reproduced here. Their writing and their concerns belong to a different era, but Knuth's comment on reading Joyce stands out as representative of something that, hopefully, will endure: 'a micro-detailed analysis of reverberations is often a rewarding experience' (10:1, 70). Such a remark should be inserted at the top of every paper on Joyce.

Unlike commissioned pieces in a stellar collection of essays, which sometimes can take in a whole field, the appeal of the *James Joyce Quarterly* often lies in reading work in progress, the first stab at an idea, even evidence of struggle. The second section of essays under Spoo's editorship is an exception in this regard, for here the focus is on judgment rather than process. This is especially the case with themed issues such as Joyce and Homosexuality (31:3) or Joyce and the Law (37:3/4). The essays by Joseph Valente and Vicki Mahaffey are companion pieces, the first focusing on Stephen's homosexual panic especially in regard to Cranly, the second, a fluently written piece contrasting the maternal idealisation of Wilde's Dorian Gray with Stephen's paternal negation. Jennifer Wicke's essay on advertising and modernity includes some well-judged remarks on nostalgia.

In what was a position statement given at a *Finnegans Wake* conference in Leeds in 1987, Attridge in 'The Dream of Interpretation' takes issue with those critics such as John Bishop who read *Finnegans Wake* as a dream. '[E]xtra-textual commentary' (191) is how we should read Joyce's famous defence of what he was attempting in his 1926 letter to Harriett Weaver: 'One great part of every human existence is passed in a state which cannot be rendered sensible by the use of wideawake language, cutanddry grammar and goaheadplot' (192). Attridge's next sentence contains the qualification 'however', but it is difficult to relegate such a considered remark by Joyce to something that is merely extra-textual, and it comes as no surprise that Margot Norris in her essay, two decades later, returns to dreams in the light of remarks by Bishop and John Gordon and others. Even if we can agree on not anchoring the *Wake* in a single dreamer or assuming it's a form of (Yeatsian) 'dreaming back' (*FW* 295.10–11), there are enough passages which sound like something from a dream or like earlier moments in a dream sequence. We need 'wideawake language' to describe such a reading experience even if all the time we are intrigued by what lies behind the black marks on the page.

Senn reminds us that symbol or *symbalein* in Greek means to throw together, and, with Throwaway in mind, one implication he draws is that 'nothing is really thrown away' (35). Kenner believes *Finnegans Wake* 'leaves us for ever uncertain what possibilities we can safely discard' (439). In spite of an excursus into the real-life, sad story of the Collyer brothers from Harlem, Moran's essay on hoarding in the *Wake* is fortunately more upbeat and gathers momentum as it proceeds. Shem, who writes the 'mystery of himsel in furniture' (*FW* 183.9–10), is in one sense 'a man without content', and, in contrast to HCE, he is 'paradoxically himself by being everything and no one' (448). The hoarding instinct can also be observed in a genetic critic such as Daniel Ferrer, whose account of the Joyce Notebook containing drafts of 'Proteus' and 'Sirens' and acquired by the National Library of Ireland in 2000 reads like an enthusiastic prospector stumbling upon treasure trove. In the 'Sirens' draft(s) he identifies 'the starting point of the parodic strain that characterises the style of the central episodes of *Ulysses*' (329), thus confirming what Groden had noticed in his essay on 'Cyclops', only in Groden's case he puts a date on it: mid-June 1919 (131).

Other essays from the third section bear witness to the anti-cyclopean stance of the volume as a whole. Finn Fordham makes a case for seeing Lucia Joyce as the hub for interpreting the *Wake*. Gregory Castle claims that *A Portrait* challenges the conventional *Bildungsroman*, although he is too ready to spy the 'colonised subject' everywhere. The scope could be widened here to include for example the ground Joyce shared with his contemporaries such a Francis Sheehy-Skeffington or Fred Ryan or Thomas Kettle or Mary Colum. In some interesting remarks on 'strangers in the house' and domestic dislocation in Ireland since the Famine, Julieann Veronica Ulin covers a lot of ground in her essay on 'A Boarding House', including how the story resurfaces in *Ulysses*. Paul Saint Amour's creative piece on Samuel Roth and copyright, which originally appeared in the Joyce and the Law volume, has an engaging lightness of touch.

Finally, Briggs's meticulous examination of how critics and biographers have played down the topic of Joyce and drinking will provide future biographers with a wealth of material and insights. What is surprising, or perhaps less so given the workings of popular prejudice, is that those outside the Joyce community have already formed their own opinion. Punch into Google search 'James Joyce' and 'alcoholic', as I did in early April 2015, and over 365,000 entries appear, including, thankfully, at the top of the list Briggs's essay from the *James Joyce Quarterly*.

CHAPTER 12

ON A PERSONAL NOTE

A PASSION FOR JOYCE: THE LETTERS OF HUGH KENNER AND ADALINE GLASHEEN (ED. EDWARD M. BURNS) DUBLIN: UNIVERSITY COLLEGE DUBLIN PRESS, 2008

In *A Tour of the Darkling Plain: The 'Finnegans Wake' Letters of Thornton Wilder and Adaline Glasheen, 1950–1975*, the companion volume to the one under review, Glasheen writes this about Hugh Kenner:

> I had a perfectly awful time with the Joycean writer, Hugh Kenner, who has sent me a book that he has written on Joyce. Parts of it were brilliant I thought—he's quite hot on *FW* and the liturgy for instance—but Kenner's is what I imagine the R[oman] C[atholic] party line is going to be on Joyce and I find it abominable. All hail to technique, damn Joyce's people.[214]

---

214 Edward M. Burns and Joshua A. Gaylord (eds), *A Tour of the Darkling Plain: The 'Finnegans Wake' Letters of Thornton Wilder and Adaline Glasheen, 1950–1975* (Dublin: University College Dublin Press, 2001), 87. Further references will be cited parenthetically in the text as *Tour*.

That was in January 1954. Three years later, in November 1957, Kenner visited Glasheen with his wife, and her tune had changed somewhat: 'As I guess I ought to have guessed from the shirty appearance of his writing, he is a handsome, stammering *boy* of 35, his nice wife's son. He was amusing & did an imitation of Ezra Pound imitating Henry James (whom he knew) speaking in his last manner' (*Tour* 171). In the new volume, whatever she asserted elsewhere, her admiration for the '*boy*' Kenner underpins nearly every letter. Indeed, in her letter to Kenner in December 1953, she has a different take on the typescript of *Dublin's Joyce*,[215] which she had dismissed in her letter to Thornton Wilder: 'Your book is a wonderful book. It is so good I know it will be published' (35). Within a short time, Kenner became her tutor and she his acolyte, but sometimes the relationship was reversed. In fact, Kenner constantly sought her approval, and presumably for that reason he sent her copies of his manuscripts before publication. Equally, Glasheen could produce the kind of naïve question that prompted something other than dismissal in Kenner. In response to a photocopy of *Joyce's Voices*,[216] for example, she asks in a voice not that easy to pin down: 'what is the Muse exactly?' (215).

While they may not have been soulmates, Glasheen and Kenner did share much in their likes and dislikes. Their attitude toward Richard Ellmann's biography and toward the man himself is not so much a form of petulance or settled hatred as a leitmotif that binds all three of them together in an historical embrace, which, in its own way, looks distinctly Joycean. On 3 October 1959, she exclaims, 'Ellmann has done it! He has written a biography that lacks time, place and characters. Hamlet without the Prince of Denmark is nothing to it!' (73). Back came Kenner's reply on 15 November 1959: 'If only he could be proved to have committed an enormous enough boner, Joyce would be Delivered from his Spell. In default of which, I see Joyce rapidly turning into a character in a book by Ellmann' (75). To Kenner, Ellmann's biography lacked 'curiosity'

215 See Hugh Kenner, *Dublin's Joyce* (London: Chatto and Windus, 1955).
216 Hugh Kenner, *Joyce's Voices* (Berkeley, CA and London: University of California Press, 1978).

about his subject, and Joyce emerges as 'a half-mad bourgeois who believed in coincidence' (75).

The charge is familiar to readers who keep up with Joyce disputes. To my mind, however, both Ellmann and Kenner, the warring brothers, were involved in forms of rescue, especially in making Joyce acceptable in the academy (which Kenner should have responded to more positively, especially when he had done so much for Pound's reputation). As we look back from today's perspective, we can afford to be more generous. Kenner's insistence on curiosity is something that I am drawn to more today than I am to the liberal-humanist portrait of Joyce in the standard biography. Equally, Ellmann's lack of care with regard to the ten years Joyce spent in Trieste is not that easy to explain whether in terms of ideology or impatience with the project. Writing about the 1959 biography, Kenner imagined Ellmann 'plotting while we slept' (75), but there is more to it than this. After spending time with Tom Staley at Tulsa in September 1975, Kenner suggests to Glasheen: 'Try this on for size—my formulation, not his [Staley's] "The Joyce of *Ulysses* was a Triestine novelist who used Irish material"' (149). Here was the 'enormous enough boner' with which to fell Ellmann, but in a sense we have already moved on, for Kenner is too restless to be detained for long by his rival (75). As for coincidence, Kenner himself is brilliant at noticing Joyce's use of coincidence (if that is what it always is), as in the dates contained in initial letters used in closing moments of *Finnegans Wake*—'*my* cold father, *my* cold *m*ad father, *my* cold *m*ad feary father, which gives us MC=1100, MCM=1900, MCM *vier* [German] = 1904'—the sacred year for Joyce (266).

The short, pithy, enigmatic remark, pushed frequently to the limits of its truth or application, as with the 'Triestine novelist' idea, is what Kenner sought, and in these letters there is something else, for he is always, as it were, trying things on for size. In another era, he might have been a speculative theologian. As it is, we are left with arguably the most suspicious mind of his generation, and—this might hurt—the least generous. 'I have steadfastly refused to have ANYthing to do with Joyceans: you and John Slocum are the only exceptions. He attracts the nastiest disciples' (61). Only his contemporaries could determine the fairness of such a remark. The triplet of 'ANY', 'only', 'nastiest', with the stress falling on the initial syllable, has a certain ring to it, but the venom is surprising when his reading public was largely composed of such people.

Europeans do not escape his onslaught either. Jacques Lacan, he writes in September 1975, is '[a] nuisance like all French intellectuals' (149),[217] while in December 1978 he admits delight at the prospect of the *Times Literary Supplement* closing down and with it '[t]hose intolerable pretensions' (359). Echoes of Pound, Wyndham Lewis, and W.B. Yeats are never far away in the attempt at one-liners or dismissive phrases such as these. Imagine describing the author of *The Four Fundamental Concepts of Psychoanalysis* as '[a] nuisance' or, by extension, a proponent of any other theory we happen to despise. Freud? 'A nuisance.' Hegel and the neo-Hegelians? 'A nuisance.' Barthes and his poststructuralist followers? 'A nuisance.' Then, by way of contrast, think of the positive gloss Kenner places on the misleading nature of Joyce's writing. One of the most enjoyable moments I ever had at a Joyce conference was in 1988 in the Cini Foundation on the island of San Giorgio in Venice and hearing Kenner, in front of an audience of some five hundred participants, with the microphones on, ask a colleague to tell him which panel he was on. Kenner, we might agree, had few followers but many admirers.

The search for one-liners leads both correspondents into different kinds of errors, which a full-scale inquiry, from a European perspective, might be able to trace back in part to the absence of the Great American Novel (about which Glasheen becomes particularly exercised in September 1976). It is as if the pithier the remark, the stronger the argument. But when one is dealing with the contexts of an Irish writer, it requires something other than an agile mind or exercises in transposition across the Atlantic. 'Ireland was the only country in Europe which never had, i.e. got convulsed by, a romantic movement. That's the key. I'm not teasing you. I[t] took me 3 years to see how it unlocked everything' (26). Such an assertion by Kenner in November

---

217 See Jacques Lacan, *The Four Fundamental Concepts of Psychoanalysis* (ed. Jacques Alain-Miller) (London: Hogarth Press, 1977).

1953 seems extraordinary given the presence of Thomas Moore in Joyce's writings or the way Robert Emmet informs the 'Sirens' episode or the many other ways the Romantic movement 'convulsed' the soul of modern Ireland. Glasheen could not have been any help on this. Years later, in June 1978, she observes that Clongowes Wood College is 'the equivalent of The Big House for Joyce' (323), an observation or conjecture that sounds emptier the more it is rehearsed. The question raised is this: what lies behind those one-liners or in what cause are they being advanced?

In the late 1940s, when Glasheen began her inquiry into *Finnegans Wake*, she defined her task as identifying characters and setting out to make an alphabetical list of proper names. In many ways, it was a good place to start since it emphasised knowledge, a sharing of that knowledge, and a way of securing the text. The result was *A Census of 'Finnegans Wake'*, which went through three editions.[218] She never, however, lost her sense that the book was fun. She explained to Kenner, 'If it isn't funny, it isn't anything, is it?' (20). That combination of applied scholarship and humour ensures a certain lightness of touch in her approach to Joyce, one that readers of her correspondence will also admire. And she is not afraid of stylistically slipping a register, as when, in *A Census*, she suggests that Tim Healy 'ratted' on Parnell (55). The correspondence in January 1955 lets us see into the defiance of that moment because the 'scholarly' Ellmann had queried her use of 'ratted', but Glasheen was moved not to be moved: 'Like Miss Dashwood I will not pay him the compliment of rational dissent' (48). In a potentially dry academic list of names, the use of casual words or phrases can remind us of the comic and subversive world of the *Wake*.

Edward M. Burns, the editor of this edition of the letters, is to be congratulated on the thoroughness of his notes. The index is less useful because it is too selective, but the notes, even when they repeat

---

218 Adaline Glasheen, *A Census of 'Finnegans Wake': An Index of the Characters and Their Roles* (London: Faber and Faber, 1956; London: Faber and Faber, 1957), and *Third Census of 'Finnegans Wake': An Index of the Characters and Their Roles* (Berkeley, CA: University of California Press, 1977). Further references to the 1957 edition will be cited parenthetically in the text.

information, are a valuable resource for the student of Joyce interested in what Glasheen, in her introduction to *A Tour of the Darkling Plain*, called 'the amateur's age of unriddling' (*Tour* xiii). In one or two passages in the correspondence when the personal criticism seems very personal, as, for example, in commenting on a person's appearance or looks, I would have cut the phrases. Personal letters are rightly a place for the personal, and, unlike the efforts of the third-person, voyeuristic narrator in fiction, they are not always for public consumption.

DAVID NORRIS, *A KICK AGAINST THE PRICKS: THE AUTOBIOGRAPHY* LONDON: TRANSWORLD IRELAND, 2012

The son of an English engineer and an Irish mother, David Norris here ranges widely over his life from birth in the Belgian Congo, childhood and upbringing in Dublin, through his time at Trinity College Dublin first as a student and later, until his resignation in 1994, as a tutor in the English Department, then onto his years campaigning for gay rights. An Irish Senator since 1987, he stood for election for President of Ireland in 2011. He focuses on his close relationship with Ezra Nawi, an Israeli activist who campaigned for Palestinian rights and who was later convicted of sex with a minor, but Norris's Presidential campaign was damaged when it was revealed he had sought clemency from the Israeli authorities for his one-time friend.

Norris is a high-profile celebrity in Ireland and *A Kick Against the Pricks* is his accompanying signature. With the bulwark provided by his (declining) Irish and English middle-class Protestant family, he mounts an unquestioning defence of his life as a politician and gay campaigner. Nothing by way of religion, class or family gets in the way. When the family recited prayers before morning breakfast, Nelly, the Catholic maid, is excused, but Norris doesn't elaborate, and we never learn of her surname. On the other hand, when asked if he is part of the Ascendancy, he quips that he belongs to the 'Descendancy'. The humour is characteristic of someone who can trace his roots back to the Kings of Ossory and Leinster and who on his English side had an uncle who served as chaplain in the 1930s to Queen Mary. Tellingly, the 'pricks' in the title is not so much a reference to life being a bitch as to the specific enemies, particularly in the press and media, who sought to bring him down.

As the list of names in the Index confirms, this is a public autobiography, and, consequently, most of the material is readily available on the net. In this sense his autobiography is a continuation of a life written in the aftermath of losing the Presidential race. People, therefore, tend to be either enemies or friends. There are ninety-five references to friends, while 'decent', as in 'all decent chaps', recurs twenty-seven times. His work as an Irish Senator widened the circle of friends and enemies, reaching out to major trouble spots round the globe, including East Timor, Iraq, and Tibet. There is a wonderful moment when on an official visit to Baghdad he tackles Tariq Aziz, Saddam Hussein's Deputy, reminding him that the torture victims he has seen in Dublin belong to the regime. Not known for his reticence, Norris can give the impression that he has been central to intervening in these disputes. He should be better known for his courage in pursuing justice for all.

In a puff accompanying *The Long Apprenticeship*, I suggested an autobiography or memoir is 'like an underground stream which comes to the surface', but there is little of this in Norris. His childhood memories resemble things filtered through an adult's eyes where too much is already in place. But, as the contemporary German artist, Martin Honert, reminds us, childhood memories are rarely like documents or photographs and are often blurry or out of perspective or come at us in glimpses or are impossibly distanced, their context emptied through time. At one point Norris wonders philosophically about the idea of consciousness, a thought no sooner raised than dismissed. It is at this stage he might have made more of his knowledge of *A Portrait*.

His view of Joyce is anchored in the one he absorbed in the 1960s. Anthony Burgess is a particular debt. 'Re-Joyce', with its conscious echo of Burgess's *Re Joyce* (1968), heads up one of his Joyce chapters, while Burgess's *Joysprick* (1973) can be heard in his own title.[219] The cover to the 1954 Signet Classic paperback of *A Portrait of the Artist as a Young Man*, a copy with a commentary by Seán Ó'Faoláin, shows the back of a young man, his head turned toward an attractive young woman, her left hand reaching down to lift her three-quarter length skirt, while in the middle distance looms a forbidding-looking church and in the background the sails of an emigrant ship. This is an image of Joyce in revolt against the world, wrestling with 'the agonies and ecstasies of adolescence', a Freudian image of Ireland's *ego, superego* and *id* which informed a generation. It is perhaps not surprising that Norris dramatically walked out of a conference in Florida in 1989 when it looked as though post-structuralism and deconstruction had done away with full-blooded authors in favour of 'the intentionality of the text'.

Norris's work on behalf of the Joyce community has been much appreciated. He details his contribution to the establishment of the Joyce Centre in North Great George's Street as well as his role in ensuring Joyce Symposia have periodically returned to their home in Dublin. The popularity of Bloomsday in Dublin is largely his creation, while his one-man Joyce shows have been performed around the world, bringing in new audiences. Whether winning medals or scholarships in his early life or running marathons in mid-career or holding court in the Senate, Norris seems most at home as a performer. His private papers he donated to the National Library of Ireland – on condition they took the lot!

LIAM HARTE (ED.), *MODERN IRISH AUTOBIOGRAPHY: SELF, NATION AND SOCIETY* BASINGSTOKE: PALGRAVE MACMILLAN, 2007

In spite of its publication prior to the 2008 crash, this survey of modern Irish autobiography still retains much of its relevance for continuing

219 Anthony Burgess, *Re Joyce* (New York: W.W. Norton, 1968) and *Joysprick: An Introduction to the Language of James Joyce* (London: Deutsch, 1973).

debates on the subject. Partly this is because the eleven essays range widely in terms of period, place, theme, and approach. Indeed, as if in keeping with the topic, the backward look is given prominence, from *The Merry Wanderer* (1725), Mary Davys's witty play on the Irish emigrant in Britain, through *Jail Journal* (1854), John Mitchel's compelling story of prison and exile, to the example set by the generation of George Moore, Lady Gregory, and W.B. Yeats. Complementing this historical contextualising is a concern with looking back to Ireland from abroad. Such concern is especially evident in the testimony of 'Mary' from *Breaking the Silence*, an archival project on migration and in her case on return, and in George O'Brien's engaging and frank reflections from the United States on how his three volumes of autobiography were received in his native country. The editor has chosen his team wisely, and the result is a stimulating collection of views on a topic which, despite the boom in autobiographical writing after Frank McCourt's *Angela's Ashes* (1996), remains surprisingly under-researched.

In his Introduction Liam Harte stresses the theme of 'self, nation and society', the subtitle to the volume, and how its most intense formulation is found in the alignment of self and nation, 'the master trope of the Irish autobiographical tradition' (3). Eve Patten, in an essay focusing on *A Portrait of the Artist as a Young Man*, rehearses an earlier, well-worn, discussion in Joyce studies, how the novel is based on autobiographical elements. For Patten, this returns us to 'life' rather than 'art' and to 'the conflicted and evolutionary Irish nation itself' (58). At one point she observes that the novel remains 'an undeniably autobiographical work, while simultaneously proclaiming its own distance from autobiography' (57). The use of 'undeniably' is troubling; it's as if a rhetorical ploy has denied a larger discussion. On the previous page she quotes approvingly the *Dana* passage from the 'Scylla and Charybdis' episode of *Ulysses* only in this case she allows a nod to the 'ludic' quality but it is the serious point that is upheld, namely how the ideas about weaving and unweaving our bodies 'bear closely on Joyce's aesthetic reshaping of his own being through both text and time' (56). It would be interesting to know what Joyce intended us to make of all this but it must be more than flattening out the irony or returning us to the autobiographical elements that make up the story. Equally, it is impossible to imagine Stephen inventing the character of Bloom or allowing him space to participate in the theme of meeting the self.

Memoirs tend to work by saying 'what was is no more'. In *Finnegans Wake*, Joyce champions the idea expressed in the awkward, telescoped phrase 'waz iz' (*FW* 4.14), how what was still is. Such a phrase can be interpreted in terms of generation and procession, with Izzy marked as the daughter; or in cyclical terms, where patterns recur or return, picking up on the 'riverrun' of its opening; or, with memoirs in mind, in terms of everything always being or existing in the present and at the same time voiced or articulated, the 's' rendered as 'z'. The phrase reminds us that one of the guiding principles behind *Finnegans Wake* is the presence of the past in the present. Unlike his previous works, where the past is always past, nothing is ever entirely lost. The river flows on. The critical and existential issue confronting such an outook or view of life can be observed in the memoir by Hugh Maxton (W.J. McCormack), a memoir which Barry Sloan considers in his thoughtful survey of Irish Protestant autobiographies. In *Waking* (1997), the *Wakean* title to his impressive memoir, Maxton notices 'Nothing is remembered as it was' (172).[220] Bereavement, he decides, is 'close to drowning. You rise for the last time, to see your life stretching not backwards but ahead' (173). Here, we might well conclude, is Joyce's legacy, a contemporary meditation on the yoking of 'waz iz' and the scene of writing.

Throughout Harte's collection, then, different aspects of the self are on display, from the performative self as in Yeats to the deflected self in autobiographies by women writers such as Elizabeth Bowen and Kate O'Brien. If cultural memory is emphasised so too is confessional culture. In this sense, the desk is a kind of prie-dieu with the reader like the priest or like God. The writer is head down, penitent, sharing secrets and seeking if not forgiveness then renewal. The editor is certain there is a master trope but the collection is telling us something else.

220 Hugh Maxton, *Waking: An Irish Protestant Upbringing* (Derry-Londonderry: Lagan Press, 1997). Page references are to Harte's collection.

In the oral narratives of emigration from *Breaking the Silence* we read of 'ghosts of other selves' (130), in John McGahern the search for a lost image, while George O'Brien muses that many Irish autobiographers are 'not quite sure what to make of their material' (233). It is a good note on which to end.

SELECT BIBLIOGRAPHY

Ackerley, C.J. and S.E. Gontarski (eds), *The Faber Companion to Samuel Beckett* (London: Faber, 2006).

Adams, Robert M., *Surface and Symbol: The Consistency of James Joyce's Ulysses* (New York: Oxford University Press, 1962).

Aristophanes, *The Frogs* (trans Gilbert Murray) (London: George Allen and Unwin, 1908).

Attridge, Derek (ed.), *The Cambridge Companion to James Joyce* (Cambridge: Cambridge University Press, 1990).

—*The Cambridge Companion to James Joyce* Second Edition (Cambridge: Cambridge University Press, 2004).

Baddeley, M.J.B. *Thorough Guide Ireland Part 1 Northern Counties* (London: Dulau, 1897).

Barry, Sebastian, *The Steward of Christendom* (London: Methuen, 1995).

— *Our Lady of Sligo* (London: Methuen, 1998).

— *The Whereabouts of Eneas McNulty* (London: Picador, 1998).

— *A Long Long Way* (London: Faber, 2006).

— *The Secret Scripture* (London: Faber, 2008).

— *Days Without End* (London: Faber, 2016).

Baumann, Walter and William Pratt (eds), *Ezra Pound and Modernism: The Irish Factor* (Brighton: Edward Everett Root, 2017).

Beckett, Samuel, *Three Novels: Molloy, Malone Dies, The Unnamable* (New York: Grove Press, 1977).

— *The Letters of Samuel Beckett 1929–1940* (eds Martha Dow Fehsenfeld and Lois More Overbeck) (Cambridge: Cambridge University Press, 2009).

Berlitz Idioms and Grammar (London: Berlitz Holdings, 1939).

Berrone, Louis (ed.), *James Joyce in Padua* (New York: Random House, 1977).

Bowker, Gordon, *James Joyce: A Biography* (London: Weidenfeld and Nicolson, 2011).

Budgen, Frank, *James Joyce and the Making of 'Ulysses' and Other Writings* (1934; Oxford and New York: Oxford University Press, 1972).

Burgess, Anthony, *Re Joyce* (New York: W.W. Norton, 1968).

— *Joysprick: An Introduction to the Language of James Joyce* (London: Deutsch, 1973).

Burns, Edward M. (ed.), *A Passion For Joyce: The Letters of Hugh Kenner and Adaline Glasheen* (Dublin: University College Dublin Press, 2008).

Busteed, Mervyn, Frank Neal, and Jonathan Tonge (eds), *Irish Protestant Identities* (Manchester: Manchester University Press, 2008).

Caldwell, Lucy, *Where They Were Missed* (London: Viking, 2006).

Carleton, William, 'The Lough Derg Pilgrim' in *Traits and Stories of the Irish Peasantry* 2 volumes (Dublin: W. Curry and London: W. S. Orr, 1843–44).

Child, Frank James (ed.), *English and Scottish Popular Ballads* vol 2 (Mineola, NY: Dover, 2003).

Cormack, Alistair, *Yeats and Joyce: Cyclical History and the Reprobate Tradition* (Aldershot: Ashgate, 2008).

Craig, Patricia, *The Oxford Book of Ireland* (Oxford: Oxford University Press, 1998).

Crispi, Luca, *Joyce's Creative Process and the Construction of Characters in Ulysses: Becoming the Blooms* (Oxford: Oxford University Press, 2015).

Deane, Seamus (general editor), *The Field Day Anthology of Irish Writing* 3 vols (Derry: Field Day, 1991)

Dickens, Charles, *David Copperfield* (ed. Nina Burgis) (Oxford: Oxford University Press, 2008).

Dickens, Mamie, *My Father As I Recall Him* (London: Roxburghe, 1896).

Dinneen, Patrick, *Foclóir Gaedilge agus Béarla: An Irish-English Dictionary* (Dublin: M.H. Gill, 1904).

Dodsley, J., *A Collection of Poems in Six Volumes* vol 1 (London: Printed for Dodsley, 1782).

Dolan, Terence, *A Dictionary of Hiberno-English: the Irish Use of English* (Dublin: Gill and Macmillan, 1999).

Donnelly, James S., *Captain Rock: The Irish-American Agrarian Revolution of 1821–1824* (Madison, WI: University of Wisconsin, 2009).

Dublin James Joyce Journal Issue 1 (Dublin: University College Dublin and the National University of Ireland, 2008).

Durcan, Paul, *Life is a Dream: 40 Years Reading Poems 1967–2007* (London: Harvill Secker, 2009).

Eco, Umberto, *The Infinity of Lists* (trans Alastair McEwen) (London: MacLehose Press, 2009).

Eliot, T.S., *East Coker* (London: Faber and Faber, 1940).

— *The Letters of T.S. Eliot Vol 2 1925–1927* (eds Valerie Eliot and and Hugh Haughton) (London: Faber, 2009).

Ellmann, Richard, *James Joyce,* revised edition (Oxford and New York: Oxford University Press, 1982).

Faerber, Thomas and Markus Luchsinger, *Joyce in Zürich* (Zurich: Unionsverlag, 1988).

Fallon, Peter and Derek Mahon (eds), *The Penguin Book of Contemporary Irish Poetry* (Harmondsworth: Penguin, 1990).

Fennell, Conor, *A Little Circle of Kindred Minds: Joyce in Paris* (Dublin: Green Lamp Editions, 2011).

Ferguson, Frank (ed.), *Ulster-Scots Writing: An Anthology* (Dublin: Four Courts, 2008).

Ferrer, Daniel, Sam Slote and André Topia (eds), *Renascent Joyce* (Gainsville, FL: University Press of Florida, 2013).

Field, Henry M., *Gibraltar* (London: Chapman and Hall, 1889).

Fogarty, Anne and Fran O'Rourke (eds), *Voices on Joyce* (Dublin: University College Dublin Press, 2015).

Forster, John, *The Life of Charles Dickens*, 2 vols (ed. A.J. Hoppé) (1872–4; London: J.M. Dent and New York: E.P. Dutton, 1966).

Freud, Sigmund, *The Psychopathology of Everyday Life* (trans Anthea Bell) (1901; London: Penguin, 2002).

Gibbons, Luke, *Joyce's Ghosts: Ireland, Modernism, and Memory* (Chicago and London: University of Chicago Press, 2015).

Gillespie, Michael Patrick (ed.), *Joyce Through the Ages: A Non-Linear View* (Gainesville, FL: University Press of Florida, 1999).

Glasheen, Adaline, *Third Census of 'Finnegans Wake': An Index of the Characters and Their Roles* (Berkeley, CA: University of California Press, 1977).

Glendinning, Victoria with Judith Robertson (eds), *Love's Civil War: Elizabeth Bowen and Charles Ritchie Letters and Diaries from the Love Affair of a Lifetime*

1941–1973 (London: Simon and Schuster, 2009).

Gregory, Lady (ed.), *Sir William Gregory: An Autobiography* (London: John Murray, 1894).

Groden, Michael, *Ulysses in Progress* (1977; Princeton, NJ: Princeton University Press, 2014).

— (ed.), *The James Joyce Archive: Ulysses Notes & 'Telemachus' – 'Scylla and Charybdis'* (New York: Garland, 1978).

Hart, Clive, 'Gaps and Cracks in *Ulysses*', *James Joyce Quarterly* 30:3 (Spring 1993).

Harte, Liam (ed.), *Modern Irish Autobiography: Self, Nation and Society* (Basingstoke: Palgrave Macmillan, 2007).

— *The Literature of the Irish in Britain: Autobiography and Memoir, 1725–2001* (Basingstoke: Palgrave Macmillan, 2009).

Hartley, Jenny, (ed.), *The Selected Letters of Charles Dickens* (Oxford: Oxford University Press, 2012).

Hayman, David, *'Ulysses': The Mechanics of Meaning*, revised edition (Madison, WI: University of Wisconsin Press, 1982).

Heaney, Seamus, *Station Island* (London: Faber, 1984).

Hobsbawm, E.J., *Nations and Nationalism Since 1870* 2nd edition (Cambridge: Cambridge University Press, 2000).

Hughes, H. Stuart, *Consciousness and Society: The Reorientation of European Social Thought 1890–1930* revised edition (1958; New York: Vintage, 1977).

Hughes, Ted, *Letters of Ted Hughes* (ed. Christopher Reid), (London: Faber, 2009).

Johnson, Samuel, *A Dictionary of the English Language* 2 volumes (London: W. Strahan, for J. and P. Knapton; T. and T. Longman; C. Hitch and L. Hawes; A. Millar; and R. and J. Dodsley, 1755).

Jonson, Ben, *New Inn* (ed. Michael Hattaway) (Manchester: Manchester University Press, 1984).

James Joyce Quarterly 50 Years Vol 50 No 1–2 Fall 2012–Winter 2013.

Jolas, Eugene, 'My Friend James Joyce' in Sean Givens (ed.), *James Joyce: Two Decades of Criticism* (New York: Vanguard Press, 1948).

Joyce, James, *The Critical Writings of James Joyce* (eds Ellsworth Mason and Richard Ellmann) (1959; New York: Viking, 1966).

— *Dedalus: Portrait de L'Artiste Jeune Par Lui-Même* (trans Ludmila Savitzky) (1924; Paris: Gallimard, 1943).

— *Finnegans Wake* (eds Robbert-Jan Henkes, Erik Bindevoet and Finn Fordham) (Oxford: Oxford University Press, 2012).

— *A Portrait of the Artist as a Young Man* (ed. John Paul Riquelme) (New York: W.W. Norton, 2007).

— *Ulysse* (trans Auguste Morel with assistance of Stuart Gilbert) (1929; Paris: Gallimard, 1957).

— *Ulisse* (trans Giulio de Angelis) (1960; Milan: Arnoldo Mondadori Editore, 1967).

— *Ulysses* (ed. Jeri Johnson) (Oxford: Oxford University Press, 1993).

— *Ulises* (trans Francisco García Tortosa) revised edition (Madrid: Cátedra, 2003).

— *Ulysses* (intro Danis Rose, John O'Hanlon and Stacey Herbert with illustrations by John Vernon Lord) (London: The Folio Society, 2017).

— *James Joyce Ulysses A Facsimile of the Manuscript II* (New York: Octagon Books; Philadelphia: Rosenbach Foundation, 1975).

Joyce, Stanislaus, *My Brother's Keeper* (ed. Richard Ellmann) (London: Faber and Faber, 1958).

Keegan, Claire, *Walk the Blue Fields* (London: Faber, 2008).

Kelly, John, *A W.B. Yeats Chronology* (Basingstoke: Macmillan, 2003).

Kennedy, Patrick, *Legendary Fictions of the Irish Celts* (London, 1866).

Kenner, Hugh, *Dublin's Joyce* (London: Chatto and Windus, 1955).

— *Joyce's Voices* (Berkeley, CA and London: University of California Press, 1978).

— *Ulysses* (London: Allen and Unwin, 1980).

Kiely, Benedict, *The Cards of the Gambler* (1953; Dublin: Millington, 1973).

— *There Was an Ancient House* (1955; Dublin: Wolfhound, 1977).

— *The Captain with the Whiskers* (1960; London: Methuen, 2005).

— *Proxopera* in *The State of Ireland: A Novella and Seventeen Stories* (Introduction Thomas Flanagan) (New York: Penguin, 1982).

— *Nothing Happens in Carmincross* (London: Methuen, 1986).

— *And As I Rode by Granard Moat* (Dublin: Lilliput Press, 1996).

253

— *The Waves Behind Us* (London: Methuen, 1999).

— *The Collected Stories of Benedict Kiely* (Introduction Colum McCann) (London: Methuen, 2002).

Killeen, Terence, *Ulysses Unbound: A Reader's Companion to James Joyce's 'Ulysses'* (Bray, Co. Wicklow: Wordwell, 2004).

Kinmonth, Claudia, *Irish Country Furniture 1700–1950* (New Haven and London: Yale University Press, 1993).

Lawrence, Karen, *The Odyssey of Style in Ulysses* (Princeton, NJ: Princeton University Press, 1981).

Lewis, George Cornewall, *On Local Disturbances in Ireland and On the Irish Church Question* (London: B. Fellowes, 1836).

Locke, John, *An Essay Concerning Human Understanding* (1689; London: Penguin, 1997).

MacNeice, Louis, *Collected Poems* (ed. Peter McDonald) (London: Faber, 2007).

McCabe, Colin, *James Joyce and the Revolution of the Word* (London: Macmillan, 1979).

McCarthy, Justin, *Irish Literature* vol 1 (Philadelphia: J. D. Morris, 1904).

McCarthy, Michael, *Irish Land and Liberty: A Study of the New Lords of the Soil* (London: R. Scott, 1911).

McCormack, W.J., *Ferocious Humanism: An Interpretive Anthology from Before Swift to Yeats and After* (London: Dent, 2000).

McCourt, John, *The Years of Bloom: James Joyce in Trieste 1904–1920* (Dublin: Lilliput, 2000).

McEwan, Ian, *Nutshell* (London: Jonathan Cape, 2016).

McGee, Patrick, *Paperspace: Style as Ideology in Joyce's Ulysses* (Lincoln, NE and London: University of Nebraska Press, 1988).

Mahon, Derek, *The Sphere Book of Modern Irish Poetry* (London: Sphere Books, 1972).

Mannin, Ethel, *Sounding Brass* (London: Jarrolds, 1937).

Maxton, Hugh, *Waking: An Irish Protestant Upbringing* (Derry-Londonderry: Lagan Press, 1997).

Melchiori, Giorgio (ed.), *Joyce in Rome: The Genesis of Ulysses* (Rome: Bulzoni, 1984).

Murray, Christopher (ed.), *Samuel Beckett Playwright and Poet* (New York; Pegasus Books, 2009).

Murray, Lindley, *English exercises, adapted to the Grammar lately published by L. Murray Designed for the benefit of private learners, as well as for the use of schools.* Third edition. (York: Wilson, Spence, and Mawman: 1798).

Nadel, Ira B., *Joyce and the Jews: Culture and Texts* (London: Macmillan 1989).

Nash, John, *James Joyce and the Act of Reception: Reading, Ireland, Modernism* (Cambridge: Cambridge University Press, 2006).

Norburn, Roger, *A James Joyce Chronology* (Basingstoke: Palgrave Macmillan, 2004).

Norris, David, *A Kick Against the Pricks: The Autobiography* (London: Transworld Ireland, 2012).

Norris, Margot, *Joyce's Web: The Social Unraveling of Modernism* (Austin, TX: University of Texas Press, 1992).

O'Connor, Bridget, *The Flags* (London: Faber, 2006).

O'Connor, Frank, *A Book of Ireland* (Glasgow: Collins, 1959).

Ó Cróinín, Dáibhí (ed.), *The Songs of Elizabeth Cronin: Irish Traditional Singer* (Dublin: Four Courts Press, 2000).

O'Donoghue, Bernard (ed.), *The Cambridge Companion to Seamus Heaney* (Cambridge: Cambridge University Press, 2009).

O'Driscoll, Dennis, *Stepping Stones: Interviews with Seamus Heaney* (London: Faber, 2008).

O'Neill, Joseph, *Blood Dark Track* (London: Granta, 2000).

— *Netherland* (London: Fourth Estate, 2008).

O'Shea, John Augustus, *Romantic Spain: A Record of Personal Experiences* (London: Ward and Downey, 1887).

Parrinder, Patrick, *James Joyce* (Cambridge: Cambridge University Press, 1984).

A Pictorial and Descriptive Guide to Bognor (London: Ward Lock, 1918).

Pierce, David, *James Joyce's Ireland* (London and New Haven: Yale University Press, 1992).

— 'The Politics of *Finnegans Wake*' in Patrick McCarthy (ed.), *Critical Essays on James Joyce's Finnegans Wake* (New York: G.K.Hall, 1992).

— *Yeats's Worlds: Ireland, England and the Poetic Imagination* (London and New Haven: Yale University Press, 1995).

— *Sterne in Modernism/Postmodernism* (co-editor with Peter de Voogd) (Amsterdam: Rodopi, 1996).

— (ed.), *W.B. Yeats: Critical Assessments* 4 Vols (Robertsbridge: Helm Information, 2000).

— (ed.), *Irish Writing in the Twentieth Century: A Reader* (Cork: Cork University Press, 2001).

— *Light, Freedom and Song: A Cultural History of Modern Irish Writing* (London and New Haven: Yale University Press, 2005).

— *Joyce and Company* (London: Continuum, 2006).

— *Reading Joyce* (Harlow: Pearson Longman, 2007).

— *The Long Apprenticeship: A Writer's Memoir* (Knebworth: Troubador, 20012).

Robinson, Tim, *Connemara: Listening to the Wind* (London: Penguin, 2007).

Sandys, George, *Ovid's Metamorphosis Englished, Mythologiz'd and Represented in Figures* (Oxford: John Lichfield, 1632).

Senn, Fritz, 'He Was Too Scrupulous Always: Joyce's "The Sisters"' in *James Joyce Quarterly*, 2:2 Winter 1966.

— 'Book of Many Turns' in *James Joyce Quarterly*, 10:1 Fall 1972.

Shovlin, Frank, *Journey Westward: Joyce, Dubliners and the Literary Revival* (Liverpool: Liverpool University Press, 2012).

Stasi, Paul, *Modernism, Imperialism, and the Historical Sense* (Cambridge and New York: Cambridge University Press, 2012).

Sterne, Laurence, *The Life and Opinions of Tristram Shandy, Gentleman* (ed. Ian Campbell Ross) (Oxford: Oxford University Press, 2000).

— *A Sentimental Journey Through France and Italy by Mr Yorick* with *The Journal to Eliza* and *A Political Romance* (ed. Ian Jack) (Oxford: Oxford University Press, 1989).

— *The Florida Edition of the Works of Laurence Sterne Volume VII The Letters Part I 1739–1764 and Volume VIII The Letters 1765–1768* (eds Melvyn New and Peter de Voogd) (Gainesville, FL: University Press of Florida, 2009).

— *The Beauties of Sterne* (London: C. Etherington for T. Davies; J. Ridley; W. Flexney; J. Sewel; and G. Kearsley, 1782).

Trench, Richard Chevenix, *The Remains of the Late Mrs Richard Trench* (London: Parker, Son and Bourn, 1862).

Trevor, William, *The Ballroom of Romance and Other Stories* (London: Bodley Head, 1972).

Trotter, David, 'The Modernist Novel' in *The Cambridge Companion to Modernism* (ed. Michael Levenson) Second edition (Cambridge: Cambridge University Press, 2011).

Ungar, Andras, *Joyce's 'Ulysses' as National Epic: Epic Mimesis and the Political History of the Nation State* (Gainesville, FL: University Press of Florida, 2002).

Walsh, Edna, *The Walworth Farce* (London: Nick Hern Books, 2007).

— *The New Electric Ballroom* (London: Nick Hern Books, 2008).

Watt, Stephen, *Beckett and Contemporary Irish Writing* (Cambridge: Cambridge University Press, 2009).

Wilde, Oscar, *The Importance of Being Earnest and Other Plays* (ed. Peter Raby) (Oxford: Oxford University Press, 1998).

Wister, Jones, *A 'Bawl' for American Cricket* (Philadelphia, 1893).

Woolf, Virginia, *To the Lighthouse* (Oxford: World's Classics, 1999).

— *Moments of Being: Autobiographical Writings* (ed. Jeanne Schulkind) (London: Pimlico, 2002).

Yeats, William Butler, *W.B. Yeats: Selected Poetry* (ed. Timothy Webb) (London: Penguin, 1991).

— and Thomas Kinsella, *Davis, Mangan, Ferguson? Tradition and the Irish Writer* (Dublin: Dolmen, 1970).

INDEX

Adams, Robert M. 53, 213
Aquinas, St Thomas 17, 173
Aristophanes xxiii
Aristotle 17
associationism 6, 32
Attridge, Derek xli, 189, 221, 235
Auden, W.H. 121
Aziz, Tariq 243

Baddeley, M.J.B. 29, 87
Beach, Sylvia 147, 158
Beckett, Samuel 99
    and attitudes to Ireland 116–117
    and correspondence 114–117
    and *Finnegans Wake* 146
    and relationship with Joyce xxxvi, 4, 147
    and sucking stone sequence in *Molloy* 15, 95
    and Tom McGreevy 117, 148
    and *Waiting for Godot* at Haymarket Theatre 125
Benjamin, Walter 132
Benstock, Bernard xviii, 223
Berger, Peter 131
Bindevoet, Erik and Robbert-Jan Henkes xxxiii
Birgy, Philippe 227
Bishop, John 235
Blake, William 161
Bloch, Ernst 231
Bloomsday (16 June 1904) xix, xl, 60, 158, 174, 215, 244
Boland, Eavan 95
Bolger, Dermot 94
Borach, Georges 144
Bourke, Angela 97
Bowen, Elizabeth xxxv, xxxvi, xliii, 118ff, 246
Bowker, Gordon 31–32
Boyce, Jackie 124
'Boylansday' xl, 216ff
Brady, Joseph 172
Bray, County Wicklow 14, 28–29

259

Briggs, Austin 232, 236
British Association for Irish Studies xiii, xxxiv
Brockman, William 232
Brooke, Charlotte 90
Bruno, Giordano 140. 162, 238
Budgen, Frank xxxii, 144, 158, 172, 218
Burgess, Anthony 243
Burns, Edward M. 241
Butler, Christopher 224
Byrne, John Francis 160
Byrnes, Robert 59, 231

Caldwell, Lucy 99
Caneda, Teresa 63
Carleton, William 82, 86, 113, 186
Carlin, Gerry 59
Carstairs, Lily 155
Castle, Gregory 236
Catholicism *see* Roman Catholicism
Celtic Tiger xxxiv
Cezanne, Paul 10
Chamber Music (Joyce) 227
Cheng, Vincent 95, 229
Clongowes Wood College, County Kildare 33, 241
Coleridge, Samuel Taylor 169
Colum, Mary 147, 158
colour symbolism 20
Collins, Michael 20, 159
Collins, Wilkie 19, 34
Comte, Auguste 12
consciousness
    and conscience 26
    and crisis of consciousness 132
    and Sigmund Freud 11, 16, 198, 229, 244
    and history xxiiff, 9ff, 38, 182, 190
    and H. Stuart Hughes xxviiiff, 22, 32, 36–37
    and Edmund Husserl xxviii
    and intentionality xxviii
    and Henry James xxviii, 238
    and John Locke 5ff, 18
    and Georg Lukács 131, 182

and Molly Bloom in *Ulysses* xxviii, xxxi, 190, 213
and national consciousness 163
and Stephen Dedalus in *Ulysses* xxxii
and Stephen's entry into consciousness in *A Portrait* xxviiiff
and stream of consciousness xxviii, 4
and subjectivity xxix, 9, 221
as a theme in *A Portrait* 9ff
Cormack, Alistair 161ff
Cosgrave, Vincent 160
Costello, Peter 214
Cricket xliii, 105ff, 173
Crispi, Luca xl, 16, 37, 68, 209ff
Craig, Patricia 89
Crofton, Mr 29, 52
Cross, Eric 80
Cubism xxx
cultural nationalism xx, xxvi, 95, 180, 222
Cummins, Maria 195
Curran, Constantine 166

Dada 10, 143–144
Dædalus, and the Minotaur/King Minos myth 16, 24, 26
Davitt, Michael xxi, 16, 21–22, 38–39
Davys, Mary 245
Day, Robert Adams 233
Deane, Seamus xxvii, 92, 131–132, 180, 222
DeLillo, Don 106
Derrida, Jacques xxxvii, 180–181, 196, 198, 202
De Valera, Éamon 20, 24
Dickens, Charles
   David Copperfield xxixff, 4ff, 34ff, 120
   and existentialism 7
   and psychology 9, 33
   and repression 35
   Joyce's attitude towards 35
Dinneen, Patrick 51
Dodsley, James 90
Dolan, Terence 96
Dooley, Maura 97
Doyle, Roddy 107
Dublin

Belvedere College 33
Brighton Square, Rathgar 25
Christian Brothers School 33
colonial context of 41, 187, 190, 226
Easter Rising (1916) 49, 155, 159, 209
Eccles Street 160, 213
and *Finnegans Wake* xxiv, 74
General Post Office 209
Grafton Street 171
Great Britain Street 41
Hill of Howth 74, 208, 215, 217
Kildare Street Club 76
National Library of Ireland 166, 210, 215, 236, 244
North Richmond Street 33–34
Parnell's statue (in O'Connell Street) 171
Stephen's Green 155
and Trieste 48, 130, 133ff, 172, 204, 239
Trinity College 114, 242
University College xxxvii, 166, 170
Wellington Monument xxiii
'world capital of boredom' 180
Dublin James Joyce Journal xxxvii, 166ff
Dubliners
   'After the Race' 166
      and 1898 Emmet procession 169
   'Araby'
      and the Araby Bazaar of 1894 168
      'blind' street in 34
      passion and desire 169
   'Clay'
      Maria's defensive manoeuvres 178
      missing stanza 77
   'The Dead'
      and Mr Browne 29
      and 'country cute' 167
      and Gabriel Conroy 15, 49
      and Irish oral tradition 188
      Joyce's *Doll's House* 178
      and 'The Lass of Aughrim' 174, 187, 189
      and statue of King William 164
      and William Rooney poem 164

'An Encounter' 180
'Eveline'
    and emigration 181
    and free indirect discourse 221
    her passivity 181
    and Belfast developer 28
gnomon 22, 234
and Grant Richards 13
and Ibsen 13, 178, 222
'Ivy Day in the Committee Room' 29, 52
'A Painful Case' 180, 185
'The Sisters'
    and Jacobite echo 164
    and rituals 74–75
    and simony 234
    title 234
    'Two Gallants' 76
Dujardin, Édouard 4
Duke of Leinster 119
Durcan, Paul xxxv, 101ff

Easter Rising 1916 49, 155, 159, 209
Eglinton, John (aka W.K. Magee) 113, 195, 199, 206
Eliot, George 129, 133, 178, 203
Eliot, T.S. xxxvii, 10, 50, 117, 177, 182, 194
Ellison, Ralph 105
Ellmann, Richard 3, 31, 130, 133ff, 157, 160, 167, 238ff
emigration 49, 100, 181, 247
Emmet, Robert 15, 166, 169, 231
Ennis, County Clare 220
Epictetus 6
Estudiosirlandeses.org xxxiv
Exiles 13, 224

Faerber, Thomas and Markus Luchsinger 143ff
Fenians xxi, 83, 124
Fennell, Conor 146ff
Ferguson, Frank 124
Ferrer, Daniel 226ff, 236
Ferrero, Guglielmo xxxii, 130
The Field Day Anthology of Irish Writing (1991) 92

Finnegans Wake
  Bognor Regis 49, 118
  closing moments 239
  and 'daintical pair of accomplasses' 151, 161
  and *Dubliners* 49
  Dublin in 54, 74
  and Dutch translation xxxiii
  and 'Dyoublong' xx1v
  and the Earwicker name 49ff, 118
  and exile 147
  experiments with sounds and language in xxvi
  HCE figure in 50, 236
  and Irish Civil War xxiii
  Irish history and politics in xxiii
  and Landsmaal xxiv
  Lessons chapter 151
  and 'mearbound' 24–25
  'The Mime of Mick, Nick, and Maggies' 178
  portmanteau words and phrases in xxiv, 16, 151, 162
  Shem in 49ff, 116, 179, 235
  and Laurence Sterne xxxv
  and swerve 74, 228
  and *Tunc* page xix
  and warping process 10, 53, 143
  waz iz 246
  and 'Willingdone Museyroom' xxiii,13
  and 'Work in Progress' 143, 157n
Fitzgerald, F. Scott 97, 107
Flaubert, Gustave 12, 59, 60, 120, 203, 222, 231
Fleischmann, Martha 144
Fogarty, Anne 166, 170ff
Fordham, Finn 236
Forster, E.M. 35, 183
Frank, Nino 135
Freud, Sigmund 11ff, 198, 229, 240, 244
Froula, Christine 230

Gabler, Hans Walter xli, 220, 223, 225
Galway xxii, 101, 117, 188
genetic criticism xl, 153, 168, 210ff
Giacomo Joyce 224

Gibbons, Luke 174, 184ff

Gibraltar xxxi, 41ff

GiedionWelcker, Carola 143, 145, 159

Gilbert, Stuart 63n

Glasheen, Adaline xlii, 229, 237ff

Gogarty, Oliver St John 158, 206

Goldberg, S.L. 202

Gorman, Herbert 135

Gramsci, Antonio 131

Great Famine, the 139, 165, 174, 186, 188, 191

Great War, the xx, 72, 88, 136, 144, 152, 155, 159

Greenblatt, Stephen 228

Gregory, Lady Augusta 94, 155, 164, 187

Gregory, Sir William 188

Griffith, Arthur xxi, xxxix, 206

Groden, Michael xlii, 193, 233, 236

Hardiman, Adrian 173

Harrison, Tony 174

Hart, Clive 212, 224

Harte, Liam 97n, 244ff

Heaney, Seamus xxviii, xxxv, 95, 110ff, 218

Hebald, Milton 145

Hemingway, Ernest 148

'The Hisperica Famina' 173

Hobsbawm, E.J. xxvi–xxvii

Homer 173, 179, 193, 194, 207, 218

Honert, Martin 243

Hooper, Conal 173

Howes, Margaret xli, 226

Hughes, H. Stuart xxviiiff, 22, 32, 36–37

Hughes, Ted 120–121

Hume, David 6

Humour xliii, 5, 15, 63, 66, 79, 80, 84, 101, 107, 118, 119, 122, 217, 241

Husserl, Edmund xxviii, 9

Huston, John 165, 174, 178, 187, 189

Hybridity xxxi, xxxiii, 41ff

Hyde, Douglas 52, 95, 97

Hyman, Louis 142

Hypnerotomachia Poliphili 228

Ibsen, Henrik 13, 178, 222
Ignatius of Loyola, St 65
Irish Civil War (1922–3) xx, 102
    and James Joyce xxiii, xxiv, 154, 181
    and W.B. Yeats xxii, 154
Irish Diaspora xli, 96, 97, 105
The Irish Homestead 17, 185, 214
Irish Literary Revival 163, 189
Irish Parliamentary Party xix
Irish War of Independence (1919–21) xx
Irishness xviii, xxvii, xxxviii, 47, 53, 105, 116, 117, 122, 163, 184
Iser, Wolfgang xxxix, 196

James, Henry xxviii, 238
James Joyce Archive 209, 217
James Joyce Broadsheet xiii, xvii
James Joyce Literary Supplement xiii, xvii
James Joyce Quarterly xiii, xvii, xliv, 231ff
Jameson, Fredric 196, 201, 205
Jesuits 33, 34, 136, 140
Jesus 8, 63, 111, 136
Jews 63, 139ff
    in Gibraltar 43, 46, 49
    in Ireland xxiii, 172
    in Rome xxxii, 130
    in Trieste 136ff
Jolas, Eugene xxxv
Johnson, Samuel 26, 50, 54, 89, 194
Joyce, James
    character xliii–xliv, 14, 141
    and classical temper 34ff, 203
    and covenant with the reader 29
    and cricket xliii
    death 145, 174, 206
    defiance in 14, 132
    drinking habits 137, 148, 232, 236
    eccentric 3, 29, 201
    education 17, 33, 194
    as a foreign language teacher 137
    and friends 28, 48, 130, 134ff, 141, 144ff, 156, 160
    Irish Catholic roots 17, 34, 111, 129, 141

and the Jesuits 17
and Jewishness 172
leaves Ireland (1904) 172
and Paris xviii, xli, 3, 49, 53, 116, 118, 130, 146ff, 160, 223, 230
politics and writing in xxiii, xxxii, 16, 38, 129ff, 180, 186, 190
and Protestants in his writing 28ff
and recycling earlier texts xli, 61, 224
social class and family background 234
Stephen Dædalus as a pseudonym 27
subversive writer xxiv, 151, 241
and values xxx, 13ff
Joyce, John (Joyce's father) xliii, 25, 160
Joyce, Lucia (Joyce's daughter) xxxvi, 116, 144, 145, 146, 160, 236
Joyce, Nora Barnacle (Joyce's wife)
    Galway accent 42
    and Irish Civil War 154
    Joyce's letters to 128
    marriage to Joyce 160
    and Molly Bloom 42
    singing 'My Dark Rosaleen' 139
Joyce, Stanislaus (Joyce's brother) 16, 136, 139
Jung, Carl 11, 145

Kealiher, Carol 232
Keane, Molly 91, 120
Kearney, Richard 173
Keegan, Claire 100
Kelleher, John V. 163
Kelly, John 154ff
Kennelly, Brendan 94, 96
Kenner, Hugh 25, 64, 212, 235
    attitude to Richard Ellmann 238
    and Dublin's Joyce 238
    and 'Eumaeus' 64
    'Molly's Masterstroke' 234
    and one-liners 239
    'The Uncle Charles Principle' 9, 194
Kiberd, Declan 173–174
Kiely, Benedict
    and asides in his writing 88
    'God's Own Country' 81

Nothing Happens in Carmincross xxii, 83ff
  and Omagh xxxiii, 71ff
  and quotation 75
  Proxopera 84ff
  and rivers 72ff
  and sectarianism 78ff
  and Irish song tradition 82
  and storytelling 75, 80
  The Captain with the Whiskers 86
  The Cards of the Gambler 87
  'The Night We Rode with Sarsfield' 78
  There Was an Ancient House 72,75
Killeen, Terence 167, 169, 170, 190, 193ff
Kinsella, Thomas 96
Knuth, Leo 234
Kristeva, Julia 196ff, 200ff

Lacan, Jacques xxxix, 17, 196ff, 240
Laffan, Michael 172
The Lamplighter (Cummins) 195
Landsmaal (Norwegian dialect) xxiv,
Larbaud, Valéry 230
Latham, Sean xlii, 231
Lawrence, D.H. 114,
Lawrence, Karen xli, 60, 224
Le Fanu, Sheridan 224
Léon, Paul 142
Levine, Jennifer 223
Lewis, Wyndham 144, 240
Locke, John 5ff, 108
Longley, Edna 96
Longley, Michael 95, 99
Lucretius 228
Lukács, Georg 131, 182

MacCabe, Colin xxxix, 131, 196
MacNeice, Louis 99
McAlmon, Robert 147–148
McCarthy, Justin 92
McCormack, W.J. (aka Hugh Maxton) 246
McCourt, Frank 245

McCourt, John xviii, 133ff
McDonagh, Martin 94, 107
McEwan, Ian 18ff
McGahern, John 75, 95, 100, 247
McGee, Patrick xxxix, 17, 182, 196ff
McGreevy, Tom 114ff, 147ff
Mahaffey, Vicki 232–234
Mahon, Derek 91, 99
Mangan, James Clarence 139, 222
Manganiello, Dominic 131ff
Mannin, Ethel 153, 177ff
Marcus, David 94
Marinetti, Filippo Thommaso 198
Marx, Karl 131, 182, 196, 205
Matthews, Aidan 98
Meaney, Geraldine 174
Melchiori, Giorgio xxxii, 129ff
Miller, Lee 170–171
Milosz, Czeslaw 110
Minotaur/King Minos myth 16, 24, 27
Mitchel, John xliii, 245
Monnier, Adrienne 4
Montgomery, Niall 167
Moore, George 95, 147, 189, 245
Moore, Thomas 76
Moran, Patrick W. 232
Morel, Auguste 63–64
Murdoch, Iris 120
Murphy, Richard 120
Murray, Lindley 57ff, 69

Nadel, Ira B. xviii, xxxii, 38, 139ff
Nash, John xxxvii, 180ff
'Nation Once Again, A' xx–xxi, 104
National Library of Ireland xl, 3, 43, 168, 215, 218, 236, 244
Nationalism xixff, 208ff
  Civic xxvii, 13
  cultural xxvi, 95, 180, 222
  ethnic xxvii
  narrow-minded xxiv, xxvii, 132, 139
  political xix, xxii, xxvi, 225

primordial xx
Nawi, Ezra 242
Neusner, Jacob 141
Newman, Cardinal [John Henry] xxv, 173, 174
Ní Dhomhnaill, Nuala 96
Nietzsche, Friedrich 210, 222, 228
Nolan, Emer 161
Norburn, Roger 131ff
Norris, David 242ff
Norris, Margot xxxvii, xl, 61, 177ff, 224, 232

O'Brien, Conor Cruise 195, 210
O'Brien, Kate xliii, 246
O'Casey, Sean 94
O'Connell, Daniel xx
O'Connell, Darragh 173
O'Connor, Bridget 107
O'Connor, Frank 81, 89
O'Driscoll, Dennis 110
O'Faolain, Sean 95, 214
Ó Gráda, Cormac xxxii, 172
O'Hagan, Sean 110
O'Neill, Christine 167
O'Neill, Joseph xxxv, 105ff
O'Shea, Katharine xix
O'Toole, Fintan 170
Oswald, Richard xxxvi, 122
Owens, Cóilín 163, 166ff

Parrinder, Patrick xxix
Parnell, Charles Stewart
    clarion call xx
    'The Death of Parnell' 52
    fall of 52, 100
    statue of (O'Connell Street) 171
Patrick, St xxxv, 112
Patten, Eve 245
Pearse, Patrick xx, 83
Percy, Thomas 90
photographs of Joyce 134, 145, 159
Picasso, Pablo 10

Pierce, David
   James Joyce's Ireland 29, 30, 96
   Joyce and Company xvii
   Light, Freedom and Song xxxi, 72, 93, 98, 106, 110
   Reading Joyce xxvii, xxviii, 74, 118
   The Long Apprenticeship 98n, 243
   Yeats's Worlds 121, 155n, 185n
Pollock, Jonathan 228
A Portrait of the Artist as a Young Man
   Christmas dinner scene 16, 32, 36, 37, 100
   and Christian Brothers 33
   and colonised subject 236
   composition of 37, 135
   and consciousness
   and Dædalus 16, 27
   and Dante Conway 21–22, 31–32, 39–39
   and Dedalus xxxii, xxxix, 27, 28, 179
   and Eileen Vance 14, 28ff
   epigraph in xxx, 16, 23ff
   French translation 23ff
   and homosexual panic 235
   and hope xix, 16
   and Imagism xxx
   and the Jesuits 33, 112
   Lynch 12
   and narrative voice xxx, 9
   and paratextual features 37
   and Ovid, *Metamorphosis* 24–25
   and 'press' 22
   punctuation 23, 37
   quotation xxx, 12, 23, 76
   and repression 33
   and serialisation in *The Egoist* 158
   and *Stephen Hero* 13, 27, 29, 36, 141, 223ff
   symbols 21ff
   title 25, 27, 28
   and 'tuckoo' 8, 14, 17, 22, 25–26
   and 'tundish' 112
   and unknown arts 17, 22, 24ff
   and 'The Well of the World's End' 23
Pound, Ezra 38, 132, 145, 157, 158, 182, 224, 234, 238

Power, Arthur 147

Pribek, James 173

Protestant xliii, 28ff, 41, 52, 79, 111, 123–124, 129, 140, 164, 167, 181, 186, 239, 242, 246

Proust, Marcel 11, 75, 230

Queen's Hotel, Ennis 220

Rabaté, Jean-Michel xli, 223, 226

Rains, Stephanie 167

Reichert, Klaus 222ff

Richards, Grant 13

Ricoeur, Paul 171

Riquelme, John Paul 223, 225

Ritchie, Charles xxxv, 118ff

Robinson, Tim 101

Rodgers, W.R. 124

Rodriguez, Liliane 230

Roman Catholicism xx, xxxiv, 17, 29, 31, 41, 77, 79, 102, 110, 122, 172, 186

Rose, Danis 60

Roth, Samuel 236

Russell, George (aka AE) 17, 185, 206

Russell, Micho 73

Ryan, Fred 97, 133, 206

Sabatini, Frederico 228

Saint-Amour, Paul xlii, 14–15, 231, 236

Savitzky, Ludmila 23, 28

Schmitz, Ettore (aka Italo Svevo) 137, 142

Schoeck, Othmar 145

Scott, Walter 82

Scroggins, Mark 59

Senn, Fritz xlii, 145, 170, 212, 232ff

Shakespeare, William 18, 49, 75, 90, 181, 199, 218, 229

Shaw, George Bernard xxxv, 94

Sheehy-Skeffington, Francis 133, 236

Shelley, Percy Bysshe 130

Shklovsky, Victor 5

Shovlin, Frank 163ff, 187

Sidlesham, Sussex 49, 118

Sinn Féin xxi, xxvii, 206, 209

Slocum, John 239
Smith, Neil 60
Spillane, Davy 73
Spoo, Robert xlii, 232, 234
Staley, Tom xlii
Stasi, Paul xxxviii, 182ff
Sterne, Laurence
  and attitude to Ireland 121
  correspondence xxxv, 121ff
  and *Finnegans Wake* xxxv
  and humour 5, 6, 67
  O'Leari, abbé xxxvi, 122
  The Beauties of Sterne 90
  Tristram Shandy 4ff
    and epigraph 6
    and marble page 12
    and philosophy 6, 9, 32
  A Sentimental Journey 19, 49, 67, 122
  Yorkshire writer 121
Stoppard, Tom 144
Stuart, Francis 81
Swift, Jonathan xxxv, 96
Synge, John Millington xxvi, 74, 121, 148, 190

Taine, Hyppolyte 206
TitBits (weekly magazine) 195
Thompson, Hunter S. 26
Times Literary Supplement 240
Tortosa, Francisco García 64
Trevor, William 104
Trieste 133ff
  and Berlitz School 204
  and Dublin 49, 136, 137
  and friends 48
  and Jews xxxii, 48, 136, 142, 172
  as Joyce's Oriental workshop 135
  as irresistible magnet for Joyce 135
  and *Triestino* dialect 134
  and *Ulysses* 130, 135
Trotter, David 20
Tuohy, Patrick 147, 159

Ulin, Julieann Veronica 236

Ulysses
  Arranger figure in 66, 195
  beginnings 129ff
  and 'A Boarding House' 236
  'Blazes' Boylan in xl, 68, 209ff
  Bloom, Leopold
    and ambivalence 200
    and P. Beaufoy 195
    and construction of *Ulysses* xxxii, 135, 211, 214ff
    and Bloom's father 41, 220
    and 'hat trick' 173
    and Henry Flower 198
    and Hungarian background xxxix, 53, 207ff
    and Alfred H. Hunter xxxvii, 169
    his imagination 67, 200, 228
    his Jewishness xviii, 49, 52, 63, 137, 142, 172
    and Orientalism 135, 169
    and 'orthodox Samaritan' xxxii, 63
    and thought processes xxviii, xxx, 15, 47, 65, 68, 195, 198, 205
    as Ulysses 69, 202, 204
    as 'Ulysses of the postal era' 198
    and 7 Eccles Street 60, 213
  Bloom, Molly
    and Boylan xl, 68, 213ff
    her consciousness xxviii, xxxi, 190, 213
    her ethnicity xxvii, 47
    and Gibraltar 42ff
    and imagined hybrid landscape xxxi, 41ff
    and Jewish looks 42
    and relationship with Leopold Bloom 42, 48, 53, 214ff
    and Lunita Laredo (mother) xxxi, 42, 217
    as Penelope 173, 202
    sexuality 67–68, 160, 200
    and Spanish eyes xxxi, 41
    and 'Major' Tweedy (father) xxxi, 41–42, 67, 214
    'Yes' at end of soliloquy 16, 216
  and Bloomsday (16 June 1904) and deconstruction xxxix, 162, 213
  Dlugacz, Moses 41, 48, 137
    Eccles Street house in 160, 213
    episodes

INDEX

'Aeolus'
    subheadings 228
'Calypso'
    and Moses Dlugacz 41, 48, 137
    and Orientalism 169
'Circe'
    as *Ulysses*'s unconscious 200
'Cyclops'
    drafts 236
    confrontation between Citizen and Bloom xxvii
'Eumaeus' xxxi, 57ff
    and the Arranger 66
    and cliché 59
    and humour of 'getup' 67–68
    and leftover quality 65, 67
    and lists 61ff
    and Morpheus 170
    and 'orthodox Samaritan' 63
    and registers 58
    and translation xxxiii, 63ff
    ungrammatical 58
'Ithaca' 15, 189, 203, 219
'Lotuseaters' 194
'Nausicaa' 144, 178, 194
    and literature as ideology 203
    and sexual difference 200
    and sickly prose 57
'Nestor' 15, 197
'Oxen of the Sun' 195, 199, 200, 223
'Penelope' xli
    and Boylan 216ff
    and drafts xl, 16, 216ff
    and Gibraltar xxxi, 41ff, 215ff
    and 'Lunita Laredo' xxxi, 217
    an opening, not a conclusion 201
    and missing wedding gifts 219
'Proteus' 19–20, 197, 205, 230, 236
'Scylla and Charybdis' 133, 195, 202
    Dana 133, 215
    and dialectical play 199
    and missing *Hamlet* lecture 230

and notes on Shakespeare 218
'Sirens' 69, 142, 164, 200
    and Boylan in early draft xl, 216
    and novel's change in direction 193, 214
    and 'Mrs Marion Tweedy' 214
'Telemachus' 65, 66, 143, 188n, 227
    an adverbial episode 195
    and cracked mirror 197
    and *Finnegans Wake* 225
'Wandering Rocks' 144, 183, 193, 203
    and subversive role for style 199ff
French translation of 4, 230
and / as 'ghoststory' 185
Gabler edition of 37n, 220, 225
Gardner, Stanley 42, 45, 48, 217
Hill of Howth in xl, 208, 215–217
and Homer's *Odyssey* 61, 219
and hope 16
'initial style' 193, 194
lunch to celebrate 4
and Mina Purefoy 170
Mulligan in 66, 68, 140, 158, 197, 199, 204–206, 228
opening sentence 194
and Rosenbach manuscript xxxii, 64, 67, 68, 209
Shakespeare and Company editions of 230
and utopian thinking 14
Ungar, Andras 207ff

Valente, Joe 225–226
Valéry, Paul 4, 230
Vallancey, Charles 141
Vallely, Fintan 124
Vico, Giambattista 132, 162, 173, 228

Wagner, Richard 222
Walsh, Edna xxxv, 103ff
Walzl, Florence L. 232ff
Watt, Stephen 216
Wawrzycka, Jolanta 232
Weaver, Harriet Shaw 148, 157, 158, 159, 224, 235
Welcker, Carola Giedion 143, 145, 159

Whelan, Kevin 163, 174

Whitaker, Thomas 162

Whiteboys xxi

Whitman, Walt 105

Wicke, Jennifer xli, 225, 226, 235

Wilde, Oscar xxxv, 21, 96, 101, 206, 215

Wilson, Richard 229

Winton, Tracey Eve 228–229

Wister, Jones 106

women

   and being stoned for adultery 78

   and autobiographies 246

   and being held as hostage 84

   and Bolivian postcard 67

   and exclusion from *The Field Day Anthology* 92

   and Irish women writers 93, 246

   and Joyce's attitude to intelligent women 148

   and Magdalene asylums 175

   and Protestant women writers 123

   and sexual desires 174

   and significance of Mina Purefoy 170

   and social oppression 178

   and subversion of patriarchy 197

   and washerwomen in 'Anna Livia Plurabelle' 178–179

Woolf, Virginia xxxviii, 29, 49, 55, 86, 182–183

'Work in Progress' 143, 157n,

Yeats, George (Yeats's wife) 117, 148, 155, 185

Yeats, Jack B. 116, 117

Yeats, W.B.

   The Celtic Twilight 74, 132, 184

   and dreaming back 235

   'Easter 1916' xxii, 155, 209

   and *Finnegans Wake* 163

   and George Yeats 155–156

   and Irish Civil War 154–155

   Joyce's relationship with 4, 159, 161–162

   and Lily Carstairs 155

   'Meditations in Time of Civil War' xxii, 154

   and performative self

   'The Second Coming' 108–109, 153

and *A Vision* 156
  The Wanderings of Oisin 120

Zurich xviii, 10, 48, 130, 143ff, 219
  James Joyce Foundation 145
  Joyce's move to 49
  Joyce in Zurich's *Who's Who* 144
  photograph of Joyce in 134, 159

Lightning Source UK Ltd.
Milton Keynes UK
UKHW05n1357200218
318187UK00002B/4/P

9 781912 224029